D0924375

CALGARY PUBLIC LIBRARY

OCT - - 2014

THROWN

THROWN

Kerry Howley

Sarabande  Books
LOUISVILLE, KENTUCKY

FOR WILL

© 2014 by Kerry Howley

FIRST EDITION

All rights reserved.

No part of this book may be reproduced without written permission of the publisher. Please direct inquiries to:

Managing Editor
Sarabande Books, Inc.
2234 Dundee Road, Suite 200
Louisville, KY 40205

Library of Congress Cataloging-in-Publication Data

Howley, Kerry.
 Thrown / Kerry Howley.—First edition.
    pages cm
   Summary: "Acclaimed journalist Kerry Howley infiltrates the world of mixed martial arts and the lives of aspiring cage fighters. For three years, Howley follows these fighters as they tear ligaments and lose a third of their body mass to make weight, and is drawn deeply into this riveting culture of violence"—Provided by publisher.
  ISBN 978-1-936747-92-4 (paperback : acid-free paper)
  1. Mixed martial arts—United States. 2. Martial artists—United States. I. Title.
 GV1102.7.M59H68 2014
 796.8—dc23
                      2014010165

Cover by Kristen Radtke.

Interior by Kirkby Gann Tittle.

Manufactured in Canada.

This book is printed on acid-free paper.

Sarabande Books is a nonprofit literary organization.

The Kentucky Arts Council, the state arts agency, supports Sarabande Books with state tax dollars and federal funding from the National Endowment for the Arts.

SOMETIMES YOU'RE WATCHING LEGIT living legends of MMA lore and sometimes half-drunk cornfield-born farmboy brawlers, but there is always an octagon, always a fence, always a path down which only fighters may walk. There is music upon their entrance. There are hard-bodied fans and fat announcers, rolling cartfuls of cold beer, laser lights that shine from ceiling to canvas. Always ring girls. Let's talk about the ring girls, please, the way they never seem to get anywhere, the way they set off, gleaming teeth and quivering thighs, only to end up back in the same cageside seat from which they alight. Round one *arrives*. Round two *arrives*. The ring girl spins in place. I used to think a ring girl's job was to be an idea of a ring girl, that is, to nest comfortably inside the memory of every other ring girl the spectators had seen, not to draw attention to herself but to the concept "ring girl" with which myriad personal qualities of her own—perhaps she has synesthetic tendencies, a deep appreciation for the late works of Schopenhauer, an engineering degree from Iowa State—would doubtless conflict. But then I found myself at a big fight out East, and the fighters were really hot on this one particular ring girl, "Britney," who, truth be told, was especially ogle-worthy as she strode across the cage. The spectators lusted for Britney by name, and this willingness to individuate forced me to reassess my position on the subject of ring girls, their function.

In the summer of 2010, when Sean was thirty pounds overweight and I was already his most persistent and devoted spacetaker, I was convinced that a successful fight had something to do not with the ring girl specifically—that would be absurd—but the chemical reaction made possible by a ring girl, an announcer, a beer cart, an audience, and who knows what else. That somehow the spectacle transformed the space; that we were watching, in action, a Theater of Cruelty, and just as Artaud would have predicted, the show sunk more often than it soared.

I myself am not a fighter, not a fan, not a shadow or a groupie or a worried wife. I am that species of fighterly accoutrement known as "spacetaker," which is to say that when the fighters leave the cage, where they are self-sufficient, for the street, where they are not, I am that which separates your goodly fighter from the common thug. As hipsters have glasses, and priests collars, and cops mustaches, fighters have us. And just as the mustache does not at shift's end quit the cop, we belong to the fighter and not the fight. Most of what fighters do, after all, is not within the purview of the octagon, and they need their entourage as much if not more on a slow Sunday afternoon when the quiet is too much to face. There is in some of them the same want that keeps cargo-shorted frat boys traveling in packs the moment they leave home, that effortfully cheerful desperation to drown out mind-traffic with the shuffle and shout of other men.

The story is this: I showed up, a spectator, to a fight in Des Moines. Moments previous I had been at a conference on phenomenology, where a balding professor stunningly wrong about Husserlian intentionality dominated the postconference cocktail hour.

"Does anyone have a cigarette?" I asked a group of skirt-suited, fading, gray-complected women, not because I wanted one but because I longed for an excuse to exit. None of them moved. I am not myself a smoker but have always preferred the company of the nicotine-inclined, and I took the aggressive health of these academics to be unseemly dogmatism.

Having nothing to do in Des Moines beyond explore Husserl with nonsmokers who did not understand him, I walked the conference center hallways. I found myself at a hotel, and then a restaurant, and then ambling along a glass corridor, one story up from downtown Des Moines. A group of young men who had fragranced themselves such that I was sure their evening had some immediate purpose passed me, and upon following them through an ever more complicated labyrinth of hallways, I landed at their destination. A framed sign standing before two closed doors read "Midwest Cage Championship." This interested me only in that it appeared to be the honest kind of butchery in which the theory-mangling, logic-maiming academics I had just abandoned would never partake.

Inside the room the lights were dim but for a great spotlight lofted above an octagonal dais, lined on all sides with a six-foot chain-link fence. A hundred male Iowans gathered in the dark on benches. Through the fence I saw that one man was beneath another like a mechanic under a truck, and the man on top had a full set of angel's wings tattooed down the length of his back. Inked feathers rippled as he punched the face of the man lodged under his stomach. A red stream dribbled down the other man's forehead, onto the canvas, where their conjoined writhings smeared the blood like the stroke of a brush. Seconds later a single hand fluttered out from beneath the wing. His fingertips touched the canvas with extreme delicacy, as if to tap a bell and summon a concierge. There was no one to inform me that this meant he had given up, so I assumed some sort of grotesque exhibition had merely run its course.

"I suppose this gives us a new perspective on angels," I remarked to my nearest, cologne-soaked neighbor, "or perhaps a very *old* perspective, given their not unthreatening depiction in the Old Testament." He stared at me and walked off, though I still think the point astute. When he returned, it was to a different part of the bench.

I watched a second fight, a third. Sometimes the men were standing exchanging shots as if in a streetfight, and sometimes they leaned against the cage clutching and clawing at one another, and sometimes they rolled about the middle of the canvas like hugging children tumbling down a hill. They tore at one another with kicks and strikes, knees and elbows. Instead of turning away from the heaviest blows, some long-suppressed part of me began focusing on the mark each left behind. I felt then that I should leave, but I did not leave, and a gloriously cut, hairless man walked out to great cheers from the crowd. His name was Kevin "The Fire" Burns and he was, I gathered from the raucous reception, a celebrated fighter from Des Moines. Twenty seconds into the fight I realized that I was not at all interested in Kevin "The Fire" Burns, but rather the misshapen man he was dismantling. That man's name was Sean Huffman, and there was not a single moment in the fifteen minute fight when he could be said to be effectively staving off The Fire's jabs to his face.

For three long and bloody rounds I watched Sean play fat slobberknocker to another man's catlike technical prowess. Jab after jab Sean ate, and with each precisely timed shot to his own mouth Sean's smile grew, as if The Fire were carving that smile into him. All the while, watching, I had the oddest feeling of a cloudiness momentarily departing. It was as if someone had oil-slicked my synapses, such that thoughts could whip and whistle their way across my mind without the friction I'd come to experience as thought itself. I felt an immense affection for the spectacle before me, but it was as if the affection were not emanating from anywhere, because I had dissolved into a kind of mist and expanded to envelop the entire space that held these hundred men.

It was the last fight of the night, and after the loss Sean lay bleeding flat and still across a row of metal folding chairs. I jumped up from the last seat I'd ever pay for, shuffled past some legs in the cheap section, snuck under a divider, lied to security, and strode over to his outstretched body to watch a doctor—well, someone with a needle and thread—stitch pieces of Sean's brow back together. I was too moved to speak, or even to introduce myself. It was weeks later, after I hunted him down in his own city, that I finally asked, "Did it hurt?"

He thought about this for a long while—I could tell he was thinking hard even though he could not, at that time, knit his stitched-up brows together in a gesture that would suggest an outward manifestation of thinking—and said, "Not entirely."

He thought then to move past the subject, but I was not satisfied.

"Well what does it feel like?"

Again he thought long and hard and let the silence linger.

"It feels," he said, "like waking up."

•

Understand that I was very excited by the spectacle, and not until my ride home, as I began to settle back into my bones and feel the limiting contours of perception close back in like the nursery curtains that stifled the views of my youth, did it occur to me that I had, for the first time in my life, found a way out of this, my own skin. My experience echoed precisely descriptions handed down to us in the writings of Schopenhauer, Nietzsche, and Artaud, in which a disturbing ritual—often violent—rendered each of their senses many times more acute, as if the dull blunt body were momentarily transformed into a tuning fork, alive, as Schopenhauer put it, "to sensations fine and fleeting." Some have called the feeling *ecstasy*. I believed in this spectacle-provoked plenitude of sensation as one believes in Pangaea and plundering Huns, but until that night in Des Moines I associated that state with antediluvian rites not accessible to modern man. Around midnight on an Iowa highway surrounded by that deep darkness only cornfields can conjure, I thought, "This exhibition, whatever it may be, has ushered ecstatic experience back into the world."

From that moment onward, the only phenomenological project that could possibly hold interest to me was as follows: capture and describe that particular state of being to which one Sean Huffman had taken me.

And so naturally I began to show up places where Sean might show up—the gym where he trained, the bar where he bounced, the rented basement where he lived, the restaurants where he consumed foods perhaps not entirely aligned with the professed goals of an aspiring fighter. I hope it doesn't sound immodest to ·say that Sean found this attention entirely agreeable, and that, in general, members of the fighter class do not mind my presence in even the most intimate surroundings. This is not to say that they long for my companionship. It is to say that they forget, with startling regularity, that I am there at all. And when something requires that they take notice, such as an irrepressible urge I might have to press a philosophical point, they react to the point itself and not to me. They don't ask about my fine hunting dog, or my well-cut cowboy boots, or my position on the Irish question. My first name is Kit. No fighter has ever asked for my last.

I remember well that first real conversation with Sean, wherein we lunched on satisfactory dive-bar burgers and I told him I thought his performance an extraordinary physical analogue to phenomenological inquiry. He cocked his head, arched an eyebrow, and said, in a way that seemed quietly pleased with my observation, "You're insane." He stirred his soda with a straw. "I just like to feel things."

We talked about backwoods Tennessee, about Davenport's rise and fall as a center of fighterly activity, about his years in the war. Every time I would speak he would stare a moment, take it in, before responding. Finally, he plucked a single french fry from my plate, which I hoped to be a gesture of impending intimacy, and thus an invitation to many more fights.

Ever since that night in Des Moines I'd felt trapped, ordered about by some base biological needs. "Eat this," my body said, "sleep now," but in the course of that fight I had spent a few brief moments—less than a minute, probably—away from this insistent yawp, and I was less given to respond. That Sean had no impending fights we might together anticipate was thus something of an ongoing disappointment, but on the other hand, this lull meant I had Sean mostly to myself.

Picture us: strolling along the Mississippi, past stretches of chain-link fence that start and stop for the ghosts of buildings no longer standing, past schools of ducks riding the waves in between stray pieces of Styrofoam. We pass a skate park recently carved out along the water's edge, where a bottle rolls noisily down the half-pipe, and three boys, two with skateboards on hand and one with his board tilted underfoot, stop and stare for a long while at my companion's half-cratered nose and mat-gnarled ears. How much more fascinated still would they be, could they see through to the sutures on the still-raw tissue between his tibia and femur, the scar tissue from a concussion, the three fused phalanges in his right hand, cracked while punching someone in the face. Sean doesn't notice the boys at all. Risk-averse Sean looks down at the Styrofoam-speckled water and says, "You know people swim in that? Crazy."

Or picture us, if you will, at The Paddlewheel, the bar where the city's fighters gather for a drink and reminisce about the old days of hard-charging Davenport glory, when a drink would have been out of the question. These are men who migrated to the Midwest because a legendary Croatian named Pat Miletich ("The Croatian Sensation") called them all up from California and Florida and, in Sean's case, rural Tennessee, but that was years ago, and none of them has even seen Miletich in a long while. There are fighters around the pool table and fighters pointing plastic guns toward a screen and fighters gathered around Sean, whom everyone adores. It's the calm, I think, that he brings to any quorum, the way his very presence drains anxiety from the room.

"Sean and I beat the fuck out of each other the other day," says a manic fighter named Brandon, "Was that not the funnest sparring session ever?"

"It was like back when we used to throw down," says Sean, "Throw. Down."

"Everyone used to throw up afterward," someone says wistfully.

"I would throw up and lay down," says Sean, "and someone would be like, 'Pat, Sean's laying down!,' and I'd have to get up again."

From the pool table we hear the crack of colliding balls chased by a string of profanities.

"When you fighting next?" asks Brandon, and Sean touches the place where his brow stitches once were, and says, with no little exasperation, "When someone offers me a fight."

June came and still we did not have one. I grew frustrated, longed for some fastidious fighting bureaucracy to oversee the entire regime, a jiu-jitsu dictatorship that would set Sean on his path with incremental pay raises and perhaps a pension. But alas, each promotion is an isolated kingdom, and one waits upon some rogue matchmaker's decision for every caged encounter. Often the kingdom would crumble after a single event, its begetter having discovered that, despite all the twenties changing hands at the door, there are too many capaciously muscled people demanding payment to make the endeavor profitable. In this way one could acquire many meaningless "championship" belts for tournaments even the winner barely recalled. Perhaps at the Big Shows you might be offered a three-fight contract, but these were not the Big Shows. The fights on which we waited were local affairs of questionable legality, which enshrouded them, to my mind, in a kind of liminal grace.

Weekdays Sean and I coexisted deep in a weather-worn house, beyond someone else's living room and kitchen, down a flight of stairs, past a washing machine, through an army-issue blanket tacked to wood paneling and skimming a fissured concrete floor, in the corner where Sean slept—the last, tiniest, most impregnable Russian doll. I liked to sit on the mattress next to some dirty laundry, stare through the single frosted window, and enjoy the deep calm that springs from a certain obliviousness to that which is most at hand.

You will ask questions. They are the wrong questions, the unfighterly questions, but I asked them myself, so I might as well give you the answers. How did Sean survive, for instance, without fight checks with which to pay rent? I asked Sean about this once, early on, and he looked at me and shrugged, as if I'd asked him why the sun was just then setting over the river. "Someone," he said, "will always have a ditch for you to dig." I never did see him dig a ditch, but there were days we spent loading tiny boxes of snack cakes onto a truck, and days he disappeared into a short-lived construction gig. Sometimes he bounced at a Davenport bar, but this was a fraught enterprise for any fighter, given that a certain kind of man made brave by drink will want to test his skills against the cauliflower-eared man standing sentry. Sean, for his part, had absolutely no desire to challenge a man outside of the cage; he was even less likely than myself, I believe—taking into account that in the third grade I pushed one Sally Mills off a swing in St. Paul—to provoke hostilities.

This was the summer when I learned both whom to follow and whom to avoid, the latter being almost exclusively the province of those men known as "shadows," for there is nothing more irritating to the devoted fighter than the nonfighters who so desperately wish to be among them. They wear the expensive branded fight-wear fighters cannot rightly afford, inform the proximate womenfolk of their supposed fighter status, and harangue actual fighters with suspect stories of their warrior instincts. So on a Saturday night Sean will be bouncing at that Davenport bar, standing by the door, quiet. And someone will notice Sean's gnarled ears, because Sean's gnarled ears attract *soi-disant* "fighters" as the bulbous red jowls of a prairie chicken attract other prairie chickens. And Sean will try to look away, turn toward the door, play with his stamp. But eventually someone will spot him through the dim bar light, and the shadow will say, "You fight?"

And Sean will say, "Yeah," still avoiding eye contact but already knee-deep in the quicksand of this man's need.

"Miletich?"

"Yep."

"Yeah," the shadow will say, "I used to train there. Before I started working for Monte," Monte being a cigar-smoking, smoking-jacketed promoter named Monte Cox, the ostentatious use of first names being a signal of inclusion meant to impress Sean, who is not impressed, but will now capitulate to the social pressure to make eye contact and reconcile himself to hearing the story of this man's One Big Fight.

"I trained nine years in Jeet Kune Do," the man will say, and Sean will pretend to look at an ID and gently stamp the manicured hand of an attractive woman, who will turn her body to sidle past, and the man, sensing Sean's impatience, will barrel toward the inevitable downfall, the reason he never made it to the Big Shows or did make it but never got a second fight. Sometimes it's an injury and sometimes it's an injury followed by an addiction to Vicodin and sometimes it's neither. Often this conversation will end with a warning—*Never fall in love with a stripper from Anamosa*—and out of a sense of mountain-country politesse Sean will feel compelled to say, "Thank you."

Let this be their one defense: so much intrafighter conversation takes shadow-disdain as its subject that their absence might occasion unwanted silence. I cannot bear their nervous energy, the ugly way their want hangs out, their unfighterly readiness to slug a stranger. Which brings me to a day in July, when I was sitting at The Paddlewheel watching Sean eat a Reuben and he got, somehow, on the subject of Thanksgiving.

"This whole country is based on a scam, just white people coming and taking things," Sean said with minimal inflection, as if explaining the inner workings of an engine. "The Indians said, 'Well OK, this is how you eat, this is how you survive,' and white people said 'Yeah, great,' and wiped them out. When you're a kid everything is so clean and simple because you don't yet understand the bullshit involved in absolutely everything."

"Look away," I said as a known shadow waltzed toward us, his toddler daughter beside him.

Sean, while no fan of shadows, was unfailingly polite, and found a good deal of amusement in my horror of them.

"Hey Mike," he said, welcoming the shadow into our space, "I have to go to the bathroom. Talk to her."

Sean got up, winked at me, and turned to the back of the bar.

"If you're into fighters," the shadow said, "I could probably hook you up with some people." I shuddered. But presently, to my relief, his young daughter began screaming across the room, and he rolled his eyes and went to her.

"Have you ever seen *1000 Ways to Die*?" Sean asked me when he returned. "There is this one episode where a woman swallowed a live fish and asphyxiated."

His phone began to buzz. He ignored it.

"Who's that?" I asked.

"Just some guy who wants to talk about St. Louis."

"St. Louis?"

"Yeah, for my fight in August."

He sipped his Coke, looked at the shadow's still-screaming little girl, now clinging to the shooting game with her head flung back in the thrall of her child-screams.

"You have a fight in August in St. Louis?"

"Oh yeah," he said, glancing at me, finishing off some fries, "Forgot to tell you I guess."

I watch and I write. My reasoning is this: If it is our job to diminish, what little we can, the space that remains between the fighter and the universe, is it not also our job to diminish the endless length of time that remains between a fighter's prime and eternity? Although I believe that a successful fighting spectacle exists in a space inaccessible to any written text—indeed, that any such spectacle is unalterably diminished by expression—so too I believe that nothing can extend the fight's temporal existence, however feebly, but a faithfully observed written record. And as I began to amass an account of each slow strike, I realized that I must also write of the world that strike would disrupt. So does one impossible task beget another, and another, until I'd produced an object even smaller than myself against an infinite expanse no man could hope to fill.

Sean – August 2010

SEAN WAS OFTEN SILENT, BUT IT WAS a particular form of silence not like other silences I had known, because it was complete, subtextless, with no electric buzzing underneath the breathing. The fact that he never asked me about myself signaled not a lack of interest but an excess of delicacy, and it was by no means in his nature to look beyond the present moment, backward toward our origins or forward to our plans. In this way we had become quite intimate without knowing the details of one another's lives. Three months into our partnership he still did not know, for instance, that both of my parents had expired before their thirtieth birthdays. And though I knew his wife had left him, I did not know her name. In St. Louis we would be removed from the site of his domestic woes, and it was my intention to come to know the other Sean, the Sean who trained and fought and won.

Sean's early victories had come to him in a pure form no longer available to the aspirant fighter or ecstasy-seeking scholar. Five, six years before my arrival, you'd waltz into a strip club, walk up to the DJ, put your name and weight on a list. "OK," a man would say, someone nominally in charge, "we'll find you someone round about your weight class," but you wouldn't expect anything like parity, because there were never enough volunteers. On the list would be lithe high school wrestlers and middle-aged tough-guy drunks and men who thought fighting their one true calling. The Amsterdam Gentlemen's Club had a cage. Admission was fifteen dollars; your compensation, as a fighter, was that you got in free. From their fold-up chairs fans leaned forward and blew cigarette smoke through the fence, behind which men fought in jeans in between beers. When the man in charge ran out of fighters he'd ask the fighters to fight again, and Sean always said yes. He never lost an amateur fight, not once. Thirty times he fought this way.

When I imagine those old fights, it's as if the Iowans were trying to reclaim some lost rites no one bothered to pass down. Because of course it's much harder to find an ecstatic spectacle in the otherwise dull and limited present than in the great sweep of historical time. If you were a fourteenth-century Latvian looking to leave yourself, you might mask up and dance through the streets reveling in Rabelaisian wonder, until the Catholic Church stopped you; were you a nineteenth-century Paiute Indian in the American West, you might try your hand at ritual millenarian dance, until the army stopped you; or an ancient maenad, join the other womenfolk in ripping apart a live goat in the Greek countryside, until exhaustion stopped you. It was the Iowa state legislature that laid waste to this particular spectacle, and so by the time our story starts all that I just described, from the sign-up list

down to the smoking, had been decreed illegal by some undereducated legislators in Des Moines. They replaced the glorious
spontaneity of old with prefight paperwork: insurance, licenses,
blood tests. Not that I'm complaining, because these paper-push-
ers only gave credence to my conviction that I'd found the true
center of ecstatic activity. It would just take a little more work to
get there.

Miletich only took you on if he thought you could be the
best in the world, and for a long while, Sean looked that way.
In 2006 his record of combined amateur and professional fights
was 37-and-1, the record of a man destined for the Big Shows.
Were I a narrator given to believe that great events stem from
a single cause; were I a narrator who relied on epiphanical plot
points; why, I might write: *And then Sean met his wife.* But I am
not that narrator. I will merely point out that four years from that
happy time, a number of less-talented Miletich protégés from
Sean's cohort were fighting before packed audiences in Vegas, had
opened gyms named after themselves, paid off mortgages by auc-
tioning off advertising space on their shorts. Sean was still fighting at promotions that staged their events in high school gyms.
He was living, alone, in a cracked concrete hole, the basement of
a friend on welfare. Between 2006 and 2010 he had lost fourteen
fights, as many as he had won in as much time. I met Sean in the
midst of a divorce-induced depression.

So I suppose you could say I came late to the fair, but that's
not how I see it. If I had missed Sean at 155 pounds and undefeated; if I had missed Davenport in the days of purest violence;
if I only saw the fearsome Pat Miletich in his gentle dotage; well,

does not every human story open midscene? It only made the chase a bit more of a challenge. Perhaps I had missed the peak of spectacle-based glory, but I had come at just the moment when Sean was ready to start climbing his way back up, and wouldn't a Kit who had come and left a decade earlier have envied the chance to see *that*?

St. Louis would be, in a sense, a glorious concordance for the both of us. Sean needed a new start, a postdivorce victory on which to rebuild his record and begin his inevitable ascent to the Big Shows. And for all the fights Sean had lost, for all the time he had wasted, I had frittered away at least as many life-years on bloodless scholastic exercises. It had taken me far too long to find a proper object of study. I hoped terribly that Sean was the man to bring me inside the world of ecstatic experience, that we might both finally be on the way to the truths we were seeking.

On the appointed day, I left my quaint little university town, drove the sixty miles of swaying cornfields to industrial Davenport, and showed up, as usual, at his doorstep. I then removed three Matchbox cars and a broken plastic Ferris wheel from the landlord's couch and patiently waited as Sean readied himself in the basement. I had of course constructed a phenom-enological theory about my odd reaction to the violent encoun-ter in Des Moines, and a predictive one relating to St. Louis, but I still knew next to nothing about what lay ahead.

"Looks like this promoter has serious money," said Sean as we turned onto the highway, toward St. Louis.

"What's his name?" I asked.

"Not sure."

"What's the promotion again?"

He thought for a while.

"Something 'MMA.'"

The news that the nameless St. Louis promoter was the kind with resources was something of a comfort, because over the summer I had listened as Sean and his friends told stories of the kind who did not. There was, for instance, the promoter who left Sean waiting hours for cash after a fight, who was preferable to the one who handed out checks not worth the trip to the bank to watch them bounce. There was the promoter who disappeared after the final bout, leaving fifteen befuddled fighters staring blankly at one another while janitors placed folding chairs on rolling carts. There was the promoter who appeared with the cash box only to fake a heart attack and be ferried away in an ambulance carrying said cash box; this had happened to Sean's friend Jason, and I took the tale to be emblematic of the degenerate promoter class.

"Where are we going, exactly?" I asked as we crossed the Missouri River and, like slow clock-gongs from some faraway town, steel plates clicked under our tires.

"Dunno," Sean said, "Brian wants us to call him when we get to St. Louis."

"Who is Brian?"

"Just a guy."

And yet there were dark possibilities money did nothing to dispel. He might, for instance, be the kind of promoter who would switch Sean's opponent at the last minute, leaving him to face a 200-pound Hispanic man who goes by the moniker "Mexicutioner," or the kind of promoter who forgets to obtain the requisite permits and is shut down by the state, or the kind to store us in a whore-and-flea-ridden crackhouse as an economical alternative to a hotel. This last misfortune had befallen a local fighter named John, as well as John's long-suffering wife Lisa, and I, for one, was afraid. But I also was conscious that to be small and openly worried was the opposite of helpful, and so I merely breathed deeply, as a therapist of Korean descent had once told me to do in such situations, and refrained from asking the obvious questions. Our immense ignorance about what lay ahead over the next forty-eight hours might just as well lead to a succession of delightful surprises, I reasoned, and thus to worry was to betray an unprofessional propensity for negative thinking.

Of course the sources of my worry extended beyond the subject of lodging. Day and night I thought of that head-clearing expansive feeling first made known to me in Des Moines. Whatever had happened in April to rid me of myself for a few brief moments—take me away from that insistent corporeal yawp ("Eat this! Sleep now!")—might never happen again, though I had passed my summer spacetaking on a bet that it would. My hope was that not only would I be subject to such ecstatic lightness in St. Louis, but that this time I would be prepared, would be studying the elements involved and watching as they fell into alignment. I wanted to capture it, subject it to close observation. I had taken to carrying a notebook in my bag, and jotting down anything that seemed relevant.

"Hungry?" asked Sean somewhere in Illinois. On the five-hour drive we stopped at both McDonald's and Hardee's. "I like *life*," Sean said, in response to an accusation I did not make.

I told him that I'd read some fighters cut weight and for weeks at a time restrict themselves to 500 calories per day, the equivalent perhaps of the Santa Fe sauce on Sean's Thickburger, and Sean cocked his head and said that a real fighter should just be able to get in the octagon and knock around people his own size. Sean had a lot of opinions about real fighters, but he also kept saying that he needed to "drop thirty pounds."

"You said that months ago."

"And they've been terrible months."

"I wouldn't say *terrible*," I said, conscious that these were the very months Sean had spent largely in my presence.

"I don't believe in marriage anymore," he said a moment later, at which point I realized that we were talking about his just-finalized divorce. He told me a story about a woman he knew who slept with her wedding caterer while still in her gown and veil. "You stand in your white dress," he said, glancing at the rear-view mirror and changing lanes. "You stand in your white dress and pretend you're a virgin and make a commitment to a God you don't believe in. For what."

"For what" did not seem the mystery Sean implied, given that every landmark in Illinois, every pit stop in Missouri, prompted some memory of a road trip taken with his wife. They'd visited the contiguous forty-eight states, even the eerily empty Dakotas. He had made sandwiches and she had fed him pretzels one by one while he drove them over the Badlands.

"Wife," I wrote in my notebook. "Prefight self-pity."

"So," said Sean, one hand on the steering wheel and the other holding his Thickburger. "This book you're writing about me."

He said this with the air of someone who had caught on to a secret. At the time I had no intention of writing a book about anyone, but he seemed gratified by the idea, and it gave me pleasure to give him some. I said nothing.

"Some kind of girl book?"

"I don't think it will be a girl book," I said.

An hour later, we pulled up to a brick behemoth gone soot-covered around the edges, the kind of building raised long ago to manufacture something now forgotten, all boarded-up windows, walls of brick, postindustrial silence. Massive cylinders shot up into a late afternoon light too sharp for a prolonged stare. We milled around, hot and squinting, until Sean located an aperture, and together we climbed concrete steps that literally crumbled under our feet, sending bits of rock skipping down the lot. Therein was a darkness full and deep, and as I reminded myself that I was accompanied by a highly trained practitioner of the fighting arts, the dark resolved itself into a room dotted with slim bodies at work. Many yards beyond them, pinpricks of light beamed from the boarded-up windows. Someone pushed a great length of extension cord out from the reach of a standing camera.

"Huffman?" said a woman with an earpiece and a clipboard, and gestured toward a boxy steel freight elevator. "Over here."

Sean paused, looked around, stripped to his shorts, and proceeded to act as if this were an entirely normal experience for him.

"Stand against the brick, by those pipes."

A man poured a translucent substance onto Sean's back, rubbed him down top to bottom. He flicked on a spotlight, and every pore on Sean's oiled body popped into view.

"Posture up," said the photographer. The oil man pointed a spray bottle at Sean and squirted.

"Dance."

Squirt.

"Hop around."

Sean's hops were earnest but far from convincing.

"Try shadowboxing."

He swiveled his shoulders and his slight paunch followed a moment later. White flesh lapped over the elastic band in his shorts. A machine kicked on, spit fog.

"Look mean!"

The fog helped. As Sean posed, two adolescents emerged in jeans and T-shirts, and I realized with some dismay that I was in the presence of two ring girls. Over the past months I had read intensely on the subject of spectacle, thinking it relevant to my experience in Des Moines, and I had formed opinions about the proper way agents of spectacle ought to conduct themselves. These women, I thought, ought not let us see them shorn of their costumes so soon before the event itself. It occurred to me that they would both benefit from a brief explanation of Heideggerian *thrownness* (the "poignant sense of having been hurled into the world without preparation or consent," to the layman) and I considered walking over to their corner of the room. But I had also, in Sean's bathroom the previous week, plucked from the crown of my head what may or may not have been a first gray-brown hair glinting in the frosted light of the single window, and I did not wish to be in potentially unflattering proximity to a pair of nineteen-year-olds.

"You're done," said the woman with the earpiece. She motioned toward a spiral staircase half-hidden by the dark, sending us upstairs for "the video component." And it was upstairs that I first met Josh Neer, who Sean said was the fight's biggest draw, tracing his finger along the curving edge of an abdominal muscle. Josh Neer was a hard-bodied fighter everyone seemed to know already, and destined to be an annoyance to me, because he was a startling counterpoint to my theory that fighters are an uncommonly intellectual breed. But Neer belonged in this circle of cameras, could have been winking as his open shirt flip-flapped in the wind. His face was board-flat with a high forehead and broad nose—a classic fighter face, run off the same mold in the fighter factory that also produced his spacetaker, Andy, who would pad after Neer to every stop in the promotional itinerary. Neer and Sean both had that stumpy neck fighters need, the one that keeps your head tight to your body instead of letting it stray willy-nilly like a windblown reed, but Neer got his unbreakable features from God. Nothing protrudes from that flat wall of a face—not a fine triangle of a cheekbone, not a slim beak of a nose. Two small eyes have tucked themselves safely under his brow. Whereas Sean. Sean's flatness comes not by God but by man. Sean is soft clay crudely pressed into shape, the curves of his nose pounded into the side of his face where it waits in a protective hunch.

"P. Diddy!" said Neer, and slapped Sean's hand. Sean didn't know why Neer called him P. Diddy, but nor did he feel compelled to question Josh Neer's judgment. "P. Diddy!" said Andy, and slapped Sean's hand. Darryl Cobb, Sean's opponent, was there too, and in the anxious silence his pectoral muscles announced themselves. He sighed and drummed the fingers of his right hand against his solidly percussive stomach. It was hard not to notice the·alarming circumference of Cobb's left bicep as he pressed it against his taut black torso, but Sean was at least pretending not to notice.

The video crew placed each fighter on a crate, against a backdrop of brick, in a space below a boom mike. I faced the video setup so as to avoid looking at a ring girl, who was leaning against a windowsill and, rather disturbingly, reading a book.

"What's going to happen Saturday night?" a fidgeting woman asked each fighter from a director's chair off-camera.

"First-round knockout," said Neer.

"First-round knockout," said Cobb.

"How do you train?" she asked Sean.

"Um," said Sean, "I should probably train a little harder."

"What?"

"Well, I'm a little heavy, you can see that. I should be fighting at one-fifty-five. I should eat better and train harder."

"OK. People don't usually say that."

"Yeah."

"Your opponent says he is going to knock you out."

Sean paused to look at the camera, eyebrows raised, and provided the audience with a long moment in which to register his skepticism. The woman in the director's chair was growing bored by the need to coax some trash-talk out of these men. Perhaps she too realized how futile this was, had sensed that fighting summons a kind of void to which words are wholly inadequate, a kind of precious prepsychological space, and that any fighter's attempt to translate the anonymous void of the octagon into words could not help but be an embarrassment for all involved.

"He isn't going to knock me out. I ain't never been knocked out and it's not going to start now."

I hadn't yet heard Sean use the word "ain't," but it felt apt in the given context.

"You guys want to run with us?" Neer asked Sean and Sean's friend Brian when the interviews were over. Neer's hands rested on his hips in a way that suggested his biceps were just too big to lay lifeless against his body.

Brian looked at Sean. "We're going to kick it B-team style," he said. Neer laughed. Andy laughed.

"Right. P. Diddy style. You're going to get a pizza."

This proved inaccurate; we did not get a pizza because Sean felt like sushi, which the three of us would find at a strip mall somewhere in a St. Louis satellite town. Before we left, Sean warned me not to bring up the subject of God; if I pointed us in this direction we'd be pulled along the entire arc of Brian's conversion narrative. Sean was tolerant of religion within certain bounds: "There's religion, and then there's being stupid" was his stated view on the matter, but he didn't want to have to nod politely all evening.

It was in the context of a fight that Brian and Sean first met, five years previous; minutes after they first laid eyes on one another, Brian laced both of his legs around Sean's neck and tucked his left toes under the back of his right knee in a triangle so tight Sean tapped. It seems to me that this kind of first meeting will lead to an intense intimacy that renders future relations uncomfortable, unless one of the participants is Sean, who is incapable of the kind of nervousness necessary to sustain an awkward moment.

We packed into a wooden booth and Brian tore the paper off his chopsticks with his teeth.

"This is my last fight before Bible college," said Brian. "I'm done with this."

"What's Bible college?" I asked. Sean tilted his head and looked at me in a way that suggested he did not want me to ask encouraging follow-up questions.

"Hold on," said Brian, "I have to tell my grandma I got here safely or she won't go to sleep."

Brian had gone on a mission trip to Nicaragua the previous summer, and while he was helping to repair a church he taught the local wrestling team some submissions. None of the kids spoke English, but you didn't need English to teach kids how to choke one another. "I had this kid in a Kimura," said Brian when he returned from conversing with his grandmother, "and it was so amazing, and I realized that this was God's plan for me. When I was a teenager I really strayed from God, from His plan for me, and that moment brought me back."

Brian was only twenty-four, in shape, quite well respected on the regional circuit, but he carried already the self-conception of a losing, injury-laden fighter. During almost every fight, he told us, his shoulder popped out of its socket like a drawer sent off its roller. He popped it back in himself.

"My shoulder hurts," said Brian as he put down the chopsticks and lifted a piece of tuna from the platter with his fingers.

"You guys, I don't even like sushi." He placed the tuna back onto the platter.

At thirty-two Sean was a much older fighter than Brian but in no sense as beaten down, as chiseled away. I knew by then all of his injuries and the way they had faded into memory. After being opened Sean's body assimilates the surgical screws and the scar tissue, and not until he presses his skin against the knurled bone underneath, like running his tongue against the pocked surface of an ice cube, does he remember quite where something split. His wounds don't call out to be remembered. Even his self-image adjusts; his nose has always been this crooked, his ears always this gnarled. This is perhaps why Brian has reconciled himself to the B-team, while Sean continues to talk about "a serious run" or "a serious go," pictures himself victorious at the Big Shows, and resists any job more long-term than bouncing Saturdays at a Bettendorf bar.

Sean would be fighting at 185, and arrived in St. Louis, like Brian, ten pounds over. They would be weighed-in twenty-four hours before the fight began so that they would have time to binge and rehydrate; starved, desiccated, brittle bodies are vulnerable to the kind of injuries for which no promoter wants to pay. It wasn't unusual to be so overweight the day before weigh-ins, Sean told me; Neer and Cobb probably had ten pounds of water to lose as well. The difference seemed to lie in the fact that the following morning, six hours before weigh-ins, Neer was running laps around the hotel, while Brian and Sean were in a hotel room inhaling marijuana smoke through a hole punched in a Mountain Dew can.

Sean's room was adjacent to Neer's, and their two balconies were separated by a wooden divider.

"Whose shorts are these?" Sean asked.

"They're Neer's," laughed Brian. "I took them off his balcony, he's going to get so mad."

"You took Neer's shorts and put them on *my* balcony? Holy shit Brian, what the fuck."

Sean clasped the corners of Neer's shorts between two fingers of each hand, and placed them, with extreme primness, on Neer's side of the divider. He twice patted a wrinkle, smoothed them out with both palms, and returned to his bong.

"You know what I'd love to do," he said after a slow smoky exhale, "but I just have no idea how to get into it? I would love to be a mercenary. You travel all around, do whatever the fuck you want. I would totally do that."

Brian scratched his knee. Light from the window fell in a thick stripe across the unmade bed.

As the afternoon wore on, and Brian and Sean gossiped about fighters, napped, smoked, and finally did some laps around the parking lot, the promoters were at work below them, transforming a hotel conference room into a stage set for the ceremonial weigh-ins they would broadcast over the Internet. I left Brian and Sean as they headed toward the real weigh-ins, to which I was not allowed—whereby the state of Missouri would determine each fighter's relationship to Earth's mass, check off some official-looking pieces of paper, and send them along—and descended to the lobby for the Potemkin weigh-ins, which would be filmed afterward.

By now several aspects of the "Fight Me MMA" situation had become clear. This promoter was quite obviously new, confused, under the impression that there was real money to be made in showcasing regional fighters to local audiences. He had hired a staff of maybe twenty people, all of whom wore their earpieces with an unnecessary ostentation, and insisted with the imperfectly arched brows of lesser tyrants that everyone badge-flash at each impromptu checkpoint. He was paying the fighters more than the going rate, paying for all the videos, paying for ring girls with uncommonly good dye jobs, paying perhaps for their matching knee-high black patent-leather boots. And he was, in the flesh, a disgrace. What I saw in Kenny Nowling, the moment he stepped into my field of vision, what I saw through his excess of exposed chest hair, his three gold chains, his product-hardened coiffure, was nothing less, and nothing more, than a shadow.

"Where's Jessica?" he asked, panic elevating his voice to a feminine pitch. "Tell Jessica I need her. Where's the Athletic Commissioner? Get me a water. No, Josh, stand there. Yes, that's great, you'll walk out last."

"The buffet is late!" Kenny shouted at no one in particular. His brother Michael, in a Rolex, alligator-skin shoes, dark glasses, and the only suit in the room, stood beside him. These were not men to inspire confidence in the making of a spectacle. They were, it turned out, a couple of Midwestern drag-racing tycoons, men who had succeeded in one domain and thought to conquer an additional realm they neither deserved nor understood. Up until this moment I had thought myself perfectly open to whatever St. Louis might deliver, but I had all along been hoping for a spare simulacrum of those early fights in Davenport strip clubs—a simple unscripted encounter unsullied by tycoons of any kind, not to mention a "video component" and stage direction.

Some sort of minor show was already organizing itself. The ring girls were in character now, posing on a dais beside a fighter. Most of the other fighters were lined up against the wall, waiting their turn for a ceremonial weight-check. The show had started, the cameras were on, here was the ersatz thing itself. Kenny thanked a long list of people, culminating in his fiancée, Jessica, and his brother, the aforementioned Michael, at which point he started to cry real, actual tears, there beside the previously positioned bare-torsoed ring girls and a single stacked fighter and the forty or so people who had come to watch, some of whom seemed to be curious hotel guests wondering why the Sheraton was full of shirtless men.

"Couldn't have done it without you," Kenny said to his brother. "Come up here."

His brother walked the two steps from his seat to the makeshift stage. A slight air of hysteria wrinkled its way through the crowd. The promoter was crying and his brother was waving and the ring girl was smiling and the fighter was flexing and everyone was stalling, because one of the twenty-four fighters was late for the photo-op. The fighter was Sean.

"Who's missing?" asked one assistant to another.

"The Miletich fighter" was the response, delivered, I might add, with a raised eyebrow, a touch of schadenfreude, a whiff of affected wistfulness for the days in which no Miletich fighter would have delayed this absurd to-do. Implicit in those three words was the entire invented history of Davenport, all the stories told in all the bars of one man's heroic defense of himself. This was not a mold Sean necessarily fit. ("I love fighting but I also love *sleeping*," Sean had said earlier that day.) Perhaps the legend was already dead. In this crowd, mention of Miletich seemed to lead to either a foggy "Is he still alive?" look, or to the conversation Sean and Brian were having on the way back from the sauna to the conference room, where Sean would finally stand before the camera and reveal himself to be an acceptably trim 185.5.

"Robbie Lawler too? All those guys are gone?" asked Brian.

"Yeah," said Sean.

"*Wow.* I can't believe that's all the Miletich guys you can name. Is anyone still there?"

"Me."

•

My theory about octagons is this: There is really only one octagon, and that one flickers in and out of existence over space and time, such that the very same octagon is summoned to consciousness over and over again. The fighters all know they have something to summon; why else the little bow at the cage door, the solemn straight-faced walk-out, the open-mouthed prayer as their brows are Vaseline-slathered. "Enter the octagon," says the announcer, and suddenly it's there. Except when it isn't, for the theory also accounts for the fights that failed: the octagon neglects to show up. These are the fights we all leave disappointed, depressed, feeling vaguely dirty for having witnessed whatever we had just witnessed. The cruelty without the "theater of." We know these fights by the way they fail to bring us outside of ourselves; rather, they drive us deeper in, make us quiet and sick and wondering whether our past ecstasies have been mere illusion.

And though I would not have put it this way at the time, what I very much wanted to know in St. Louis was which were the elements that brought forth the octagon, and which that kept it away, and how one kept the elements in sync such that the integrity of the spectacle might be best protected. I would have liked a spreadsheet or a bulleted memo to this effect.

I bopped along to the music Kenny Nowling was blasting as he forced us to stand in the August heat. I believe it was some kind of rap. In addition to his musical selections Kenny wished us to admire the full-size bus he'd slapped with the logo "Fight Me MMA," before which he stood as he addressed the fighters in the parking lot beside the arena, a few hours before the fight.

"We want you to come back and fight for us," he said, smiling, oleaginous in the summer sun. The fighters were confused by all the ceremony; perhaps they were being buttered up for some cruel letdown, something about the lack of funds to pay them. Instead we were led to a locker room with a television that took up half the wall, the screen filled with the still-empty octagon, and a dozen lockers labeled with the fighters' names. The lockers, upon further inspection, each contained bags bursting with swag. Their names were sewn into the sides.

For a moment the only sound to be heard in the locker room was that of zippers unzipping. Hands breaking into packages: an iPod, a mousepad, a pen, T-shirts, cologne.

"Fight for you?" Sean said, tearing plastic from the iPod, "I will *hook* for you."

"I can use this pen for Bible college!" Brian said.

We were meant to stay in the room afterward, listening to the referee recite the rules. The fight would end when a man tapped the canvas in defeat, or the referee decided that one of the fighters was not adequately defending himself (whether out of exhaustion or because he had lost consciousness), or the doctor Kenny Nowling was legally obliged to employ felt an injury particularly grievous, or, alternately, the three five-minute rounds ran their course, at which point a panel of three judges would consult their notes and determine a winner. There was to be no "small joint manipulation," which meant that one could not bend an opponent's finger backward until he tapped, no eye-poking, groin-kicking, head-butting, skin-pinching, or hair-pulling. There was to be no "fish-hooking," or sticking one's finger in the other man's mouth. Nor, as the rules have evolved thus far, is it permissible to strike a man in the back of the head, the spine, the throat. It is illegal to knee him in the head while he is on the ground. This last prohibition is controversial, and it is often noted that such a knee would be perfectly permissible in Japan.

We were *meant* to stay in the room and listen to a recitation of the rules, but Sean is not a man in the thrall of authority. It was six o'clock, well before any ticketholders had arrived. On the ground someone had pasted sets of blue footprints leading we knew not where. Wordlessly Sean and I followed them past the other locker room, a snack stand, a "Fight Me MMA" T-shirt kiosk, and through some double doors, where we stopped and craned our necks in unison. Terraced walls sloped up on all sides, 10,000 seats planted in them. Four prodigious flatscreen TVs—these, I surmised, for the "video component"—faced each side of the arena. The octagon waited, inert. From its far side a fireball shot into the air.

"What the hell was that?" Sean asked.

The twin fire-coughing propane tanks the promoters had apparently procured were attached to an elevated ramp, on which fighters would make their entrances. There would be revolving laser lights. There would be dry ice. I felt offended by the lack of delicacy. Sean, whether out of nervousness or disgust, fell silent and walked back to the locker room. I took a seat by the cage and stayed as the arena swelled with fans, until each terraced wall was half-stippled with faces, until all the earpieced assistants materialized, clipboards in hand, until the ring girls assumed their cross-legged pose. There are those who feel smaller in a crowd, but I felt part of an intuitive elect, each of us driven here by the impulse to gather and be given access to something I could not name.

The lights went out, and the screens flipped on; it was time to see what had become of the video. What first came across were just pictures—crisp images of men against brick, all the clean visual work you'd expect, montages of men lifting iron things. Someone was beating a tire with a sledgehammer, and then someone was punching a bag, and then someone was just standing in front of some wooden beams. It wasn't until the sound kicked on that I woke up and began to wonder whether I had misjudged the entire enterprise. A fighter stared at the camera. Hideous noises poured from his open mouth, and from the mouth of the next fighter, and the next. The audio system was broken, distorted beyond all recognition. Thousands around me put their hands over their ears, closed their eyes. The sounds were complex variations on a long low moan, so loud as to be physically painful, the soundtrack of a bloody war waged underwater. I left myself open, put my hands at my sides, parted my own lips. Each time a man moved his face, this low prehuman music blasted out, a cry just outside the decipherable. Oh, auspicious malfunction! For five long seconds Kenny Nowling, who was standing between me and the cage, stood shocked in terror-stricken stillness. This moment had not been in the script. Then, lifting his arms over his head, he crossed and uncrossed them, until someone somewhere sucked the voices from the men so nothing at all issued from their lips, which went on parting and meeting and parting again.

Now everything seems to click, as if the final element has been righted such that a waiting spectacle might spring forth. Now the face of the announcer is beaded with sweat, the light beams spin in tandem, the beer carts creak with melancholy. The one element that does not shift, that seems incapable of shifting, is Sean, who walks out, when summoned, looking exactly as I had left him. He strolls slowly toward the octagon, eyes downcast, as if taking a solitary walk on a spring day.

The fighters of St. Louis, we are soon to discover, eschew the elegant minimalism of their Des Moines counterparts for some over-costumed vaudevillian mime. In a moment Darryl Cobb will walk out—"*The Devastation Darryl Cobb*"—wearing a construction vest and a camouflage balaclava, will pause at times on the ramp with his hands on his hips, as if modeling said vest on a runway, will bring men to their feet. In Sean's case the ramp merely seems like a long way to get to the cage, and his utter lack of affect renders everything else bizarre, like a dancer stopping midperformance to have a smoke as the rest of the company swirls by. The propane tanks do not start shooting flames until he is halfway down the ramp. Sean strolls along, looking down, and does not appear to notice the balls of fire rising in his wake.

"It is very evident," an announcer will say during the commentary added to the fight when it airs, weeks later, on local television, "that Darryl Cobb, you can see there, is a much more fit fighter than his opponent."

Cobb stands two inches taller than Sean, hairless and hard. Deep creases line his upper body, articulate shoulder from biceps, ripple across his abdomen. Musky light bounces off his head. The ring girl rises from her seat, all teeth and confidence.

Sean's arms, which I have heard him describe as "T. rex arms," are so short they do not seem to serve the same animal purpose as those of Cobb, which are uncommonly long; Cobb's biceps rise almost comically from the small of the elbow. He seems to slide through a different substance than Sean, every tap quicker, arms extending from and snapping back to his compact torso like the searching tongue of a fly-hungry frog. He jabs Sean, kicks him, jumps into and out of Sean's reach in a single hop. And yet it is Cobb pressed against the fence, crowded by Sean, who glides toward Cobb even as he eats shot after shot. Sean moves like a fat man on hot coals, never still for a moment but each step fractions of an inch off the ground. Cobb jabs. Sean's back is to me and he vibrates hard twice in time with the glorious unfurling of Cobb's arms. They dance in my direction; Sean has gone red in the soft skin under both eyes. When Cobb leans into one leg and shoots the other across Sean's white calf I hear the knock of bone against bone and feel the crowd hear it behind my back, the small parts of 3000 ears vibrating in tune. Brian pours water into Sean's mouth and kneels close to whisper his counsel. Now there is a third slash on Sean's face, this one on the nose, a red so deep across the bridge it's almost black.

When the ring girl is through her second cycle, Cobb tries the same side kick. Sean catches Cobb's ankle in his hand, and for a long moment holds him still and tilting on one leg, before yanking it hard and sending Cobb flat on the mat. Sean pounces, and now they are both on the ground facing one another, Cobb struggling from the bottom. Sean spreads his whole self prone atop Cobb's flat body, shoving his bloody eye into the other man's chest. Both men are soaked in sweat; as Sean holds Cobb down they slide this way and that, two jellyfish jockeying, and then all at once two black legs and one arm emerge from the bottom to spider around Sean's back, and it seems that Sean, still on top, is a piece of meat inside a hawk's spindly talon. Cobb twirls out, all length and grace, and Sean stumbles to his feet. I have forgotten myself entirely; if any mortal part of mine is calling out for attention, I cannot hear it.

The men, standing now, pause for a breath. Cobb throws that same kick, and this time Sean absorbs the blow while slamming his right fist into Cobb's cheek.

Cobb backs up. He turns his head side to side theatrically, as if to shake off the punch. He smiles wide.

"You've got a nice right," Cobb says.

"You've got a nice left," Sean says.

"I think a lot of people," says the TV color man, careful to steer clear of self-incrimination, "would not have expected Huffman to last this long."

Both men are smiling now, their eyes wide as they lunge into one another. Cobb's arms swing right up the middle, one-two, jabs that would take another man out; Sean's face trembles slightly and he hops out of the way, swinging with great loping hooks from either side. He seems not to register kicks to his thigh, stomach, calves; Cobb grimaces more as he throws a punch than Sean does as he receives one. Sean was bleeding from the brow a moment ago, but the bleeding has stopped altogether, as if the seams on Sean's body were something you could rip only temporarily before the flickering surface of his skin fuses back into a single unbroken sheath.

It isn't until the third round that Sean's skin begins finally to tear. First it's a stream from one eye and then the next; the blood dribbles onto his chest, draws itself into a strange webbing along the front of his torso. When Cobb knuckle-digs the deep cut along the bridge of Sean's nose blood falls thicker, in dark waves. Sean is still absorbing blow after blow, barely quivering at Cobb's hardest, straightest jabs, but it is as if his skin is conceding where he will not; Cobb is still hard and unbroken while Sean leaks onto both of them, still smiling, still in the center of Cobb's range. My thoughts slide by with the same whistling clarity of that night in Des Moines, but this time I feel pulled toward Sean with the painful, pathetic gratitude of a person who knows herself to be incurring a debt she'll never discharge.

Sean huffs hard as the bell rings, as the judges judge, as Cobb's arm is raised in predictable triumph. Cobb looks mildly pleased in victory. Sean is perfectly delighted in defeat. He walks out into the crowd, smiling hugely. "Feels good!" he says to no one. "A fuckin' war!" In the locker room the other fighters fist-bump, slap his ass, lay large hands on his sweaty shoulders. "I got more gas at 170!" he laughs. They all congratulate him at once, their voices lost in the sweep of praise, the words "warrior" and "monster" floating up through the sweaty mob. Sean hops into the shower and sings loud happy syllables that bounce off the walls. "Where's the doctor?" he asks Brian as he towels off. Later there will be needles, anesthetic, thread, but the doctors are nowhere to be found at the moment, and Sean is too adrenaline-drunk to feel anything; he slips back into the crowd to catch some fights, but so eager are people for a piece of Sean that he doesn't get to watch a single one from the floor. A boy of maybe twelve walks up to him and asks for his autograph, and, having revealed Sean as generally amenable, unleashes a stream of kids with pens at the ready. A stout blonde pretends to have a question for him, kisses him on the cheek, and runs away in heels that click on the sticky arena floor. When I turn from the fights to Sean, I realize that I am standing in a line of people waiting for an audience. A man in a suit waits behind me, and as I step out of the way puts his arm on Sean's shoulder. "I would like to invite you," he says, "up to our skybox."

As Sean jogs up a flight of arena stairs, I stay close so everyone knows I am of his party. A Hispanic woman in high heels blocks our passage; she holds up a camera, raises her eyebrows, and smiles shyly. Her husband snaps the picture.

"Thank you!" she gushes. "Oh, thank you!"

People crowd around Sean, shoulder up against one another to better hear his chatter. As a man places a Bud Light in his hand, Sean is as garrulous as I have ever seen him. He is telling them about Miletich, about his game plan, about his time in the Navy. He is telling them about his plans, about his comeback, about how he is going to make a go of it this time for real, about how he really is going to get into shape. I can see our future clearly now, a trimmer Sean, bigger fights, the two of us thrown together into an exalted dissolution each time he elects to take us there.

From the skybox we have a perfect view of Josh Neer pounding his fist into the face of his opponent. The shock of Cobb's beating has only just begun to register on the soft surface of Sean's face, which is bubbling up in odd places. As he talks a purple egg swallows more and more of his forehead. The skin under his eyes has gone bulbous and yellow. Dried blood in the moon above his right eye has clotted to black. His left ear is deformed as ever, the top half shiny and round as an eyeball. "Hey," Sean says, taking notice of me for the first time since the fight, "did I tell you that I'm going to be a dad?"

Erik – Summer 2010

GRANTED IT IS NEVER LOOKED WELL UPON for a spacetaker to take on more than one fighter, and for months I resisted doing so. But every time I told myself that Sean deserved my undivided devotion, I had some dark vision of his potential demise: an illness of the sort that felled my parents, a brain injury in the octagon, a drawn gun at the bar where he bounced. And where would I be without Sean? In my home, near the university, I mostly studied the lives of great fighters and waited for him to call.

"We are united," I had written in a long email to the Department of Philosophy Listserv, "by an interest in the nature and structure of experience. I have recently had reason to reconsider everything I know about what it means to make contact with the noumenal realm. Great experiments in consciousness are being regularly conducted in our region."

Though the email ended with a generous invitation to join me at Sean's next fight, the only response was from the program secretary, asking that I restrict my use of the listserv to information about student housing. And yet so bored and lonely was I, on a night when Sean was bouncing, that I made an appearance at one last postlecture cocktail party. "Do you think," said a portly, well-liked Floridian epistemologist unable to disguise her obvious disgust behind a show of academic inquiry, "that you have become desensitized to violence?"

It wasn't meant, of course, as a question. With that I abandoned them, and on the walk home, as I passed by the New Pioneer Food Co-op, was struck with that particularly frustrating case of *l'esprit de l'escalier* to which only those of us capable of pulling long quotes from memory are subject. It was Nietzsche who said that a certain type of ghostly, corpselike wretch turns away from Dionysian revelry in a spirit of "healthy-mindedness." I would write my fighterly thesis, but I would not fraternize with the healthy-minded; better to leave them to their prenatal yoga, their gluten-free diets, their dull if long lives of quietest self-preserving conformism. Without Sean I would be completely outside the fighterly ecosystem, a spectator once again, no more privileged than any curious passerby. Alone.

I had heard tell of Erik Koch long before we met, in that tossed-off way local fighters refer to men with whom they crave proximity. ("Oh yeah, I trained with New Breed a while back," an associate of Sean's said, using Erik's nickname to further insinuate a familiarity I was sure he did not have. Note too the lack of temporal specificity typical of garden-variety dissemblers.) Three times he had competed in the Big Shows, and twice he had won, though he was only twenty-two, a decade from his prime fighterly years. I knew he'd be besieged by spacetaking applicants, men whose capacity to take space greatly outstripped mine, and so for months I kept my distance, only, say, showing up at fights I thought he might attend, or driving the thirty miles to the decrepit corner of Cedar Rapids where lay his gym. I never caught so much as a glimpse. Then a kind soul pointed out New Breed's roommate, and I followed the roommate home. Should there be any amateur spacetakers among you, might I hazard a suggestion? Timid permission-askers are doomed to fail at a profession that requires a silently assured shoring up. Here is what I did: I knocked.

"Hi," said Erik, and realizing that he expected an explanation if not a pizza, I presented myself as a student writing a paper on great fighters of the present century, having once heard of a thirteen-year-old gaining access to a reticent John Lennon in precisely this way. Moments later we were leaning back in two adjacent arm-chairs, lacking only pipes to puff on. I swiftly abandoned the student ruse, which was fine with Erik, who mostly wanted me to admire pictures of past meals on his phone. There was a roast beef sandwich, big as a baby, glistening with grease. There was video of an entire three-foot hoagie being consumed in one sitting. "I went to Panchero's after this fight," he said, leaning forward in the chair, walking around, plugging in his phone, sitting back in the chair, "and I got a burrito four times the normal size. It's four tortillas, equal to four burritos. I ate it in eight minutes and I wasn't full. I was not full. There is a video of me eating it."

He got up again to unplug his phone, which he did with the utmost grace. Erik was tall for a fighter, white, hairless, clean. I leaned forward as he held the tiny screen to face my armchair. The burrito was very big. "The biggest thing I always crave—I'm a big bread fanatic—bagels. I'll go to Whole Foods—do you know Whole Foods Market?—oh my god, I love it. I go there and get this really good deli meat. They give you five-hundred bucks for food so like I'm not using my own money, I'm gonna get the best, top-of-the-line, right? So I get some good wheat bagels."

Because I did not yet know Erik well and did not understand that I had saved him from a rare and frightening moment of solitude, I interpreted his monologue as a generous affirmation of my new role as spacetaker. At this juncture I tried to make an exit, fearful that I was overstaying my welcome, but Erik simply kept talking, pacing, and rubbing his thumb along the face of his phone to flick through food-related pictures. He did not want me to leave. It went on like this for an hour, me and him and the pictures and the Cedar River rushing past ten stories down.

How *new* he was. In Sean I had an unbreakable, unflappable veteran, rock-hard and lumbering; here was a slippery-fast blossoming prodigy. Not a shorn tendon in his sprightly form. Nose straight, undereyes unlined, skin taut and unbruised. He was a decade younger than Sean in civilian years but in fighter years that's far longer, because a fighter undergoes more wear in a year than you or I might in five. There was something beyond his youth; the fact, perhaps, that he did not look like a fighter, lacked the stumpy neck and high brow, lacked the thick trunk. He did not have a fighter's compactness; he extended rather more over the earth. And seeing this for the first time, I was struck with a thrilling fear at the thought of his fragility. What would happen,

I thought, if a rock-hard slobberknocker caught this feather-light hummingbird of a man? Perhaps nothing would happen; punch a feather and it goes on floating. Or perhaps he would collapse, bones cracked, the flicker gone.

A girl in jeans shorts and a bedazzled tank top arrived at the door.

"Your girlfriend?" I asked.

"No," he said. Then, "KayLee, get me a soda," which she did.

"To be honest," Erik said as KayLee fetched the soda, suddenly switching gears, "I believe I'm one of the best in the world. I look at José Aldo. I look at Urijah Faber. I can compete with any of them. I'm a big forty-fiver. You see these little guys on TV and the cage looks huge. The first time I got into the cage, I was really intimidated, and then I realized I could see over it! I was like, what the hell. Those guys are so small."

I speak of Erik with the utmost respect, and had at this time been attempting to intercept him for quite some time, which should give you an idea of the esteem in which I held him. But this talk of competing with the Brazilian José Aldo could only be taken as unmerited braggadocio—not that I disapprove of a certain fighterly swagger—for Erik was a novice unknown outside of Cedar Rapids, and José Aldo the best 145-pound fighter in this or any other universe, having already defended his belt once, and destined to defend it again and again and again. The very idea of someone who lived in Cedar Rapids fighting someone resident in Rio de Janeiro, the greatest fight city on earth, amused me. Though I suppose it must be admitted that Erik had two inches on José.

Erik asked no questions of me, not my name or address or astrological sign (Scorpio), and even if he had I would not have told him that over the previous months my longing for a fight-induced state of being—that expansive burst of clarity—had grown immoderately, such that one fighter no longer seemed enough. I merely listened, until Erik, shadowboxing, said, "Well, I'm moving to Milwaukee at the end of the week, so."

I struggled to remain calm. Having finally made Erik's acquaintance, having been welcomed into his home, I found a man preparing to move three hundred miles northeast, to the state that was my least favorite of the fifty and the one in which, not incidentally, I'd been born.

I must have looked stricken, though Erik, texting as he delivered the news, did not notice. And certainly it was odd for a fighter of any renown to be here in Cedar Rapids, a small gray unfighterly city most notable for a burning saccharine scent wafting off the Quaker Oats factory, a full eighty miles west of Davenport. It made much more sense for a fighter to leave home, first of all; and to leave home specifically for Milwaukee, where truly great fighters gathered to train at the royal camp of one Duke Roufus. Duke, a former kickboxing champion, had discovered Erik six months prior, anointed him, granted him access to the Big Shows and thereby the small screen; through Duke's connections, Erik had twice appeared on Pay-Per-View. One could not possibly hope to compete with the best in the world, diminutive as they might be, whilst resident in Cedar Rapids. There were no Dukes here, only far-flung freemen who staged brawls in the stale basements of downtown bars.

Yet Erik did not, in fact, leave for Milwaukee, for reasons I could not yet understand, and so the next week I did my best to be the audience I thought Erik required. His eight or nine space-takers were mostly fellow fighters, and likely not champion listeners. Here I saw an opportunity; for though I would not roll, and preferred to be invisible, I could feign membership in the active, head-nodding, sympathetic-sound-making school of aural witness. I knew when to ask the right question—*How big was the burrito?*—when to widen my eyes with astonishment. And sure enough, that very weekend when I called Erik to initiate an ingratiating session of listening, he asked for a ride to Valhalla, the gym to which I would pretend not to know the way. I let him direct me through uptown Cedar Rapids, hot air wafting in open windows, past the blocks of hospital, past the homeless shelter, past a series of rundown homes with lawns gone to seed. "Right here," said Erik at the small storefront wedged between a nursing home and a house with toys strewn about the yard. The place was all window on one side; I had been this far, peering inside that window, but never beyond it. On the glass yellow letters curled in the heat, threatening to peel off onto the curb:

VALHALLA COMBAT CLUB
WHERE DREAMS O E TRUE

Erik was already stripping as he walked into the storefront, sliding off his shirt and shoes, down the stairs, up the stairs, to the blue-matted room in the back of the building, where we found the rest of the team, so quiet we could hear cars rumble past. It was eighty degrees outside, some constant in which one could trust, but it was at least a hundred once you got through the door. The first room was wet with sweat but utterly empty: a jury-rigged boxing ring, a pink plastic chair someone's little girl outgrew, a tree stump on which to sit, brass knuckles nailed to the wall. Like pages of an open book, pieces of ceiling flapped down over our heads. A great gilded mirror in which Erik enjoyed staring at himself was perched along a wall pocked with crumbling plaster. We sidled past the boxing ring to the second room, where we came upon the gym's innermost sanctum. In a space the size of a furnace room, six pairs of men turned over one another in silence like gears churning in the service of some larger machine. One pair paused, stuck; another tumbled over and over until they too latched into place, jammed. There was a thump, a gasp as one man's weight pushed the air out of another man's lungs, the dull sound of two locked bodies as they pivot. In the far corner, by the wall that was also a window, a man corkscrewed his way from under his partner's planted knees. Erik picked a partner and found a rhythm.

The men called their collective "Hard Drive," and most had "HD" tattoos somewhere on their sculpted persons. Perhaps it was the way the heat held its grip on my lungs, but I felt as if I had been led to the catacombs of a heretical cult. They were more careful and solicitous with one another's bodies than might be you or I, perhaps because they knew exactly how it was that bodies broke. When it came time to complete a choke or bend a joint, the men would merely pretend to do so with broad theatrical gestures. I hid on a wooden bench beside a hanging bag and watched twelve men play.

Erik is lissome porcelain limbs, bloodless grace, a body that does not move as you expect bodies to move. Imagine clean white arms sweeping back and forth, slim muscle making itself visible in flashes, long torso turning with every sweep and snapping back so quickly the flicker of an eye is not fast enough to follow. Erik is of the generation of martial artists who can do everything well, and among those he is one of the few with a sense of flow so natural—and I mean natural at its most etymological; the flow he channels is *of nature*—that it is as if he travels through jump cuts; it is as if you, his audience, have missed some connective motion, some kinesthetic preposition.

I was, through careful study, beginning to see that the most talented fighters are those who can transition seamlessly between fighting arts. They launch the encounter as boxers, erect, until the man with the better judo throws down his opponent and holds him flat with the leveraging gifts of the well-taught wrestler. The trapped man will perhaps spin out, pop back up erect, lean on one leg and swing the other, Muay-Thai-like, in the direction of his opponent. They will stumble and clutch one another against the fence in a way reminiscent of quarrelsome lovers; one man, looking for the best position from which to throw the other, will thrust his forehead into the other man's chest, as if listening to his heart. The fight will change not only in style but also in mood—from playful hops about the canvas, and a minutes-long quiet as the fighters hug against the fence searching for a position of advantage, to the terrifying moment when one fighter finds his opening. The second someone well-trained in Brazilian jiu-jitsu has trapped, over twenty well-chosen moves, another man securely underneath him, the writhing turns to pounding, the playful taps to brutal strikes, an elbow to the eye. The flurry endures until the victim taps the canvas in defeat or a referee hurls his body between the men, one of whom may have, at that point, slipped from consciousness. And at the close of a truly violent encounter, in which one man has struck and broken another, the mood changes yet again. Fractions of a second after the referee backs off, the men will smile broadly and touch hands, as if they'd just together purged themselves of some demon and might now part ways in peace.

It was Erik's fortune to be gifted in not only all the necessary arts, but to slip with grace from one to the other. And like any great fighter, he relied most heavily on the most superior of them.

Of course the undereducated in the many arts of MMA will have trouble separating the Brazilian jiu-jitsu experts from the novices; are they not all squirming on the floor like writhing centipedes? But here is how I tell the true jiu-jitsu master from the false, and it has nothing to do with belts, which are just a boastful way to fasten one's pants. The well-trained jiu-jitsu artist looks lost on his feet. He walks with a kind of sad resignation, ever ready to throw his back to the floor, his legs in the air, because the jiu-jitsu artist has of course remapped his body, such that his legs are another pair of arms, the small of his back an axis to pivot upon. How strange it looks when, after practice, all the men rise onto their feet, forcing all their muscled weight on those two small, pathetic pylons. What a weak base most of us—the tottering untrained—accept without a thought!

The untrained man—and it's always a sad thing to watch— looks natural on his feet, and thrown to the ground, knows not how to conduct himself, such that he generally gets down on all fours like a canine after a squirrel. There the novice simply waits for a better man to jump on his back, wrap legs around his waist, press a forearm into his neck, and choke him. Or he just lies there with his back to the mat until a man pins him to the ground with knees on either side of his chest, then falls back on the novice's arm and bends the unfortunate elbow backward. Eventually the novice will learn that jiu-jitsu is in part the search for vulnerable angles; after expertly isolating an arm from the body, a black-belt will bend the elbow backward, or if it's a leg he has in his clutches, the knee. The neck is another vulnerability, all jiu-jitsu artists being amateur anatomists who will, with doctorly precision, pinpoint your carotid artery and proceed to press upon it.

And yet all the artery-pressing intensity is, in practice, softened to play between friends. I watched Erik gently torque the arm of a man named Jared, Erik's legs across Jared's chest, Jared's wrist in Erik's grip, until the elbow hinge straightened and Jared tapped. Nothing looks violent or forced here; the men, careful to protect one another against fractures and laceration and ligamentary tears, play with a cerebral placidity. The way to that armbar was some twenty movements tried and countered, twenty deceptions tendered until one stuck and Jared relaxed into the elaborate trap set for him. "Like chess" is the dull analogy of the unimaginative, but more like snake-charming, the job being one of drawing out, wooing a body from its tight clenched coil into a single yielding line.

As Jared and Erik separated only to entangle themselves once again, I noticed a man with an odd white complexion. The two were sheathed of the same material. Erik and Keoni were not white as pale pink, but truly white, porcelain, alabaster, and without a single blemish across the entire visible expanse of skin. One feels around the brothers a sense of unnatural cleanliness, a certain unworldly hygiene. In the beginning, in my great naiveté, I interpreted the fact that they never spoke to one another as evidence of a fraternal telepathy.

"Break!" someone said twenty minutes in, at which point Valhalla was soaked in what I would later hear Keoni, the most poetic member of Hard Drive, describe as "sweat so deep you wish you could just slip under the surface and swim away."

They were slow to pull arms from legs, untwine their thighs from one another's torsos, except of course for Erik, who sprang up squirrellike and began shadowboxing even as everyone else poured outside, where the air was slightly cooler. He followed them, walked by as they spread themselves along the curb, and began again to shadowbox. One of the men disappeared entirely into a dented garbage can Erik's brother had filled with ice water.

"You gotta talk it up a little bit," Erik told me in an instructive tone while the others rested, continuing a previous conversation about his recent fight. He was hopping from foot to foot as he sparred with the ghostly other. "So, everyone in the division is short next to me, right?"—jab, jab, hook—"So I call them midgets. I said to my last opponent, 'I won't throw a high kick at you because it'd go right over your head. It'll be more like a midkick that I knock you out with.' People like that. The way I look at it, you're not just a fighter, you're an entertainer."

Men were lying flat on the sidewalk, huffing, hands on their chests. From the ice-filled garbage can the man shouted, "Erik is a badass," and some ice water splashed from can to curb. Erik smiled.

"Erik is a prodigy," someone said.

"Doesn't telegraph anything."

"He's a beast."

"A warrior."

"A warrior beast."

When Erik prepared himself for the cage he whittled himself down so dramatically that he looked severely malnourished, all bone and shadow, skull too visible under the flesh of his forehead. He spent an enormous amount of psychic energy repressing elaborate culinary fantasies such that when he finally got to eat, he binged with panicked atavism. Having gained thirty-five pounds since his last fight, he was restored to a slim, tall, first world twenty-one-year-old. He pushed out his small stomach the way you would a quivering beer gut, and the hard curves of muscle almost disappeared.

"I am a husky boy!" he shouted, slapping skin laid over abs like moss on rock.

"Embrace the husk!" said a fighter named Lonnie.

In life though not in myth we grow more not less aware of ourselves as we fall under the influence of any particular spell; we do not forget but feel ourselves peeling from our original objectives toward whatever siren calls us, as aware of every misstep as can be. So it was with Erik, the beauty with which he moved. I listened, at first theatrically, but then my head was nodding and I was watching with authentic fascination at this body so perfectly obedient to Erik's will. To watch Erik move was to watch Cartesian dualism disproved.

"Cartesian dualism," I wrote in my notebook. "Disproved."

"You're some kind of writer?" asked a fighter.

"Not exactly," I said, but someone was already speaking over me.

"She's April O'Neil!" shouted another fighter, in what I would later identify as a reference to the Teenage Mutant Ninja Turtles.

"Is April O'Neil coming to Rocky's house?" someone asked Erik.

Friday nights at Rocky's were a Hard Drive ritual. Other fighters spoke about what they did there; it was assumed to be some kind of hardcore, secret training regime.

"I don't know," said Rocky, squinting as he leaned against the window. "Women aren't really invited."

Rocky was a heavily muscled Iraq veteran and preschool teacher who wouldn't fight because he'd been punched in the face once and found he didn't care for it. He was, that summer, Erik's best friend.

"Well," said Erik, "she's different."

My heart flopped so hard in my chest I thought I might pitch over. I heard in those words the right to stand by his side, wait in locker rooms, sit so close to the fight I could slip my fingers between holes in the fence.

"The reason I am so good," Erik said later that night, when eight of us were together seated in Rocky's basement, "is because I literally—I'm crazy. I don't have a job. I don't have any way of making money. I just decided to train six or seven hours a day."

As Erik spoke he kicked at a standing bag that shot out of Rocky's floor. "Most people won't do that," Erik said. *Thwap.* "They're like, 'You need a backup plan, you need something to fall back on.' But if I have a back-out plan then it's easy for me to back out." *Thwap.* "My parents are like, 'Go to school.' Well if I go to school maybe I'll be like, 'Well, I'm gonna do this instead.' Playing it safe. I won't do that. So maybe"—*thwap*—"I'll end up in the gutter. I'll take that chance."

Rocky and Erik kept their distance from intoxicating substances, but the rest of the men were passing around a rolled stick of cannabis, of which I partook solely in the interest of behavioral camouflage. The conversation turned to a legendary fighter named Mauricio Rua, popularly known as "Shogun."

"Lonnie is obsessed with Shogun," said Rocky. "Lonnie thinks Shogun could beat Jesus."

"No," said Lonnie. "What I said was, if anybody could beat Jesus, it *would be* Shogun."

"Jesus didn't exist," said Rob on an exhale. "I was watching this thing on the History Channel; they don't have any evidence."

"Come on," said Rocky, the group's only believer.

"They don't even have—"

"They got shit," said Rocky. "Records and stuff."

"What movie should we watch?" Keoni asked more out of a sense of ceremony than anything else, because there was only one movie they watched on Friday nights. "*Pumping Iron*," Erik said. *Thwap.*

We filed upstairs to collapse on the sofa, the floor, a long fuzzy couch. Erik lay in a recliner, legs hanging over the side. The bottom half of Erik's HD tattoo was visible from under his T-shirt sleeve. Demian's peeked out from the hem of his shorts. Jared slid in the VHS tape, which hummed until something clicked and Schwarzenegger popped onscreen.

"C-Can we smoke up here?" asked Jared, who had a serious stutter only cannabis cured.

"No, just downstairs," said Rocky.

"Have you tried blueberry muffin tops?" asked Keoni of Demian, passing over the box.

"No."

"You haven't lived."

Arnold Schwarzenegger and his competitors stood onstage and transformed themselves into Greek statuary turned steroidal. They stared into the distance and pushed out sinew, swollen balloons of muscle choking on the body's fibrous webbing. Tendons popped thick as electrical cord. Schwarzenegger looked as though he had been skinned and painted orange.

"Let's say you train your biceps," Schwarzenegger said in everyone's favorite scene. "Blood is rushing in to your muscles and that's what we call the pump."

"Da pump," Erik said.

"Dats what we call da pump," Keoni said.

"Your muscles," said Schwarzenegger looking straight into the camera, "get a really tight feeling like your skin is going to explode any minute and it's really tight and it's like someone is blowing air into your muscle and it just blows up and it feels different, it feels fantastic. It's as satisfying to me as cumming is, you know, as in having sex with a woman and cumming."

Erik laughed, doubled over.

"So can you believe how much I am in heaven?" continued Schwarzenegger, "I am like getting the feeling of cumming in the gym; I'm getting the feeling of cumming at home; I'm getting the feeling of cumming backstage; when I pump up, when I pose out in front of 5,000 people I get the same feeling, so I am cumming day and night. It's terrific, right?"

Erik laughed so hard he spilled his Gatorade. The men had watched this scene dozens, perhaps hundreds, of times. Rocky rewound it and they watched it again.

On that couch, surrounded by those men, a strange warmth radiated through me. Rarely have I seen a group of people so comfortable with one another, so easily intimate. They would be laughing that entire night, leaning into one another, sharing muffin tops and trading movie lines. It is with only slight embarrassment that I admit how I ached to be more securely among them—to share with a dozen people the same tattoo, the same stories, the same hot sweaty days engaged in some physical endeavor. They even shared a similar build, though some were black and some brown and some, like Erik, blindingly white. With the exception of Rocky, no one was noticeably muscled, because Schwarzeneggerian muscle was worse than useless in an actual fight; it starved the rest of the body of oxygen. No one in the room looked particularly like a fighter, either—no broken noses, no flat faces, few mat-gnarled ears—and least of all lanky long-necked Erik. In jeans, alone, in a bar, each would be just a boy too small for football.

"Are you coming with us to Adventureland tomorrow?" Rocky asked Erik after the second viewing. Rocky and Erik spent their few hours away from the gym alternating between trips to the casino and trips to the amusement park.

"No," Erik said, "I'll be in Milwaukee by then."

Here was the evening's only uncomfortable moment, a slight tightening, a collective intake of stale air; I began to realize that Erik's talk of leaving was a source of great frustration to these men, who considered Erik theirs. If he stayed in Cedar Rapids, remained theirs, he would remain but a novice fighter making absurd untested claims about his capacity to face José Aldo. The silence between Erik and Rocky lingered.

Erik was on his feet and shadowboxing again. Steve ordered a pizza covered in ground beef and cream cheese, then collected money from everyone but Erik, who started talking about shadows posturing at a bar in Iowa City. "The other day Wes and I were at Union," he told everyone, "and Wes was talking to this girl and these guys came and interrupted, talkin' about how they're fighters who train with Erik Koch, yadda yadda yadda."

"Of course," said Demian as he was taking a slice of pizza, lifting it up high above his mouth so as to catch swinging strands of hanging cheese.

"So Wes came and got me and was like, 'Hey, these guys say they train with you.' So I go up there. And what happens when I show up. Never seen them in my life. They're like, 'Oh my god! Erik Koch. You're awesome, yadda yadda yadda.' That shit is offensive to me. I got nut riders everywhere. People I don't want on my nuts."

I cannot say I often saw these "nut riders" myself, because these men so rarely ventured out in public, and when they did, as to a bar, they did so as a single covey clearly uninterested in mingling with lesser members of lighter flocks. Much more likely was it that I would find myself with two or three of them preparing for a fight, as I did the next day, squeezed between Rob and Erik as we drove in Lonnie's truck to a place Erik knew. Our knees touched as we knocked along. It was two weeks before the fight; Lonnie and Rob were hungry and miserable and mostly they spoke of how much more hungry and miserable they would become.

"Look at my abs," said Lonnie, pulling up his shirt on abs turned flat by denial. "I hate my abs. My abs mean my life sucks."

"I'm going to be so angry by July fourteen," said Rob. "If you want to be around a Debbie Downer, hang around me."

Erik pointed to a field by the highway in the shadow of the backside of a billboard and Lonnie pulled the company pickup onto the grass, leaving tracks in soil made soft from yesterday's rain.

When Rob and Lonnie fought Erik would be there; all of Hard Drive would be there, for every fighter came to every HD fight in driving distance, crowded the locker room, walked as a fist-pumping entourage to the cage door, and none of them would ever, under any circumstances, fight one another; to seek that kind of penetrative intimacy with one's brothers would be to commit a crime as old as crime itself. Thus Hard Drive fought Miletich, and Miletich Miletich, but never Hard Drive Hard Drive. There were also the Catholic boys in Dubuque and the Tai Dam in Des Moines, descendants of refugees from Vietnam. The Tai Dam would stage the fights Lonnie and Rob had coming to them in a West Des Moines dance hall.

Now while every Saturday night brings staged encounters to every American county, coast to coast and most especially in the soft prairie middle, the fights of which conventionally minded fighters dream are not those in West Des Moines dance halls but those staged in big cities and broadcast on Pay-Per-View. Much as we might hope for the fighters' dream to remain clean and pure, it will in fact be driven by the exigencies of cable television. One may start, as did Erik, with an encounter in a Cedar Rapids convention center, but one does so in the hopes that some guardian angel is waiting, someone who will pluck you from your obscurity. This is what Duke had done for Erik. And at that point, unless you are stuck as Erik is stuck, you will kiss your mother goodbye and move, as fighterly men once moved to Davenport, to one of three currently ascendant camps in Albuquerque, Miami, and Milwaukee, from which you will ascend to the Big Shows. Then, provided you are conventionally minded, you will dream of your title shot, of the day when they deem you fit to challenge the fighter of highest status. Even Lonnie and Rob dreamed of this, though Lonnie would continue to be a house painter, and Rob a paralegal, and both would lose their fights against the Tai Dam, at which point they would turn, as they always did, to Keoni, who would know just what to say.

Of course even as we dream, we know there are dreams beyond our capacities; and the fighters of Hard Drive, being especially intellectual men Keoni handpicked, tended to see more clearly than most. Rob was a single father who drove a full hour back and forth to Valhalla every weekday after work. Nothing came naturally to him, and no one would ever suggest he ought to be fighting in venues bigger than the Cedar Rapids convention center. What he had, in Hard Drive, was the right to tell anyone that his best friend and coach was the fighter Erik Koch; that when he fought, Erik Koch was in his corner; that when he lost, Erik Koch would help him rebuild for the next time.

Erik pulled the kettle bells from the back of the truck. He stood in between Rob and Lonnie against the sun and took a big step, pushing the weight behind his stretched body before bringing his arm forward as his hip turned in time and the bell flew fifty feet over the grass before it rolled and landed on a tilt like a planet. He ran to the weight, picked it up, launched it again. Rob tried to do the same with his weight—lift, swing, hurl—but let go slightly too late. Lonnie released too early; both of their weights slopped into the grass. "His doesn't sink," said Rob as he jogged left. "Yeah, it just like rolls," said Lonnie, breathing hard. Rob and Lonnie crisscrossed the field, veering left and right, while Erik cut a perfect landing strip straight through the grass.

I cannot tell you exactly when it was that the uneasiness began to manifest within me; but this was about the time I noticed that something I had taken for granted in Sean was here, in Hard Drive, lacking. Sean projected an aura of sustained bewilderment; he was willing to be lost and alone. I could sense no such bewilderment in Erik, no such courage. One had to be ready to receive the octagon, were it to ever show up; and Erik did not seem ready to receive, so safely was he sewn into the fabric of Hard Drive, so apparently unwilling was he to bear the wound of leaving home. What I am trying to say is that I was certain, in the summer of 2010, that Erik Koch was a thing of great and rare beauty, and not at all certain that he was, at heart, a Fighter. And so instead of trying to keep him in Cedar Rapids, as Hard Drive would, I began to root for him to break free.

Erik – Fall 2010

IN REGARDS TO THE PRESENT NARRATION, I feel compelled to defend myself against a certain sort of prejudice endemic to our times. "You," my gentle detractors will say, "who purport to tell the stories of these real men, are but a work of *fiction*." This I do not deny: I stand before you every bit as fictional as longitude and latitude, as the Roman calendar, as the sixty-second minute, and I encourage you to dispose with all of these to the extent that they offend you. The Prime Meridian, an act of imagination, runs over Arctic sea ice, Mediterranean waters, the sands of the Sahara. Do you doubt the sand because you doubt the line? For be assured, in the world I describe, space *was* taken. The fighters were heard by human ears, each word faithfully recorded. Real fingers ran over the stitches in Sean's brow. Real tears fell down the face that watched him fall.

Now those who ask that I be as real as Sean have a curious faith in the ability of people with birth certificates and tax IDs to free themselves from the fetters of deception. My (admittedly neurotic) progenitor, on the other hand, is so conscious of her own tendency toward self-confabulation that she hesitates to call anything she says of herself a fact. She has never known a real person who saw herself with even passable clarity; never known a storyteller who could tell of a trip to the supermarket without self-gratifying sins of omission. All narrators, I say, are fiction. *All.* The reliable ones have the decency to admit it.

As summer turned to fall I, Kit, was only beginning to understand the stories Erik and Sean told themselves that they might continue to be artists of abandon. I shuttled between Cedar Rapids and Iowa City and Davenport, mill town to university town to river town, Erik to home to Sean. I had found through the fighters a new way of communing with the natural world, and driving through bucolic Iowa I imagined that the fields favored me for having achieved a higher relation to them. In September the six-foot walls of corn vanished overnight, as if swallowed by sky, and the horizon moved south to meet the soil. I thought myself graced with an extra slice of firmament.

It was my intention to split my time as judiciously as possible, never mentioning one fighter to the other unless omission entailed deceit of the kind no right-thinking spacetaker could countenance. If Sean asked where I had been, and I said that I had been "with Erik Koch," Sean would smile and narrow his eyes and say, "You know he has never fought anyone serious, right?" or sometimes just "Cedar Rapids?" followed by a high-pitched and endearing "ha!" If Erik asked where I had been, and I said, "with Sean Huffman," Erik would pretend not to have heard, change the subject, and perhaps talk to someone else for a while.

This last response encompassed something of the difference between spacetaking for Sean and spacetaking for Erik, for Erik had someone else to whom to talk. He kept always two or three friends in his immediate vicinity, and was frequently in the process of texting more, padding the buffer between himself and the possibility of solitude. And while all these men would gather around Erik so as to soak in his fighterly aura, I was beginning to see that it was Keoni, not Erik, who could keep them from drifting away.

When Keoni Koch walked into a room the room went quiet; when he made a joke the whole room erupted in raucous laughter. Whereas I felt that I could be contentedly invisible among the other men of Hard Drive, Keoni responded to me with a somewhat grave attention I could only find unsettling. On our second Friday night at Rocky's, a fighter named Rob asked me, not unkindly, why I preferred to be in their presence rather than that of other scholarly types in Iowa City. He was playing a video game at the time. I replied, after a moment's thought, that I respected "the fighter's refusal to surrender to the dulling impulses of self-preservation." Rob kept playing, as expected, and Erik tapped texts into his phone, as expected, and the other fighters continued a conversation about a nutritional supplement. Keoni, packing a bowl, looked straight at me, nodded sagely, and said, "It's interesting to me that so many people are out of touch with what it means to be alive."

I knew in that moment that I had to speak to Keoni, very likely at great length. And yet I said nothing, because I also knew that to show undue enthusiasm for Keoni's company would dismay his sensitive brother. It wasn't until Erik went downstairs to kick the standing bag, and the others were gathered around a pizza in the kitchen, that I asked Keoni—somewhat timidly, conscious of the deference with which he was typically treated—whether we might meet, alone, to discuss his previous comment. In the living room we could hear the thwap of a kicked bag one story down. Keoni, looking rather pleased, assented to a date and time.

Every Dionysian tribe requires its Apollo. Hard Drive's was of average height, which is to say shorter than his brother, with a strong jaw, blue eyes, and an HD tattoo on his bicep. We discussed his past for a full three hours in his front yard, with his two children playing before us. When speaking, he maintained an eye contact I could not take, so I looked down to his clean porcelain fingernails, the way they were precisely cut, without a single cuticle in view. I realize, reader, that this will sound odd—but it is very unusual for a man of twenty-nine years to have perfect nail beds, and I think you too would find it striking.

As previously stated, I do not approve of epiphanical plot points or stark narrative shifts; even the greatest and most truthful moments, moments of ecstatic bliss, leave the lay of fate, as far as I can tell, largely undisturbed. But there is a moment I think perhaps worthy of considering here, as generative of each of the rope-knotted bodies, every smooth mount, every taut triangle, of which I caught view in Valhalla.

Picture Keoni Koch, age fourteen, a short bright boy born to an evangelizing liberal pacifist father—a Baha'i preacher, no less, so enamored of peaceful synthesis that he believed in the next life Buddha, Muhammad, and Jesus would walk together holding hands, or whatever the deific equivalent of holding hands may be. Keoni believed every word his father said and also, to his father's enduring confusion, that hand-to-hand combat was the only subject on earth worthy of serious study. "What is with all this *violence*?" Doug Koch would ask, descending the stairs, hand on the banister, upon discovering his strange small lonely son with yet another bloody film.

Now the martial arts film as a fictional genre is a not-unvexed subject among practitioners of the fighting arts, such films being agents of embarrassing mythologies adopted by especially entrepreneurial shadows. I speak here of *Bloodsport, Kickboxer, Enter the Dragon* and their ilk. One only need think of real-life dojos and the fictions they exploit—senseis who speak only in aphorisms, grand fighting "secrets" passed down through generations, the purported mysticism of the much-touted death touch. Absurd, truly; an embarrassment. At the end of the climactic tournament that ends every such film one martial art always emerges victorious and it is always the art, you will have noticed, native to the country responsible for producing the script. As an adolescent, Keoni saw through these clumsy plot points to the propaganda, being dispositionally skeptical, but he continued to watch. Erik, at six, preferred to play outside in the manner of children the world considers well-adjusted.

In 1994 a short chubby fourteen-year-old Keoni slipped what he thought was such a movie into that VCR—a film betokening yet another tournament, yet another chauvinistic promotion of a single martial art. Boxers will fight sumo wrestlers will fight masters of Muay Thai, promised the plastic sleeve. The moment of which I am talking, the moment that suggests itself as a moment of fate-changing mind-shifting import, is the moment Keoni notices something is amiss with this film. The pauses between scenes are of odd and varying lengths, the graphics resemble clip art, the announcers are bewildered and, because no one in this country is yet conversant in the martial art that will win the contest, are of limited help to the audience. There is no backstory, and fighters called upon to comment say things like "I'm not very good at interviews." The slim Brazilian man—not the Sensei of Japan or Kung Fu Master of China or Playboy Bodybuilder of Belgium—is winning every fight.

The glorious tournament Keoni was watching had been conducted by jiu-jitsu mad Brazilians in Las Vegas in 1993, and this was the authentic audiovisual record. Keoni, in search of a fiction, had landed upon a history. It was as if a couple intending to watch a romantic comedy had by some misunderstanding stumbled upon unedited documentary footage of human copulation. This was the scientific method applied to thousands of years of empty martial grandiloquence. Should a master of any martial practice wish to claim his art form superior—as his predecessors had, unquestioned, for centuries—this tournament required that they provide some evidence. "Could a sumo wrestler defeat a kickboxer?" asked an announcer, and a sumo wrestler was left crying in the cage, two teeth missing, one of which was lodged in the kickboxer's foot. Could a shootfighter wrestle down a karate master? A submission artist submit a jiu-jitsu champion? As the matches continued Keoni fast-forwarded past the clumsy graphics, past the shifty-eyed interviews, paused to watch a hulking Olympic wrestler look up, desperate, from his position between a small Brazilian's snaked legs. He fast-forwarded again, paused to watch a 'roided-up brawler fall unconscious, his head tilted against the grip of the same Brazilian's right arm. It is in watching Royce Gracie, master of a practice called Brazilian jiu-jitsu, that the true limits of Keoni's world are finally drawn. Royce Gracie defeated all of these men by mastering an art superior to theirs. So did this encounter with reality vivify all the old fictions; because there *was* a secret fighting art, passed down through generations, and with it small men could smite large ones.

These encounters, the progenitors of the Big Shows to which Erik would eventually ascend, preceded even the classic fights I so wished to have seen in Davenport strip clubs; so early and pioneering were they, in a time before the term "mixed martial arts" came into being, that they embraced a certain roughness even the strip clubs would never have tolerated. Those were times when one could pull an opponent's hair, stick an index finger in a man's mouth, elbow a man in the spine. They lacked a certain dignity, but here was an art form in its infancy, and infants must be allowed their clumsy explorations, must hurt themselves to know what it is they cannot tolerate. Most, watching these early spectacles, would have seen only bar brawls transplanted to a cage, which is what only the most unlearned people, such as certain tragically ignorant epistemologists in Iowa City, say even now of mixed martial arts. Keoni, being of a more refined nature, could see hazily how these encounters pushed backward into biblical times and forward into his own future.

Thus began Keoni's momentous familiarity with Brazilian culture; the same obsession that was overtaking Pat Miletich in

Davenport and Chuck Liddell in Nevada and Frank Shamrock in San Jose. Royce Gracie, having abandoned jiu-jitsu-saturated Rio to seek his fortune in the United States, ventured to the Midwest. He invited the most ostentatiously muscled and self-regarding men in every town to fight him; he slithered about their bodies, held them helpless, and then leapt into a choke that left two options: tap or lose consciousness. He offered to teach them, for a price, and the men who came to dominate the Big Shows were the men who said yes.

Royce hosted and competed in further primitive shows, and after every tournament a new tape appeared at the Cedar Rapids Blockbuster. Brazilian jiu-jitsu, in its fluid formlessness, is not easy to describe in something so static as a sequence of words; it is no easier to learn by mere observation, as Keoni heroically attempted to do from the tapes he played and rewound until the ribbon thinned with wear and the picture wavered, bounced. The Brazilian Keoni was watching came from a fertile fighting dynasty, that dynasty trained by a Japanese fighter of a long Japanese line, whereas Keoni's father was a pacifist preacher and his mother a university chemist. The problem before him was not merely the lack of instruction but the lack of partners with which to train; he had no bodies on which to act; it was as if Keoni were a student of surgical medicine in a world of floating spirits. He filled notebooks with tiny scrawls that described, step by step, whatever he could glean from the tapes, until the tapes stopped coming.

Keoni, too sage for traditional instruction, quit school at seventeen, whereupon his baffled father kicked him out of the house. The Koch brothers would never again share a household. Forced to find employment, Keoni turned to a telecom company. Getting hired was not difficult. The challenge of his young adulthood was not finding employment but finding fellow playmates, because the kind of person willing to play is harder to find than the kind of person willing to work, paid work being the province of the anxious, the routine-bound, those seeking safe harbor in a single static wooden desk. Even the word Keoni uses to describe the practice of jiu-jitsu—*roll*—suggests the very opposite of fixity, an openness to the universe, a making vulnerable. The aimless aim of rolling was to be never still because to stick in place was to stop the game and everyone knew that no moment was meant as an end to itself, that every position—guard, mount, half-guard—was a phase on its way to a new one, some self-contortion he didn't even notice until he found his body passing out of it and into some new form he may or may not have a name for. Positions were something to pass between, brief moments that happened to occupy semantic categories.

Do you suppose the bodies of civic order, in their infinite love of the hard and fast, the writers of written rules, approve of this slippery ambiguity? I do not myself approve of newspapers and their sad preoccupation with the near-at-hand, but were you perusing one in 1998 and you came across the phrase "decline of western civilization" or "everything that is wrong with men" or "slack-jawed children whose parents must be cretins," you were probably reading an article about these early fights. And had you continued to read that paper day after dreary day, you would have found that eventually a senator from Arizona named John McCain pushed Royce Gracie, and all of the men he regularly submitted, off of Pay-Per-View, bankrupting their noble enterprise. The blackout lasted years, until some cigar-smoking Las Vegas moguls bought Royce's promotion and figured out how to accommodate the ruling class. During the long interim, when Keoni was most hungry for knowledge, new tapes no longer arrived at the Blockbuster on the west side of Cedar Rapids. Keoni, an innocent, did not know why.

From the office where he sold telecom services in Cedar Rapids Keoni would drive to the house his pregnant girlfriend had just found for them, a fenced-in two-story detached single family home at the intersection of two quiet streets. The house had a small basement, empty but for a washing machine, a dryer, a rusted-through pair of pruning shears, an empty plastic bottle of weed killer, and a kicked propane tank. The way out was a wooden staircase with a missing riser and half a handrail. Keoni spent everything he had on a wrestling mat. He laid it up against three concrete walls, around a metal pole. He lined the mat with wood and drilled the wood into the concrete floor.

By day he was serious and professional and infallibly prompt and it seemed that he ought to be in charge of people, so the corporation gave Keoni three underlings.

"Want to come train in my basement?" Keoni asked a kid named Devon.

"Train for what?"

"Ultimate fighting. UFC."

A few months later, Devon had an underling of his own.

"Want to come train with us?" Devon asked Beau.

"Train for what?

So it was that Keoni found, at work, men with whom to play. When Devon and Beau knew a few things, I am given to understand, the moments of instruction diminished into hours of bloody revel. Sweat hung so heavily in that basement the pads never dried and pieces of vinyl flecked off like pie crust. Keoni blasted house music; between songs there were the sounds of heavy breathing and Velcro being torn from itself and the shuffle of his wife's feet on the floor above. The frosted window fogged. Hair collected in the cracks of the mat. The pocked walls bled water. Heads and toes slammed into the metal pole. They rolled with the gentle, attentive respect of men who did not want to lose a partner to injury—no one ever suffered even a broken finger—but they also hugged one another hard against the wall, and as they dragged each other to the ground the concrete scraped the skin from their fingers. When he needed something—ice, water—Keoni climbed the stairs, opened the door, and crisp cold air slammed his wet body. He hurried back down. Devon and Beau, now completely devoted to Keoni, came three nights a week, then four nights a week, and they brought friends.

How quickly some men, by the force and purity of their vision, can turn a mere activity into a kind of institution. These men had no thought of fighting in staged spectacles; they longed merely for this playful absorption, this reprieve from the healthy-minded world of annual reports and sexual harassment training. They played thusly for three years, seven nights a week, two hours a night. I did not believe this seven-nights-a-week business myself when Keoni related the fact, thinking it the kind of exaggeration that sprung from his natural intensity, but Devon and Beau and

Erik independently insisted that they kept to the same schedule. For years they were all scabbed from the concrete, a semipermanent physical state to which Keoni referred as "chewed up."

During that period, which we might in the interest of categorical precision call the "early basement period," Keoni rarely saw his brother outside of family holidays. Such distances allow admiration to grow unchecked; as a sixteen-year-old high school dropout Erik worshipped his older brother, whom he considered unassailably tough. It was Thanksgiving, the whole family gathered at their parents' house, when Erik worked up the courage to say, "I want to try." And in response, one day soon afterward, Keoni permitted him to join the group. In full view of the others he held Erik down for three humiliating minutes, letting Erik thrash until he tired. To everyone's surprise, Erik returned the next day.

For the first months Erik seemed no different than Beau, Devon, or Jesse—especially Jesse, the natural athlete—and he was just another body with which to roll, dropped off by his father at nine in the evening, picked up at eleven, the youngest member of a growing coterie of Keoni-trained players. He was perhaps most notable for the way his proper playful aspect could, in a moment of disadvantage, turn to petulant anger. Caught three times in three rolls, Erik might ascend the broken steps, slam the door, and sit outside until his father arrived to ferry him home.

For the first five months he had struggled along with the rest of them to learn the choreography of each complicated submission; just where to exert pressure as you wrapped your legs around another body, just how to cross your ankles so the neck between them couldn't twist out. Certain submissions required the memorization of ten, twelve steps, each of which had to be perfected; and a decent martial artist will know how to pretend he is going for one choke or armbar or leglock while actually going for another, or how to transition to a new strategy when an opponent's body type or strength level makes a particular submission untenable. In this sixth month suddenly Erik picked up a sequence after seeing it once, precisely as a prodigy trombonist might hear a tune once and reproduce it perfectly forevermore. Keoni had taught many boys, with extreme patience, how to follow a long chain of moments leading to a choke, but only Erik picked up the whole chain like there were no choice points in which to get lost. And it was as Erik discovered his own freakish muscle memory that he became the hardest working among them, the first in the basement and the last to leave. To this day, with all of the darkness Erik has left behind, every member of Hard Drive will assent to the fact that Erik trains harder than do they.

Thus it was that they trained in Keoni's basement, then in the parish hall of a defunct Lutheran church. Locals responded to the ·Pennysaver ad expecting, perhaps, a salubrious aerobic workout, and never came back. Fifty or sixty people cycled through the parish hall, but only Rob and Erik stuck. Sometimes Keoni would be inspired to attempt a new exercise; he might put eight men in a circle and make them punch one another in the stomach. The next morning, his total enrollment would regress to two.

It was when they rented that husk of a building, Valhalla, that they found more than a few people willing to embrace an intimate athletic sect. By then Brazilian jiu-jitsu was no longer a secret art for which Keoni had to evangelize, and the men he trained wanted to compete inside octagonal cages. He brought them to fights at fairgrounds and cattle congresses where the canvas, exposed to the sun, burned the tender bottoms of the fighters' bare feet. He brought them in contact with his brother. When people outside Hard Drive's intimate circle had heard of Valhalla, they had heard of it because of Erik, and this quite limited recognition brought Keoni no small satisfaction. He had given Erik the gift of fighting, and by remaining in Cedar Rapids, Erik bestowed on Keoni's little gym an aura of legitimacy.

Others, watching the way Erik pretended not to hear when Keoni addressed the group, and the way Keoni sighed heavily with every mention of Erik, thought they understood the situation. They had seen films in which a younger brother surpassed in skill his older sibling, leaving the lesser brother sad and alone and very possibly addicted to crack-cocaine. But Keoni had no taste for ecstasy. He was a civilian of a quieter class, a vessel through which Brazil arrived in Iowa. Keoni loved to be at the center of a group of men growing hard. He loved that he was the first contact these men had with the most perfect fighting system ever devised. He loved that he was owed.

"You seeing that girl?" Keoni asked one post-*Pumping Iron* Friday that summer, meaning Ashley, a girl who drove Erik to fights and seemed to aspire to the kind of spacetaking we all associated with KayLee. "No," Erik responded, which surprised everyone, but then, it was a time when Erik was trying very hard not be associated with any nonalienable aspects of the local landscape, because he was halfway to Milwaukee. "OK if I hang out with her?" Keoni asked, to which Erik said, "Go ahead, I could care less." Thus it was that recently separated Keoni, a twenty-nine-year-old father of two whose wife had just had an affair at the Cedar Rapids Marriott with their mutual coworker in middle management, asked a girl out for the first time in thirteen years. At 8:00 PM on a Saturday night she knocked on his door. He had already cued up a movie. "Can we watch something else?" she said immediately, perhaps because the date movie Keoni had chosen was *Capitalism: A Love Story*. "Why?" asked Keoni. "I don't even know what capitalism *is*," she said, and he, striving to be solicitous, said, "Sure you do," and she said, "I'm only nineteen, I don't have to know," which is when, according to Keoni, he knew this relationship was already dead, and switched over to *Hot Tub Time Machine*.

In the morning, when Keoni woke up alone to make some coffee, he leaned by a window. In the backyard, something white and translucent shimmered off an evergreen. The whole yard was, in fact, looped round in white strands, as if mummied over and recently unwrapped.

What first occurred to Keoni was that Erik, angry about an aborted liaison for which he had given Keoni explicit permission, had draped his own brother's yard in toilet paper. It occurred to him also that Erik did not have a day job, could not pay his own bills, and was currently driving a car that Keoni had loaned him, and so it seemed that Erik had driven Keoni's car to Keoni's house using gas paid for by their father and proceeded to throw seven or eight rolls of toilet paper, also paid for by their father, over the foliage in Keoni's yard.

That was Keoni's version of events, told to us at Rocky's house one day when Erik was elsewhere training. He and Erik would never mention the matter in one another's presence; they almost never spoke in any case. When Erik decided to tell his side of the story, the day after he papered the yard, it was to the team, in the gym, at a practice to which Keoni did not come. That he was the guilty party was now so established he did not try to deny it. He delivered his speech in the now-familiar form of a farewell. "My brother is forcing me to leave," he said, by which he could only have meant that in spending a few hours with Ashley, Keoni was making Erik's life so intolerable that he could not stay in Cedar Rapids.

"I'm sorry, because I love all you guys," he continued, "and I won't get into it again, a lot of you have heard about it already, but basically, he doesn't respect me. So I'm going to Milwaukee, even though I made this gym, because I can't stay here. Things are different now. And it's a shame, because if I leave, people are going to start losing."

When various fighters relayed the story of Erik's speech to Keoni, they either did or did not mention the part where Erik announced his departure. Erik was either calm or unhinged, either spoke for three or five minutes, and either did or did not call Keoni a traitor. Only four words in Erik's speech remained unwavering in the retellings, the words the men found most singularly offensive. *I made this gym.*

There were stories that kept rising to the surface, incidents from before my time meant to demonstrate Erik's hypocrisy in threatening to abandon his own team. It was recalled, in this period, what Erik had said of Jesse Lennox on a night when he'd had more to drink than his frail, long-suffering metabolism could endure. Deep in the basement era, Jesse Lennox started showing up four days a week, then three. Then two. He told Keoni that he was training at Miletich, the Iowa camp people had actually heard of, the camp with branded T-shirts and mandatory HIV testing and what was called, rather extravagantly, a "sponsor acquisition program." Ever even-keeled Keoni told Jesse, when Jesse asked permission, that "you write your own book," that "nobody can tell you what your destiny is." Erik said nothing of this until his twenty-first birthday, when people were handing him shots that self-respect demanded he take. The men were canopied around a table at a bar near Rocky's house when someone brought up Jesse Lennox and Erik began a tirade the fighters tended, now that Erik was threatening to leave, to recall. "Fuck Jesse Lennox," began Erik, in a speech that lasted minutes and left the rest of them stiff-backed. Keoni had made Jesse, said Erik, Hard Drive had made Jesse, and yet when Jesse finally made it to his first Big Show, it was Miletich in his corner and "Team Miletich" sliding across the Pay-Per-View chevron. He had taken what he could from the fighters and forgotten them. "Jesse Lennox," said Erik, "is a traitor."

I suppose in relating these tales, which I picked up mostly by sitting behind a hanging bag, I leave myself open to charges of provocative gossip-mongering for my own dubious amusement, or, worse, to sate some kind of vulgar thirst for meliorist moral instruction. But since the men were so well-walled, the letters HD burned into their limbs, what seems gossip was more like the political tumult of a small island nation-state, a Singapore on the swirling Cedar River. I could not read the minds of these men, but I came to know what memories had congealed into anecdotes, and what narratives they knew by heart.

August turned into September and September into October.

Erik still did not leave and would not articulate a reason. I, for one, did not need him to. From my dealings in Davenport I knew plenty of fighters who would never leave home, and knew too that their aspirations would remain just that. Erik was so comfortable in the company of his friends, so given to a laugh over anything at all, and he had never known anything but Iowa.

All that summer he drove Keoni's car from Keoni's gym to Wes's apartment, where he was living, to a pizza place that never made him pay. He could not smell the churning grain—didn't know what people were talking about when they described the sticky-sweet cloud hovering over the city. The wide empty streets of downtown seemed to him neither wide nor empty, merely streets, the way one drove over the city-splitting river, which did not strike him as particularly gray. He drove Keoni's car from the pizza place that did not make him pay to Wes's apartment to Keoni's gym to the movie theater, where three or four men jumped out of line to ask him when he was fighting next and the guys who did not approach him explained to their girlfriends that this was Erik Koch, the man they'd seen fighting on TV, and then he watched a movie with Wes and on the way home his dad called to say I put some money in your account and I will see you this weekend and Erik said I love you dad and Wes thought this was cute.

"You're a leech," Steve screamed at him once, at Keoni's house, in the midst of a fight whose origins no one can remember.

"It's a lifestyle," said Erik.

I would not call it leeching myself, any more than I would accuse Sean or Erik of parasitical dependence on services I willingly provided. How delicate is our little ecosystem of reciprocity; how easily men are hurt when the unstated terms of their exchange shift beneath them. Erik was not leeching, I say, but exchanging. He was a most generous provider of proximity to himself. So he provided himself to Rob, who drove him everywhere he asked. So he provided himself to Rocky, who fed him day after day. So he provided himself to KayLee, who gave him we know not what when we weren't around. So he provided himself to Wes, who let Erik live with him rent-free. All that was asked was that Erik be physically present, which did not seem to anyone, with the possible exception of Erik, too much to ask.

Fiddling with his computer one day between workouts, Rocky found a make-your-own-movie time-waster with which to waste time. One just typed bits of dialogue and watched them spill forth from prefab animated puppies. He named a puppy in green overalls Erik and a puppy in a yellow dress Rocky, placed them in a bright green meadow, and screened his film—*Milwaukee,* he called it—as a bonus feature on a Friday, just before the ritual viewing of *Pumping Iron.*

"Well, I am moving to Milwaukee tomorrow so I thought I would take a stroll through the park," says a bulbous Erik puppy without inflection. "Are you fucking kidding me dude?" responds Rocky's equally round, inflectionless counterpart.

ERIK: Jesus Christ Rocky. I am fucking serious this time.
ROCKY: Oh I'm sorry man. I didn't realize you were serious this time. So that pretty much means you're leaving for sure since you were serious the last eighteen times too.

ERIK: Whatever dude. Tomorrow morning I will be on my way
   to Milwaukee and you will look stupid.

ROCKY: Man. You do sound more serious about this than before.
   I believe you now.

ERIK: You do? Thanks man. Because I am really not fucking
   around this time.

ROCKY: There's no chance in hell you're leaving tomorrow.

ERIK: You cock suckin' son of a bitch, I have to leave tomorrow.
   And besides, things are different now. I can always have
   KayLee give me her car while I live there.

ROCKY: You're right about that. That bitch is pretty much
   retarded. We should pull a circle jerk on her and that
   Ashley chick. How does tomorrow night sound to you?

ERIK: Motherfucker Rocky. You know damn well I will not be in
   town tomorrow.

Rocky's film was received by all, Erik included, as an accomplished piece of documentary filmmaking. Erik shook his head as it ended, smiling, charmed, and to an extent I was only then beginning to realize, trapped.

Sean – Fall 2010

I AM NOT A BORN TRESPASSER, AND I don't know that Sean is, but when you spend your days in a concrete hole you will tend to spill out into spaces unsanctioned. Thus Sean appropriated the local Sheraton, where he crossed the long lobby staring at the carpet and hoping no one had the will to remove a man with ears so obviously deformed by consensual violence. The business center was a place to print his bloodwork, the shared kitchen microwave a place to mold his mouthpiece, the sauna to shed weight prefight. Once, long after the months I want to tell you about here, Sean emerged from a half hour in the Sheraton sauna, huffing, eyes gone dead, and lowered himself to lie flat on the concrete floor. A hotel employee walked through the pool area, shot us a look, continued on. Sean splayed his arms and legs and stared up at the ceiling and lay there recovering until finally he said, "I don't have much direction. Life just kind of flows through me."

When Sean says he knows no direction, I hear him talking of a grace particular to his kind. To be a great fighter, I came to believe, one had to be naked before the clash, which meant not cluttering one's life with other people, petty distractions, emotional armor a violent encounter need penetrate. Sean clung to nothing. And so when something in the universe did happen, he was wide open, a gaping hole, an instrument alive to tuning. Feelings had him. When he was hungry he ate, and when he was tired he slept, and when he had need of a woman, he found one online and had her. The future made and unmade itself in the space of a single conversation. "I should become a Navy SEAL," he'd say, packing a bowl with his thumb, and a moment later, "Nah, I don't approve of what we're doing over there," and riffle through his pockets for a lighter.

There were no fights to be had upon our return from St. Louis, no encounters to encount. I found my position vis-à-vis Sean elevated, for I was still his only spacetaker, and here were fightless days and days in which Sean's status required shoring up. It was those long stretches of sameness, unraveling over many months, that justified this entourage of one. I attended seminars as seldom as possible—Sean being my Yale College and my Harvard, as I was fond of telling him—and we toured the city: to the art museum, to The Paddlewheel, up the steep hills, back down to the bank. He led, I followed, and even during the dampest, drizzliest November day, this had a feeling of ceremony. A two-person parade, if you will.

What this was like is not easy to describe. To be in Sean's aura was to be in a suspended state of unpreparedness; it wasn't just that anything could happen, but when it did happen, you would be empty and unready for it and without resources to react, which was, in the end, just another kind of readiness. Sean's very presence in this place was a contingency laced with various misfortunes: when he left Tennessee five years before, he headed for Team Miletich instead of to an equally celebrated team in New Mexico because he thought his '89 Chevy Blazer was more likely to make it to Davenport than to Albuquerque; and when his catalytic converter grew clogged in Illinois he hadn't had the money to fix it; and when he was told the car could not go over 30 mph, he said OK, and drove it at 29 mph on the highway ("Was it scary? Fuck yeah, it was scary") until at last he arrived. Thus the most mundane events were laced with a kind of unknowing. The world would provide or it wouldn't, destroy you or move on.

Thoughts came unbidden, and often late, as did the news that he would be a father at the end of our time in St. Louis. On that occasion I pressed not at all, hoping the moment would pass and I would never hear tell of it again, but he continued the next morning in the car on the way back. We were speeding across mile upon mile of barns and cattle and empty stretches of green soybean carpet followed by more barns and more cattle and very occasionally a white fence with lilies planted by the posts, as we let our arms hang out the windows into the heat.

"She wants money for it," he said. He was shouting so I could hear him above the wind. "As soon as she told me she was pregnant she started asking for money. Like, it's yours, give me forty dollars."

Sean had slept with nineteen-year-old Alexis twice, eight weeks previous to the fight in St. Louis, and a mere month after his divorce was finalized. His knowledge of the basic facts surrounding her existence struck me as rather limited in scope, though he had met her sister. At some point between their lurid tryst and the fight in St. Louis, Alexis moved to Omaha, notified him, by text, that she was pregnant, and demanded cash. The story had certain holes in it, I thought.

"I hope I can get custody," Sean said. "At least for the weekends."

"What?" I asked, alarmed at the fact that this fetus, which I took to be an imaginary agent of blackmail, had suddenly become a human child with weekend plans.

"I want to be in its life, take it camping back in Tennessee, that sort of thing."

The side of Sean's face was purple with bruises.

"Little kids are amazing," he said.

"But—"

"It's going to need to spend time with someone more educated than Alexis. Her grammar is terrible; she's just really ignorant."

"You sent her money?"

"Just a little, she said it wasn't enough."

I quite doubted that this woman was pregnant at all. But my strategy here, if you could call it that, was to let this comment hang and hope it swelled into a portentous suggestion Sean might assimilate. We were quiet for a while; I turned on the radio. He turned it off.

"She smokes," he said. "That's crazy, right? It's so risky."

From this conversation I do not mean it to be inferred that Sean was particularly credulous; indeed, Sean's Pyrrhonian skepticism and anarchic antiauthoritarianism was of the sort only afforded those so strong in body and mind they haven't need for fragile elaborate delusions carefully balanced, like stacked glass, upon the delusions of others. One of his favorite expressions was "running a scam," an accusation he flung at almost everybody with a broad-minded enthusiasm that knew no boundaries of class or status. Sean doubted not only the architects of the war he'd fought in but also the presumed authority and easy sanctimony of the men with whom he fought. He doubted women, promoters, bartenders, anyone remotely involved with the UFC or its television show, car mechanics, the people at Legal Aid, the staff of the University of Phoenix, and landlords. He doubted the President. "You suddenly find and kill this guy in an election year?" he said when Barack Obama announced the murder of Osama bin Laden. "Right. Yeah. Very convenient."

Truth be told, I thought little of our Alexis-related conversation during those months, its uncharacteristic fixity. I paid attention instead to all the jobs Sean liberated himself from just a few weeks in, the way he escaped from the office stapling OSHA manuals, walked out one night of the bar where he bounced. One job was becoming very regular—a job at a construction site, six days a week, seven hours a day for two months—and it was this regularity that made Sean stop, one day, halfway through his morning commute. He stopped the car. He started the car. He drove back home. "I don't want to build stuff for a living," he told me later that day.

"Wouldn't it be easier to just keep a job?" someone asked him once at The Paddlewheel, and Sean said that would not be easier at all, because he was a fighter, and to pretend to be otherwise was to struggle against himself hour after hour, day after day, though, that being said, this was not a period in which Sean demonstrated much interest in working out. Sean's fluidity was such that he had taken on a kind of phantom quality; he slipped between houses so quickly one could not expect to find him where one had last seen him, though through each move—from the concrete hole, to the first floor of a Motel 6, to a studio, to a shared apartment above the gym—if one were to find him, one could be sure he'd be planless and happy to wander outward.

Nevertheless, I felt inspired by his determination not to let life interfere with his artistry. I was inspired enough to email the Director of Graduate Studies and explain that I was engaged in some exciting experimental philosophy, and that I supposed my ongoing study of the phenomenological basis of ecstasy to be more important than taking a few survey courses at what was, after all, a midranked philosophy program. I felt that they should make some allowances on my account. He responded with a rather abrupt note informing me that the requirements of my degree would remain in force. I did attend my classes on occasion, most often a course on the Philosophy of Language, taught with some competence by a Professor Knowles who, when told of my project, deemed it "a possibly interesting revisionist study of nineteenth-century Francophone aesthetic theory." I took this to be an expression of enthused support tempered by twenty years of imprisonment in the Department of Philosophy building, which, thanks to an era of university architecture principally inspired by fear of rioting youths, quite literally resembles a bastille.

Thus buoyed, I responded to Knowles's assignments with the rigor of a scholar rather than the craven parroting of a student. He assigned a paper on the antirealism of Hilary Putnam, who believed that the only independent reality is beyond the reach of our perceptual capacities. I did not see much point in rehashing Putnam's various casuistic maneuverings, and offered instead ten pages explaining that there was a way, even in our time, to intensify the body's poor perceptual capacities, if only for a fleeting moment. My examples required some illustration of various martial-arts stratagems so I included, for Knowles's benefit, graphics meant to convey the meaning of "rear-naked choke" and "leglock."

One afternoon Sean and I parked right up against the Mississippi and together walked up the limestone bluffs, where a few whimsically turreted mansions endure. This was the Davenport of Gilded Age German landowners who covered the hills in wrapped-porched Palladian-windowed well-columned homes perched high above the river. It was September then and chilly but as we ascended we shed our jackets and held them in hands that swayed with our long climbing gait. There were some places where it felt a little odd to have a companion whose face had been reshaped by his profession, but then Davenport's industrialists were dead and its fighters very much alive.

Sean was telling me about his latest job; his boss told old ladies that the earth beneath their homes exuded an invisible toxic gas, then installed tubes to suck the poison out of the earth and fan it out into the atmosphere. Then his boss told the old ladies to rest easy: problem fixed. Sean was paid in cash.

"Is that safe?" I asked, breathing hard. The cold made my knuckles ache.

"Well I can die now," he said. "I've already passed on my seed."

The mansions' current inhabitants had arranged their expensive cars to angle just-so against the curves of their long black driveways, as if to pose one still life against another. The lawns had been edged, planted, trimmed. The only movement was a man mowing the edge of his lawn where it met his neighbor's. The mower of lawns looked us up and down, registered that we were not of this neighborhood, but, being that this was Davenport, probably understood that we were together of the fighting class. We walked on.

"If there is one thing I'm afraid of," said Sean, "it's lawn mowers."

Sean was texting the whole way back down the hill. He was shaking his head.

"What is it," I asked.

"The mother of my child," he said, "thinks ammonia is a disease you can get."

It was clear now that she really was pregnant, though no one could say by whom, and that she was living in Omaha with a boyfriend named Kris. Had there been a delicate way to suggest to Sean that he was very likely not the father, I might have ventured forth into such awkward territory, but he seemed to have shut down the skeptical elements of his cognition in all matters Alexis.

A long, curt, increasingly antagonistic written correspondence swallowed the months that lay ahead. Every time he brought up the subject of Alexis, I would try to change the subject, but he insisted upon reading her texts aloud. I have no record of their correspondence, as it is not the kind of thing with which I would have sullied my notebook, but what I can reconstruct from those dramatic readings goes something like the following:

> Boy or Girl?
> Send $
> Boy or Girl?
> 2 soon
> Stop smoking
> Dont tell me what to do
> Boy or Girl?
> Boy
> Sending $$
> $60? Its your SON
> Stop smoking
> Send $

In the end Sean always sent money. I suppose in retrospect the birth of a living distraction might have worried me even more, the lack of attachment being something I so admired in Sean, but because nothing else changed—there was no fixed job, no permanent house, no pattern to any given day—I could see this emergence only as a kind of infatuation that would pass when Alexis disappeared completely, one hoped, into a dark textless pocket of the earth. But it got to the point, somewhere around December, when every conversation terminated in the imminent birth of a child at the hands of a demanding adolescent.

Need $80 to see doctor
Don't have it
How can u do this to your son?
Will get it. Want 2 b there when hes born tho
Hell no ur just a sperm donor
yah MY sperm

In January Alexis sent Sean a picture, by text, of a boy she had named Josiah. She said the sister was there when the doctors put the baby into her arms. A writhing creature revealed himself to them. "Yep," said the sister, laughing as she touched Josiah's fist and welcomed this permanent fixture of the world into being. "Sean Huffman."

Erik – Fall 2010

I HAVE ALLUDED BEFORE TO THOSE WHO think fight-dwellers to be toothless cretins and backwater voyeurs, who take us to be sadistic thrill-seekers atrocity-hopping our way across the Midwest, who think we've grown so cold and hard that nothing but raw violence will penetrate our thick-headed daze. Who think us the perfect enemies of the polis. I will not object on every front; I won't plead innocent on every charge. Fighters are not, it is true, on the side of civilization, and nor, by extension, are we. Fighters on the side of civilization are called soldiers, and soldiers do not fight only with those who freely consent, or pull back when a bell sounds, which may or may not have something to do with why the man who came closest to destroying MMA was a war hero popular among the people. But what I find very strange is that these very same detractors—war hero included—describe the sport of boxing in the most elevated terms: It is poetry, it is ballet, it is chess. Boxing, they say, has a history.

I consider it a strange concept of history which omits the fact that boxing is an eighteenth-century invention, and that in order to invent it the British banned, in the ring, wrestling and kicking, which is to say they elevated boxing from a *mixture of martial arts*. And a strange conception too that passes over pankration, the ancient Greek mix of grappling and fistfighting known to scholars of sport, and with which Theseus successfully slew the Minotaur. History begins wherever you start searching for it. If you look hard enough at the King James Bible, for example, pausing in the thirty-second chapter of the book called Genesis, you may find Jacob, who is being subjected to some obscure sacramental test, grappling, in the sporting sense, with a physical manifestation of God.

And yet I won't disagree with this impulse, this drive to wipe clean the historical record. Spectacles shouldn't have makers, nor miracles first-movers, and it seems to me that a fighter in his purest form has no history. Perhaps then we must imagine the sport sprung fully formed around 1990, as the haters will have it, and simply accept this inevitable prejudice against the new. But all this about our being bloodthirsty—"Isn't that like dog-fighting?" a Baltimore heiress once asked me when I tried to explain the concept of mixed martial arts—well, let us be judged by what we see. When heads are bowed, do you see the great sweep of belief converging upon a Midwestern dinner table, or do you see pork chops getting cold? When a hearse passes, do you see the American dead connected in long bars of black, or an inefficient mode of postmortem transport? And look, now, at a young fighter flying through the air, picked up and slammed down by the brother to whom he taught this very throw, now registering the shock of the fall, now curling into fetal position, now clenching his jaw to avoid crying out in pain. Do you see an entire enmitical fraternal history winnowed to a single act? Do you see dog-fighting?

I speak, obviously, of the time Erik tried in earnest to leave. The decisive impetus was Erik's parents; who, upon seeing their sons locked in anger, all Erik's relationships in a state of degradation, and having heard, like the rest of us, daily promises of a move to Milwaukee that did not come to pass, sat down their son for a gentle intervention.

"You have to do *something*," his mother said.

"You can come visit every weekend," said his father, who had, due to Keoni's persistence and Erik's success, finally come to see the inherent nobility in his sons' vocation.

Erik was not ungrateful for the push. The next night he packed his television and a duffel bag into Wes's car, and Wes drove him northwest toward Milwaukee, five hours away, simply because Erik asked. Wes was not a member of Hard Drive, and existed apart from the team's collective psychology; in Wes's reading of the situation, Erik was a victim of their pathetic, insidious jealousy.

Erik found he had, after a long summer of verbally distancing himself from Cedar Rapids, the courage to break free, though not without a good deal of fear. He passed the drive posting messages on the Internet to tell the fighters how much he loved them; how they were his true brothers. "You all own a piece of me the way I look at it," he wrote, "I love you," and as Wes approached the

Wisconsin state line, "Can't help but burst into tears." The fighters wished him well and teased him. "Quit cryin', pussy," wrote Lonnie. Erik did not want to arrive. Wes dropped him off at an anonymous apartment building in a Hispanic neighborhood, across the street from a closed brick bar and a soon-to-be-evicted storefront church with the words *camino de santidad* scrawled on paper and taped to the door.

Now, as you have begun to see, each promoter has his petty kingdom. But not all kingdoms are created equal, and to walk into the world of Duke Roufus, who was tapped into the vast glittering network of the Big Shows, was rather different than standing shoulder to shoulder with a couple of tawdry St. Louis drag racers. Duke Roufus had stars in every weight class, a gleaming capacious gym, a minor press corps that hung on his every whispered word. The moment Erik moved to Milwaukee the fightwear he could not formerly afford began arriving at his new home in boxes: twelve shirts, fifteen hats, to be given away by him as by some Winsconsinite Evita apportioning gold to a grateful peasantry. Now there was a machine in place to project his image across the nation, a team of top-tier coaches with prepared notes on his next opponent, a lineup of sponsors happy to pay for a spot on the shorts someone had sent him unbidden.

I did not venture myself to Milwaukee, and not only because I had academic obligations in Iowa. The very thought of Wisconsin was singularly distasteful to me. I was born in a place called Baraboo, and resided there until the age of sixteen. I hold no particular ill will to the place beyond the fact that it is my place of origin; and no person ought to return to the place from which she sprung, unless she wants to risk being stuck in time. What happens when you go home? You see your cohort—all the rooted fearful fools with whom you were educated. You see your parents, and the room in which you spent lonely nights as an adolescent, and the distant suburbs in which you are expected to live. You drop into the matrix that tried to create you, until you left it, and found your true set of contemporaries, the people with whom you choose to commune. My people are not Jane Banks or Peter Smith of twenty-first-century Baraboo, but Simone Weil of Depression-era Paris, and Georges Bataille of midcentury Reims—the people who sustained me during the long period of study that preceded my time as a taker of space. Should I ever decide to spawn a nuclear family and enjoy their dull companionship between bouts of desk-ridden drudgery—to live, that is, in what Sartre called "Bad Faith"—I shall return with all due haste to Baraboo. But until then, I resist the temptation, lest the comfort and simplicity of a conformist life suck me back into its maw.

Thus it was that Erik and I spoke on the phone, developing a sort of patter, a back-and-forth by which I took space from afar. "How are you doing?" I would ask, and elicit the invariable response: "Just livin' the dream."

Milwaukee was not a fighterly city; it was merely where Duke happened to land, and Duke was on the grid, one of many such men who mostly peopled places like Vegas, Rio de Janeiro, Tokyo, and Seoul. Such men, I had discovered, could live anywhere; what mattered was that they had one another's numbers and the power to pluck fighters they favored from the backcountry, raise them up to Pay-Per-View. It was less that Erik had arrived at some physical space than that, in coming to Milwaukee, he signaled some readiness to belong in the world of the Big Shows, not merely to show up and go home.

It was much on his mind in those weeks, how readily the people of the grid dropped you right back into the hovel in which they found you, should you lose twice. That particular fate was made clear by the countless fighters who had fought in Big Shows, lost, and come back down to, say, a high school gym in downtown Davenport. These were the leftovers, the class of men who went to The Paddlewheel to tell over and over the story of their One Big Fight. Some of these men had gotten as far as Erik only to find that their bodies were too fragile to handle the force of a truly studied striker, or to find that they lacked the intelligence to transition from boxing to Muay Thai to jiu-jitsu to wrestling with the fleetness befitting an artist of martial collage. Sometimes they hadn't even lost; they'd gotten hurt, or gotten hurt and then addicted to Vicodin, and in the interim the men who ran things ceased to care.

Erik did have one recurring injury, an ache in his elbow that called to him when he was tired and hungry. In the long history of Hard Drive, and all the boys Keoni ushered into the circle, there had been a single glaring mistake. His name was Joe Vedepo, and he did not play with the gentle scrupulousness of the others; when he had another man by the arm, even in practice, he would pull until it hurt. In this way he tore the fragile tissue in Erik's left elbow; and Keoni, incensed, banned Vedepo from the gym for life. This was what happened when people who did not belong in the gym were permitted to play. It was also a story about how to leave Valhalla, forever, and transform a bunch of brothers with whom you shared a tattoo into strangers.

Erik had lost exactly once in his career, back in March, to a wrestler in Ohio who held him down for three rounds. He could not, then, lose in Las Vegas in November, a mere two months away. And so he was training four or five times a day: a run, a boxing session, jiu-jitsu, weight-training, and another run. Yet there seemed, he complained to me, much time left over in a city he did not know. All of that time was spent with the room-mate Duke had selected for him, Anthony "Showtime" Pettis, Milwaukee's most celebrated fighter and a twenty-three-year-old half-Mexican half-Puerto Rican man who did not want to spend his Saturday nights watching *Pumping Iron* on repeat.

Milwaukee was not yet a place where Erik had an audience, but a place where Pettis had limitless spacetakers constantly jockeying for fighterly proximity. Often these men would follow Pettis to a bar he owned with Duke, a bar they called Showtime, as part of Pettis's ambitious branding strategy. At Showtime, I am given to understand, Pettis would converse with girls in Spanish while Erik sat idly by, tolerating Pettis's shadows and their questions about him. Very early in the morning—so went their routine—Erik and Pettis would return home with which-ever Hispanic girl Pettis chose for the provision of nocturnal intimacies, and the friend of that girl, who would provide par-allel services to Erik.

Erik took all of this to be constitutive of adult life, having had no experience away from the fraternal nest of Hard Drive, and he is far from the first man to venture to a new place and mold himself to the given shape of things. The apartment they shared was a one-bedroom, and so these intimacies tended to be somewhat exposed, with Erik on the couch and Pettis in a loft that itself afforded no privacy. It went on this way, night after night, until one particular evening when it finally occurred to Erik that he and Pettis were not of the same world.

One September Saturday night, a week and a half into Erik's move, Pettis and Erik departed from Showtime and returned home with the requisite two girls. Following this party was Pettis's uncle, a Hispanic forty-year-old man in a T-shirt, sneakers, and low-slung jeans. He was thickly accented and always around, making the most of his fortuitous blood relation. He smelled of drugstore musk. Erik treated him with a distant courtesy he thought owed to anyone over thirty.

I hesitate to relate the following Pettis-instigated vulgarities, and do so only because Erik related this story to me not once but three times, as if retelling it helped explain something he was not otherwise prepared to articulate. The men gathered in the kitchenette, while the girls—shy, silent, grateful to have been selected—waited in the living area. It was Pettis's desire that both he and Erik be intimate with both girls. His exact words, I believe, were: "Let's bang them, then switch."

Erik led his assigned paramour to the couch, taking it as given that Pettis would disappear into his room and Pettis's uncle would show himself out. The girl he had been assigned peeled off her vestments one by one until she was completely bare-skinned, visible in the weak light of the window above the couch. Erik could hear Pettis and his uncle laughing, though by the time he realized that they were laughing because they were watching from the dark kitchen, he too had disrobed entirely.

He found this extremely uncomfortable, but the thing was already in motion, and the girl didn't seem to find the situation unusual. That he was being watched merely made him feel pressured to do precisely as Pettis had instructed, and so he dutifully performed the act Pettis expected him to perform.

"He's drilling her!" Pettis reported, laughing.

Erik turned his face away from the kitchen, back toward the couch. Something smelled odd. Like musk. He turned his face back toward the kitchen to see Pettis's uncle, pants unzipped, standing before him. He had exposed himself inches from the girl's mouth. The girl screamed. Erik jumped up.

"What the fuck?" Erik shouted.

Pettis laughed and playfully shoved his uncle. "What the fuck, Reynaldo?" To Erik, he turned, slightly conciliatory. "You guys can take the bedroom," he said.

For Erik this particular incident could not simply be assimilated into the rhythm of his new life. Some line had been crossed, and he wanted to talk about it. "I am just a farmboy from Iowa," he told me soon afterward, which was not, strictly speaking, true. "I'm used to getting to know girls. In Cedar Rapids it's like, hey, wanna go on a date, wanna go see a movie?"

Following this experience, Erik stopped padding after Pettis night after night, though he had no car and feared the neighborhood; Pettis's brother had told him casually of a man recently stabbed to death on the block's southeast corner. This left Erik isolated and awake. In his new life there was no one with whom merely to be. Alone, he listened for the first time to the worried chatter in his own head.

Now were you to ask the average person what stands in the way of fighterly excellence, what is most likely to short-circuit a fighterly career before it launches, well, he might say a weak chin or a lack of intelligence or insufficient discipline. The spacetaker knows otherwise. The fighter's greatest enemy is homesickness, and you cannot spend more than a week in any fight camp without watching weak men wilt for want of their own beds. It strikes the aspiring fighters on the reality television shows—at least one will drop out because he misses his mother. It robs fight camps of half their new members, which is why no one will take an aspirant seriously until he stays put for a month. And it was, in September of 2010, very near taking down Erik. He could see that this was coming, was, indeed, expected of him by his brother and his team.

Erik had been in Milwaukee for thirteen days. He closed the door to his room. He flipped the television on and off, fought the urge to eat forbidden carbs, picked up laundry off the floor, went outside to sit on the steps, came inside to sit on his bed, turned on TV once again. Were he home he would have been somewhere with Rocky and Jared and KayLee, the casino maybe, laughing about a favorite line from a movie they knew by heart. He picked up his phone and thought about asking his father for a ride home. Instead he texted the team with an altogether new hostility.

Over the next week he texted the team hundreds of times a day, calling them stoners and losers; he told them, to their amazement, that they owed him money; he threatened violent retribution for various offenses. He had heard that Rocky had said something rude to Wes, for which he told Rocky he would "beat his ass." He also accused Rocky of hitting on KayLee, at which point Rocky told Erik he was going to get a restraining order, at which point Erik questioned Rocky's manliness. Erik accused Jared of being jealous. He told Keoni that Keoni owed him money for a burrito, which Keoni claimed was the one time Erik had paid for anything in the thousands of times they had eaten out together. And so on, for days.

I did not see why Erik's absence should prevent me from enjoying the other fighters' company on Friday nights at Rocky's house, and so it was that I watched these sentiments received in Cedar Rapids. That particular evening, the remainder of the team declined to watch *Pumping Iron*. "I don't want to talk about Erik," Rocky kept saying by way of bringing up the subject of Erik, "but I will say that he is one injury away from being nothing." It was again recalled that Erik had called Lennox a traitor. The subject would move briefly to food, but even then it would swerve back to Erik, and Rocky would say Erik was one injury away from being nothing, and a new slew of anecdotes would be unleashed. Everyone was standing, leaning against Rocky's countertops or hovering around a fresh pizza.

"Man that cereal's fuckin' good!" said Jared, digging into a bowl of Rocky's Kashi granola. He had to stay away from the pizza because of an upcoming fight.

"Isn't it?" said Rocky. "I eat that cereal every morning with a fuckin' banana."

"I could kill that whole box," said Steve. "At Matt's house I used to go apeshit on their fridge when I got high, then I'd come back the next day with fuckin' bags of groceries to replace everything."

"Erik would do the same thing, right?" Rocky joked, and everyone laughed at the idea that Erik would ever pay anyone back.

"He'd pay 'em back someway, right?" joked Rocky. "He'd teach 'em how to do some shit or something?"

Everyone laughed.

"They owe *him* actually, right?"

"We should have just refused to give him rides," said Jared, "just left him somewhere."

"Wes would have picked him up," said Rocky.

"I really think if I had a chance to talk to Wes," said Rocky, "I could make him see things the way they are."

"I don't know," said Keoni, "Wes is pretty smart. I think Wes just likes to have a good time."

"What's he get out of that shit?"

"He gets a jockstrap."

Keoni, citing the toilet papering of his backyard, believed it to be probable that Erik suffered from a chemical imbalance beyond his control. Jared strenuously agreed with this hypothesis, as did Rocky. They turned to the Internet. Did he suffer multiple personality disorder? Was he bipolar? By 11:00 PM they'd lighted upon their diagnosis: sociopath. The Internet offered thirteen warning signs. It was Keoni's earnest opinion that Erik exhibited all thirteen.

"I don't want you to take this the wrong way," Keoni texted Erik, "but you exhibit thirteen classic signs of sociopathy."

When Erik had left, Keoni predicted that he wouldn't last two weeks away from home. In fact Erik was to last three. That Friday night he called his father in an all-out panic. He said that he didn't feel like himself, was afraid of what he might do, and was terrified that he had lost all motivation to fight. The chatter in his head was growing louder, he could not sleep, and he was thinking of checking himself into a mental hospital. Erik's father drove five hours there, five hours back, bearing an anxious Erik in the cab of his truck.

•

Months before his departure for Milwaukee, that day we first met in his apartment, Erik, by way of introduction, I suppose, imparted his philosophy. "You gotta be crazy about it," he said. "I don't know if you've ever seen the movie *Pumping Iron*. With Arnold Schwarzenegger. You've never seen it? Arnold Schwarzenegger used to be Mr. Olympia. Arnold Schwarzenegger was the best body builder in the world. Best in the world. Two weeks before a competition his father died, and his mom called and said, 'Your father died, you have to come out here for the funeral.' And Arnold Schwarzenegger said, cold as hell, he said, 'I can't. I'm doing this, I gotta worry about this right now.' He hung up on her. She tried calling back, he didn't pick up the phone. Put it completely out of his mind. It's the people who make sacrifices like *that*, the crazy ones, the ones who are dedicated. Great fighters are great because they sacrifice."

I suppose many will find these sentiments immoral. But

would you truly have, in the final accounting, an artist of bodily transformation pack his toothbrush and truck off to an Austrian funeral? Though none of us would want to live in a universe peopled primarily by Schwarzeneggers and Eriks; though we actively seek to ostracize the will to destroy unchosen bonds of familial duty; nor, I think, would we want to live without such sentiment, or without genius, such as it is. The price of engagement with the eternal is perhaps heavier than we like to admit in the bright light of day. By all means, we say, sacrifice health and money and stability and carbs; rehearse your lonely tragic dance in the cheap hotel room by the train tracks; succumb to your artisanal narcissism, until the moment it makes us uncomfortable because a progenitor's corpse is involved. I say the world needs genius, and genius is jealous.

Now for every city dweller there is the city itself and then the city that is properly yours—the few blocks you regularly walk and the few stores you properly patronize. Erik's personal Cedar Rapids, given the proud obsessive narrowness of his own focus, was smaller than most. The places that were places in which to be were Wes's house, Rocky's house, Hard Drive, and perhaps in the cab of his father's pickup. He drove his father's truck, that Friday afternoon, through the city he had only managed to half-leave. There on the side of the split highway was his pizza place, and there the Blockbuster from which his brother rented the video with which he discovered MMA, and there the high school from which he dropped out, and the convention center at which he fought before he was discovered. And then habit, as much as anything else, has him driving past the blocks of hospital, past the homeless shelter, past the rundown homes with toys in the yard and tall grass creeping through wrought-iron fences, to the place "where dreams o e true."

Erik walked into Valhalla as if nothing had passed between any of them, and everyone tacitly assented to live by this fiction. Most of them said something mundane by way of welcome; they were not surprised to see him because they didn't believe he had the strength to stay away. Rolling in pairs, arms snaking through legs, heads bowed in that tiny heaving room, they soon became deeply entangled such that I could not tell without effort whose limbs were whose. They seemed one capsized organism struggling to right itself. Beside me a fighter slick with sweat wriggled onto another man's back, nearly slipping off but steadying himself by twining his legs round his partner's wet waist. When Keoni blew the whistle one fighter flicked sweat from his belly button onto another, who retaliated by wringing out his shoulder-length hair on the stomach from which the sweat was flicked. The room was misty, the low afternoon light through the long windows overbearing, and a few fighters crouched low to catch their breath. Erik and Keoni were distracted as the men paired up for sparring, and then they were the only two men unpartnered, and no one was watching, but everyone was.

Keoni approaches Erik, both of them so similarly complected that the boundaries between their bodies blur, though Erik is shadowed about the collarbone, under the ribs. Erik weaves and strikes, but Keoni easily dodges each jab and comes inside his brother's arms, hugging Erik, holding him for a long time, as if to wait for the others to cast glances in their direction, as if to stretch this brief moment of struggle into a long show of impotence. When Erik breaks free, Keoni charges, head low, to sweep Erik and lay him flat, but Erik is too fast to be swept. He twines his arm around the neck of Keoni's bent body, such that Keoni is stuck bowing as Erik stands erect. What happens next is so quick as to be invisible: Erik releases the neck slightly, threads his arm in between Keoni's legs, and hoists his brother like a suitcase soon to be lofted up onto a high shelf. Keoni is five feet off the mat, perpendicular to Erik, suspended there, expressionless, waiting for his brother to have his long victorious moment and slide him gently back to the mat.

Fighters are not soldiers; they are not on the side of family, or country, or civic pride. And if they are self-conscious pursuers of ecstatic bliss, they cannot even be said to be on the side of the self. The self is always the thing you're fleeing, and if your self seems mired in a history, maybe that's got to go too. Everything about this room and the people in it is too close, too constitutive, too historical. And were Erik to place Keoni down feet first with the gentle care expected of him, Erik would not be told that he was never again welcome at Valhalla, and he would not leave, tomorrow, for Milwaukee, and he would not there stay. In the history of Hard Drive, there had been one man who successfully left the team behind, and his name was Joe Vedepo. Erik lacked the fortitude to keep himself in Milwaukee when he knew his fellow team members would welcome him back; he also knew well how to make himself forever unwelcome, and thus make Milwaukee possible.

Erik slammed Keoni onto the mat. We felt the windows shake, the floor tremor, and heard Keoni moan, curled up on the floor, something in his shoulder torn. We closed in around his bent body, all except Erik, who walked away, grabbed a kettle bell, and stared out the window into the street.

I said nothing to him the night he finally broke all ties with home, but silently pledged to be by his side for each and every of his fights, no matter where or when.

Sean – February 2011

February in Iowa is not like February anywhere near an American coast. These are days when we Iowans slip our way up sidewalks so long frozen the very concrete has cracked beneath. When we wrap ourselves in futuristic, highly advanced textiles even as we hide within brick-steel-stone homesteads, pondering in pyramidical silence the cruelest expression of enmity between God and man.

Sean still was not training, but he did finally have a fight, which he said was "in the bubble," and though I did not know what this meant I did not wish to show my ignorance by asking. Allegedly, he also had a child—a child Alexis would not let him see until he had sent her money he did not have. Whoever was victorious in the bubble would walk out with $1000 cash, and while I was more than a little skeptical about Baby Josiah's genetic provenance, to Sean, this meant that winning the fight would mean the opportunity to make his son's acquaintance. I longed for a glorious and transcendent encounter, but I was not entirely sure that I wanted Sean to win.

I arrived early at his doorstep on a snowy Saturday evening, ready to drive him to the bubble. He answered the door with a glass bong in his hand.

"It's good you had your drug test yesterday," I said.

I stood by the door, thinking that in hovering I might impel Sean to hurry. If we were late, we would miss the rules meeting and prefight physical, which, if the promoter were tightly wedded to legal procedure, would mean instant disqualification. An hour later, after Sean had secreted the remaining marijuana somewhere, changed, and found a momentarily missing glove under a pile of books about Bruce Lee, we trudged back to my car in silence. Dirt-flecked snow crunched beneath our feet.

"I really should have trained for this," he said in the car. "I have to get serious about my career, before it's, you know, too late."

By "too late" Sean meant his midthirties, when a fighter was often on top but also on his way out. Thirty-two, thirty-three—these are the years in which a fighter is old enough to have absorbed all the necessary skills, all the wrestling throws and boxing skills and squirrelly jiu-jitsu moves, and the body has not slowed down so considerably that it is as if he is practicing his perfect form underwater. Fighters who still fight at thirty-two and thirty-three are men enigmatically impervious to injury. The tissue that connects femur to tibia is in them not prone to shearing; their neurons are not given to disruption when slammed against their skulls. Sean was thirty-two. "How old are you?" he asked me once, during our first days together. "Twenty-five," I lied.

As I drove, Sean informed me that while he had had all the required blood tests necessary for a fight in Davenport, he had taken them so long ago that they were out of date, as was clearly marked on the paperwork in his hands, and so he perhaps would not be allowed to fight at all. I was finding it hard to see where the street ended and the sidewalk started. I hit a curb. Sean laughed.

"Take a right at Curan Street," he said.

I squinted to make out the sign, but caught it too late.

"Oops."

"I think," he said, "that you might need glasses?"

"It's just the snow."

What I could not miss was the bubble, a great, bulbous dome in the distance, the top half of a gargantuan soccer ball. When Sean and I walked in together it was as if we had entered an active digestive tract. Giant fans kept the place inflated. It was the idea of a man too cheap to build a proper arena and, though we did not know it then, too poor to pay the taxes on even the balloonlike structure he managed to buy. The bubble's fluttery walls flapped on borrowed time.

In its fluidity, at a time when I was hoping to record a moment of transcendence, the bubble seemed most promising. And yet having crossed the structure's threshold, been taken into its peristaltic flapping, I was disturbed to find that the atmosphere inside felt startlingly like the atmosphere outside. February is a poor time to hold a fight inside a glorified tent. I shivered inside my coat, clutching my notebook to my chest. Two hundred fight fans huddled together. EMTs covered themselves in blankets meant for downed fighters, and cornermen slipped their arms out of their zipped coats so that the sleeves hung like vestigial limbs. Sean didn't seem to notice, but then he was high.

Some graceless amateurs were already tussling in the cage. "Sean!" said Spencer "The King" Fisher, walking toward us with Jesse "The Ox" Lennox. "Sean Huffman!" said Joe "The Triangular Strangler" Pearson. "You fighting tonight?" I was reminded again of how much other fighters thought of Sean. He was that rare fighter who did not pass on fights he was likely to lose, who fought anyone he was asked to, which is part of why his record was, in the winter of 2011, sixteen wins and eighteen losses, and part of why he had not ascended to the Big Shows, where men rather more careful than he would land. It might take only five spectacular wins in small fights for someone to notice Sean and pull him into the spotlight, where he might fight beside men such as Erik. But every time he accepted a fight he had no chance of winning, he set himself back at least a year of reputation-building.

"Have you seen a fight card?" Sean asked me, and I went in search of one. Teenage boys hugged their girlfriends, who were hugging themselves. A couple of firefighters claimed the space under the bubble's single, toaster-sized heatlamp. On the floor beside a fireman's boot, I spotted a fight card and plucked it from the floor. Sean was one of those seasoned veterans who fights second to last or third to last or, on a card especially "stacked," fourth to last, so I was not at all expecting what I found there printed.

"Sean," I said, when I made it back to the locker room, "you're the main event."

He exhaled and rubbed the back of his neck.

"Shoulda trained," he said. Sean handed two folded pieces of paper—his long-outdated blood test results—to a mustachioed middle-aged fight doctor watching the match then in progress. The doctor took the pieces of paper and tossed them, still folded, into a cardboard box full of other pieces of paper.

Sean's opponent, Miletich protégé LaVerne Clark, was just then gliding through the interior of the bubble with a dozen spacetakers who spoke to the paucity of my spacetaking ability, all amply muscled black men with tattoos. LaVerne Clark didn't have to go broken-record on his One Big Fight because LaVerne had had five Pay-Per-View fights, four of which were wins. Clark hadn't been thrown out of the elite so much as aged out of it; those wins came to Clark a decade ago, when the MMA was still an unformed thing rife with hair-pulling, crotch-kicking. He was by this time in his late thirties, likely low on gas, but he remained as lean and muscled as he was in his prime, and he remained too a man who attracted a thick aura of half-admiring rumor. He was, according to whom you asked, "unhinged," a "crack addict," "bipolar." He was terrified of housecats, I once overheard Sean telling another fighter, and had been known to run from them, room to room, at other people's parties. Even without his spacetakers I would recognize LaVerne by his too-small head, too-large pecs, and the small scar that dips into the hairline of his left eyebrow.

"You know this is a title fight, right Sean?" asked Chris, the nervous, twitchy promoter none of us had noticed lurking in our collective shadow. "It's five rounds." His T-shirt said "Blueblood MMA" against a backdrop of wings and splattered paint. The winner of this fight would be Blueblood MMA welterweight champion. This involved a pleather belt with a cast-iron buckle. So is our little subculture stippled with petty kingdoms and their tweaker kings.

"Oh. OK," said Sean, who had expected only the usual three.

Another firefighter had joined the first two under the heatlamp, which was definitely not going to burn down the bubble. LaVerne, in shorts, looked miserable, even close to crying. It has often impressed me that the most highly trained fighters display toughness only against that particular element of the world they're trained to fight, which is to say, other men. They wheeze helplessly in the cold and go to pieces at the slightest sign of sickness. I once made the acquaintance of a fighter who emerged from the cage with a grotesquely broken nose, and displayed not the slightest sign of displeasure until hours later, when an emergency room nurse flashed an anesthetic-filled syringe and he sprung squealing from the doctor's chair.

In the ring two young men tumbled in the harmless ineffectual manner of playing puppies, while approximately half of the crowd shivered in the beer line. I attempted to record the details of my surroundings, with the idea that those elements immediately preceding that strange perceptual intensity I associated with fights might be always in common, but it was extremely awkward to write with a gloved hand, and as a result much of what I wrote is sadly illegible. I quite remember being unimpressed with all of the fighters, and deploring the way their encounters dragged on as the rest of us suffered in the cold. Men who lack the knowledge to submit an opponent and the power to knock him unconscious cannot bring a fight to a close; it must endure for the full fifteen minutes, at which point the decision will go to the judges, who will deem some barely bruised boy the victor.

Late that night, Sean was the first to walk down the carpet, and the shivering crowd fell silent for his slow ascent. The quality of the audio was not spectacular, but the melting of Metallica's drumbeat into the harsh flapping of the wind-blown walls did strike me as auspicious. When LaVerne shot out, all those gorgeously cut men behind him, and the ring girl swung her ceremonious hips round the ring, and the announcer drew out the "a" in "Huffman" like a spinning record momentarily stuck, and some especially perceptive nerve in the back of my neck began to twitch—then, I thought, in concise paraphrase of Nietzsche, "order vies with chaos at the point where the orders of beauty collapse." That's when the taunting started.

"Kick him in his fat ass!" shouted one of LaVerne's men sitting cageside.

"This is a three-round fight," the referee told Sean and LaVerne.

"I thought it was five rounds?" said Sean, looking around for the promoter, who had disappeared.

"No, three."

What followed was a fight unlike any of the eleven previous. There was a man well practiced at dishing out bodily harm, and a man as impressively capable of taking it. Sean took a jab that would have broken his nose had his nose not already been permanently pounded into the side of his face. The body blows came hard and fast and tight, and Sean was merely standing with his arms at ninety degrees in front of his bleeding eye. Except for the gasps that followed every snap of Sean's neck, the crowd was silent. Sean got under a hook and took LaVerne down, but LaVerne squirreled out, stood up, and began again to pound. Round one, Round two, no one here would remember the difference. During round three LaVerne began to loosen with exhaustion, to breathe hard, to lift his hands with effort. Even tired, LaVerne had a beautiful elasticity about him, so loose in his bobbing stance, and Sean, surging with something, could see LaVerne's lines more clearly now. The black of the ref's shirt looked suddenly blacker. The give of the canvas under Sean's feet seemed to deepen. Sean had lived in Davenport long enough to know that LaVerne Clark's weakness was the hard right jab; thus the scar. But Sean did not throw a jab. He wiped some blood from his forehead, a motion less desperate than expectant, as if readying a stage. The fight had just begun; the octagon's arrival, I felt sure, was imminent.

The bell rang, and LaVerne raised his right hand in victory.

"It's five rounds," a seated state official said. He had a binder and in it the contracts Sean and Laverne signed. "It's a title fight."

"Oh," said the ref, "five rounds."

"Five rounds!" said LaVerne. "You are fucking with me." He was pacing back and forth in the octagon. "You are fucking with me," he said, this time directly to the ref, who looked at Sean, who looked down.

"Fatass!" someone shouted.

The bell rang.

LaVerne tripped Sean and began to elbow him, repeatedly, in the spine.

"Watch it," said the ref. "Watch it."

LaVerne looked directly at the ref, looked at Sean's back, and elbowed Sean in the spine. Twice.

"That's it!" said the ref, waving his arms back and forth. "That's it, it's over! Disqualification."

LaVerne wailed, punched the canvas, and stood up.

There was a moment in which none of the officials, and no one in the crowd, acknowledged that the fight had ended. The cornermen stayed seated. The official with the binder did not move.

"OK," said the promoter, breaking the tension, walking toward the octagon from wherever he'd been hiding, "that's it."

The ref raised Sean's hand, red with Sean's blood. Boos rose up from every side of the bubble.

Despite this surface failure and the subsequent public humiliation, Sean did not look in the least displeased as we made our way back to the locker room. He was in fact wearing a tight close-lipped smile that looked to be suppressing a much bigger smile. With the few men waiting to congratulate him on the $1000 he had just, somehow, won, he shook some hands, then walked into LaVerne's half of the locker room, where a spacetaker was pulling bloody gauze from the fighter's outstretched hand.

"Hey, man," said Sean, "I just want you to know that you won that fight."

"My problem is not with you," said LaVerne, holding out the other hand now. "They are fucking with me in here."

"Yeah, you weren't hurting me," Sean said quickly, and paused, looking over his shoulder to make sure the ref wasn't in the room. "We could have gone two more rounds. Bad break. Rematch, right?"

"Yeah, that's right, that's right," said LaVerne. "Anyway, I can't give you the belt. I left it at home."

Sean smiled politely. What could matter less to him than a belt? He walked outside the locker room, where I was waiting.

"I did *not* want to go another two rounds," he whispered, pulling the gauze from his own hands. "I gotta start running hills."

Until that moment I had not seen a fight successfully launched simply collapse upon itself, its wiring exposed, its architects not just unmasked but openly bickering in the aisles, all the concentrated energy we'd summoned suddenly dispersed like a monsoon turned to vapor. I'd never seen the thing so naked. And then there was Sean, perfectly pleased though the encounter had gone nowhere; simply happy, as if taking a good beating was an acceptable substitute for transcendence.

The feeling of money in his pocket had Sean chattering, all that night, about how he'd start training again, running, biking twenty miles each and every day. He had to get down to 155 pounds and "fight smarter," he said, find the right fights, and start planning his ascent to the Big Shows. He had a great chin, he said, and all the skills, and just needed to finally commit to his career with everything he had. "I've sparred with some of the best in the world," he said. "I've gone three rounds with Jake Ellenberger. I need to start running hills, training, you know. Stuff athletes do."

Josh Neer called, I thought perhaps to congratulate Sean, but in fact, to coax him toward another encounter. "He's *how tall*?" Sean said into the phone. "Two-twenty? Are you kidding me? Ha!" He shook his head, looked at me. The fighter, it would turn out, was a foot taller than Sean, forty pounds heavier. "I don't know," Sean said. "I don't know."

And a moment later, "OK."

"I'm a fighter," Sean said to me. "I fight whoever, I don't pick fights like some of these other guys."

It is strange what tricks memory plays, because while I well remember feeling cheated and toyed with by a universe that promised release but could not release deliver, I somehow remember this evening with a faraway fondness. It had a frigid purity, that February night; for it was only weeks before something corrupt crept between Sean and me, and the harborless giant I knew fell to the entangling mundanities of the ordinary world.

Erik – November 2010

"Four eggs," I instructed the waiter at the finest restaurant in The Palms Casino Resort.

"Egg salad?" He was in a starched suit, pouring water into a delicately lipped glass.

"No, four hard-boiled eggs."

"Four eggs."

The waiter returned with four eggs huddled in the slight depression of a sizable dinner plate, as if to further diminish the sad feast through a trick of scale. Each egg had been shelled, which was, I supposed, the benefit of ordering hard-boiled eggs at the finest restaurant in The Palms. Erik was a few flights up in his hotel room, showering after a workout with Duke, but he had asked that his meal be ready when he descended, and I feared displeasing him.

Though Duke, Pettis, and Erik's manager could be found dispersed among the card tables and slot machines, not a single member of Hard Drive had ventured with us to Las Vegas. Following the momentous schism between him and his brother, Erik had been "banned for life" from the gym and its environs. That Keoni framed this as a measure he was taking for the safety of his fellow fighters may have masked his quite reasonable anger behind a show of enlightened concern, but then again it was true that Rob and DJ were openly afraid of rolling with the team's most volatile member.

Banished, Erik returned to Milwaukee, to his warm, fast-talking Italian-American coach, to his potential as one of the youngest men in the most prestigious promotion open to men who weighed in at 155 pounds. From their offices in Vegas, con-nected people continued to call him in Milwaukee, and it was as if he had never made the mistake of going home. Would he like to be in the official UFC video game? They would fly him out to L.A., take measurements, and then boys everywhere would fight their friends in the avatarical form of Erik "New Breed" Koch. Pettis was asked to be a judge for the "Miss Wisconsin USA" pag-eant and in declining the offer, sent Erik in his stead. Erik met, at the event, the manager of a *Jersey Shore* cast member. Would Erik like to be on an episode of DJ Pauly D's upcoming reality spin-off show? He said he very much would like that. He was unat-tached, alone, free to make commitments to as-yet-theoretical reality shows as he pleased.

Erik at last arrived at the restaurant, sat across from me with-out a word, unrolled from the napkin his knife and fork, and began the surgical egg procedure with which I was, by then, familiar. I would have liked to discuss our surroundings, as it was my first encounter with a professionally run promotion and I had many astute observations on the subject, but he ate with an air of sacral solemnity I did not wish to desecrate by speaking. It was my twenty-ninth birthday and I had not told a soul in the world.

You may think that a starving man on rations, faced with the few calories he is allowed, would proceed with survivalist immediacy to incorporate whatever was laid before him. But the rationed man is all precision—he sees, in his allowance, fine nutritious distinctions you do not—and so when Erik finally raised his knife to halve his egg, he did so with great deliberation. With his knife he hollowed the half-yolk from its white skin and deposited the caloric yellow mass onto his plate, where it sat uneaten like a pat of butter. He scraped offending yellow flecks from the egg's gelatinous walls. He slid the flat of the knife against the plate, shedding shavings of yolk onto the porcelain, put his knife down, and placed the white in his mouth. He approached the second half of the first egg. This would be Erik's last watery wisp of permitted food before weigh-ins; he would not eat again for thirty-five hours. Erik's frame had already cratered into a landscape of shadows and white skin stretched tight over bone.

It would not have occurred to most 180-pound fighters that they might, through force of will, gain admission to the 145-pound weight class. Certainly the Californian Cisco Rivera, a full two inches shorter than Erik, would not be losing a fifth of his body weight. Erik had, back in Cedar Rapids, informed me that he could lose thirty-five pounds, weigh in, binge like a feral labrador, and feel ready to fight a day later simply because he was twenty-two years old. Self-starvation was the biggest challenge of his chosen vocation, every prefight diet was more painful than the last, and two years hence, Erik said, the drop would be impossible. His ability to boomerang from 180 to 145 back up to 160 would diminish unalterably with age; he would be impelled to fight amongst a slightly more substantial group of men, the "lightweights," which included his roommate Pettis, and so was something neither of them deigned discuss. Thus it was that one of the youngest fighters in the promotion saw only days slipping away. Two years he had in which to get a title shot and win the opportunity to fight the invincible Brazilian José Aldo, who would probably still be champion at 145. This was, of course, absurd, given that Erik was nowhere near title contention. But thoughts of the title pushed Erik through the long days of his weary yolk-scraping existence.

After the eggs, Erik opened his eyes a little wider, and we took the casino elevator up to his room.

"This is what you got?" I asked.

"This is Whole Foods peanut butter, they make it in a machine there," Erik said. I had been talking about the branded T-shirts and laptop bags and hats, but did not interrupt him as his focus shifted back to food. He pulled a plastic tub out of the shelf under his bedside table, where it lay next to bananas and a loaf of bread.

"*This* is chocolate peanut butter from the machine. This granola," he said, holding a plastic bag of cereal, "is sick." He replaced the granola and seized on a bag of chips. "Cheddar and Sour Cream Ruffles. These are *the shit*."

I eagerly assented to their excellence, as if I were quite familiar with them. I very much wanted Erik to feel buoyed by the fact of my company, and had been watching for signs of annoyance ever since one October night at Rocky's, where I had continued to pass Friday nights even after Erik decamped for Milwaukee. The abandonment of Jared and Rocky, Keoni told the team that night, was in no way a departure from Erik's usual approach toward long-term relationships. Erik had had a succession of best friends he'd cut off suddenly and without explanation, inventing supposed slights he would never forgive. It was part of a pattern, Keoni insisted, integral to his personality, and quite likely attributable to his sociopathy as diagnosed by the Internet. "Anyone who doesn't expect to be dropped like that," Keoni said, with what I took to be special attention to me, "is being naive."

The thought that Erik might at any moment terminate our relationship so thoroughly haunted me during our trip that even now I associate casinos with insecurity. Should he decide to stop answering my calls and requesting my presence, I would have wasted five months on a man of no use to my project, a project of importance not only to me but to future students of descriptive phenomenology. And I simply could not abide the idea that some other spacetaker—someone larger, and more given to Midwestern colloquialisms—would take the space I had so carefully reserved for myself by Erik's side. That someone else would be sent to order his eggs, someone else privileged with the knowledge that the old Vedepo-induced injury in his elbow hurt more intensely as he grew more slim; this was enough to make my stomach turn, which was in itself a silver lining, because it allowed me to share, on that trip, something of Erik's distance from the possibility of food.

I had arrived in Las Vegas the day previous, anxious to see the American city considered most fighterly, but underfed Erik did not want to see the Cirque du Soleil or the Hoover Dam; he wanted to go to Walmart, and so to Walmart we went. Outside, on the mountain-edged expanse of pavement cooking in desert sun, Erik was all angles and shadows, bounceless, frail, a dusting of hair over his shaven head. Walmart fluorescence added a yellow cast to his white skin, turned olive those undereye pockets of gloom. Raccoon-eyed and ravenous, Erik slothed through each aisle, his gallon jug of the day's permitted water consumption hanging low at his side, dragging him down, slowing his advance. He needed baby oil, he'd said before we left. But then I followed him into the hardware aisle, walled in by dozens of varieties of sandpaper, and we did not appear to be progressing toward the aisle marked "baby" at the far end of the store. He hitched up his jeans with his free hand as he walked; they slipped again down his sharp hips. He was walking away from the baby section and toward the chip aisle, where he stood for a moment staring at the Cheddar and Sour Cream Ruffles. While he described the slow throb of his esophagus I imagined the whole pipeline glowing as in some educational film about the digestive tract. He picked up the Ruffles and made it halfway to the register before remembering the oil for which he had come.

"What," Erik asked the taxi driver on the way back to The Palms, "is the best buffet in Las Vegas?"

Back in Milwaukee, Erik told me, the Hyundai Elantra Keoni lent him was papered with oil-stained wrappers—Burrito Supreme, 100% Beef, BK Stacker—remnants of forbidden foods vicariously enjoyed.

"I'm buying you a burrito," he'd say to Pettis. "Eat it. I want to smell it."

The fast food Erik purchased friends ate slowly, wafting ground-beef-steam toward their skeletal driver, leaving the paper crumpled and the scent hovering. This seemed to me deranged culinary masochism, but Erik insisted that he could not possibly starve himself so effectively were he to take his mind for a moment off of food. And in this, Vegas was cooperative, for to the starving man Vegas offers comforts one does not necessarily associate with the city. At the Rio Resort and Casino, for instance, if you can see past the seamlessly linked rooms for poker and keno and slots, past a singing girl in sequins, a stream of light, a wisp of smoke, if you can see past plastic neon-lit flames leaping over paisley carpet and the "future Chippendale fan" pink onesie featured in the giftshop window, past the spiraling staircase up to the heavily curtained Italian restaurant meant to evoke fine dining but suffering in that regard from its direct adjacency to Wetzel's Pretzels, if you can gaze beyond the gargantuan goggle-eyed head hanging from the Masquerade Room, or if, you are, like Erik, quite literally starving, you will notice that this city is not merely a purveyor of monetary risk but a purveyor of food. You will notice that this food is marketed chiefly through the promise of quantity, specifically through the provision of casino buffets. It is these buffets that interest Erik, their promise, their hideous abundance. For $39.99 one can in fact purchase an all-day pass to many buffets, a package known as a "buffet of buffets," inclusive of seven—as in wonders of the world or deadly sins, but pertinent to only one sin, that of gluttony—in-themselves-perfectly-adequate self-serve experiences: Le Village Buffet, the Emperor's Buffet, Spice Market Buffet, Flamingo's Paradise Garden Buffet, Lago Buffet, Harrah's Buffet, and the "world's most acclaimed buffet," the Carnival World Buffet at the Rio.

"The best buffet in Las Vegas," said the taxi driver, "is the Rio Buffet."

Erik smiled and leaned back into the pleather. He had never been to the Rio Buffet but nevertheless qualified as a Rio Buffet expert, having taken the virtual tour but more importantly having spent many hours visualizing his sublime deliverance from self-deprivation. In the twenty-four hours between weigh-ins and the fight, Erik would gain twenty pounds, and he took great pleasure in imagining of what those pounds would consist. The Rio Buffet, he informed me, offered 300 distinct dishes, seventy varieties of pie, an array of "bars," including a sushi bar, a taco bar, and a stir-fry bar. He knew its small army of friendly spoon-holding servers, its fifty yards of curving black countertop, its unaccountable progression from sausage pizza to cocktail shrimp to scrambled eggs to lentil soup to crab legs to fried fish to sushi to green salad to gravy-slathered pork chops to honeyed ham to flank steak to barbeque ribs to burritos to tacos to waffles to spring rolls to dumplings to sweet-and-sour pork to eggs benedict to bacon to one giant vat of ketchup to croissants to cubed mango to green bean salad to seven kinds of lettuce to the gelato-and-pastries bar whose delights are too many to enumerate, but which Erik would attempt to enumerate if given the chance.

The Rio was only one part of the plan, which also included spaghetti and meat sauce and an entire loaf of garlic bread from

Battista's, subs from the local Jimmy John's and twenty-four German chocolate cupcakes being mailed overnight from Milwaukee by a pair of baking groupie sisters who had arranged for a courier to hand cupcakes to Erik the moment he stepped off the scale.

"I am a fighter," Erik told the taxi driver. "I am planning what to eat before the fight."

"You shouldn't overeat," said the driver.

"Anderson Silva eats two Big Macs before every fight," said Erik. "It doesn't matter that much."

The conversation paused as traffic crawled past the MGM Grand, hulking and soot-stained in the midmorning light.

"Have you tried the NASCAR six-pound burrito?" Erik asked. The NASCAR Café's six-pound, two-foot burrito was also part of the plan.

In the hotel room that night, watching The Food Network and fiddling with his phone, Erik shivered, skeletal, in his hoodie.

"Let's go to Rio," he said, heavy-lidded, grim. "I mean just to see it."

It was 10:00 PM. Had it been Sean making the suggestion, I would have voiced a preference to take in a late film at the casino's movie theater, but I did not want to risk being on the wrong side of Erik's Manichean inclinations.

Erik and I left the room, descended in an elevator with Erik's picture hanging in it—"Tickets on Sale Wednesday"—passed a young crowd at the blackjack tables and a not-at-all young crowd at the slot machines, exited into the pedestrianless abyss that was the space between off-strip Vegas casinos, and walked to the Rio. Beyond the Mahjong and Keno tables, the poker tournament competitors in cowboy hats, Erik pointed to a sign: "the Carnival World Buffet." We passed through swinging doors into a vast shellacked cafeteria.

"It's closed," I said.

The food had been vacated. What was left was all fluorescent light, clean steel, and frosted glass. The only person in the room was a man behind the counter, wearing what looked to be a gas mask and pouring steam out of a tube. Erik attempted to penetrate the mask by shouting.

"I am a fighter," he said, pointing to himself. "I want to come here tomorrow."

The man in the mask nodded a quick, deferential, non-English-speaking nod.

Affixed to all fifty feet of the gleaming counter were black plaques etched in white. Erik began at the north end of the room.

"Pizza," he read off the plaque, and paused, staring at the aluminum heater and readjusting his grip on his jug of water. A light on the far end of the room flickered.

"Shrimp scampi."

I walked into the expanse of rag-wiped tables and sat down to endure Erik's fantasy with what I think to be commendable patience.

"Poached eggs," said Erik. His face had regained its yellow pallor and seemed to recede into his hoodie. "Scrambled eggs."

Twenty minutes later Erik reached the gelato. The steam-cleaner had left.

"Let's go," said Erik, and we padded back through the casino, where at 11:00 PM on a Tuesday night only the committed or addicted remained.

Erik spent the next morning resisting the intake of liquid. It was then that I recognized perhaps the only salutary psychological side effect of self-starvation, for Erik was about to weigh in beside his opponent, and he had not, as far as I could tell, thought about his opponent at all. He had seen Cisco by the blackjack tables a while back, and briefly in line at the in-house movie theater, and the moment Cisco left his field of vision was the moment Erik's thoughts returned to the Rio Buffet or gourmet granola or a single chocolate cupcake, though he was even beyond that now, because now he was dreaming of water. The thirst, Erik said, was worse even than the hunger. It made his teeth ache. Desiccated by forced dehydration, Erik's skin had taken on a new solidity; pinched, it would pause before flattening back into itself. His ligaments had turned brittle. His elbow hurt. He sneaked, at some point, a sip of Crystal Light, but the powder at its base stuck to his teeth in his dry mouth and made his teeth hurt so intensely he regretted the transgression. He slathered himself in baby oil and stepped into the sauna and sweat, tensing hard as if he might will a few more drops of water from each straining muscle, until the sauna scale read 145.5. At his last fight, Erik had been so weak at this weight that Keoni had had to physically support him on the walk from the sauna to the scale.

In a packed hotel conference room later that afternoon Erik watched Cisco play with the chains around his neck. There were reporters present from legitimate media organizations, which itself distinguished this entire endeavor from any fight I had yet experienced, and they came flanked by cameramen. The fighters were surrounded by teams of coaches in matching T-shirts; all were supported by sponsors more eminent than their local tattoo parlors. The fight would air on Pay-Per-View, and whoever won the main event would win fifty times what he might at one of the marginally legal fights in which I had taken space with Sean.

Cisco and Erik both stared out past photographers crouching and clicking around the dais. When he heard his name called Erik stepped onto the scale, which scrolled up to 146, the maximum allowed weight. His face went slack and his lips parted slightly. He flexed both arms. It was a less than convincing show of strength, a bizarre accumulation of protrusions popping under a translucent sheet of skin on his arms and abs. When he flexed, his two tattoos, "HD" for Hard Drive on the left and "Z" for Zombie Nation Army on the right, gleamed black and clean. He was nauseated and shivering with cold.

Erik stepped off the scale and posed for some shots with Cisco, who stood two inches shorter than Erik. Cisco was thin but not very, fully capable of fighting at 135 should he find within himself half of Erik's willpower. They faced one another with fists raised, and Erik equalized their heights by forcing his head forward so his neck shot horizontally from his shoulders. He had started doing this a few fights ago, he had informed me, and someone said that he looked "like an alien." Now he was doing it every fight, and shaving his head to augment the effect.

"He looks like an alien," I heard one of a dozen sportswriters tell the gentleman sitting next to him.

Erik stepped off the stage, and a girl in French braids handed him a large Tupperware container containing twenty-four German Chocolate cupcakes.

Off-scale, backstage, I watched Erik slump against a wall and rip the top off a small plastic bottle of cherry Pedialyte: "Helps Kids Feel Better Fast." He downed it quick as a shot and opened another, and another. Twenty other fighters were drinking the same thing. Smiling teddy bears stared from between their thick fingers, then gathered on the floor in a growing mass of crushed plastic.

Erik ripped open a black duffel bag, inside which he had packed food and drinks that he knew from experience his shriveled stomach would not immediately return: cornbread, a single banana, V8, and a small turkey sandwich. He forced a large square hunk of cornbread into the round of his mouth and closed his eyes. Other fighters were staring. No one else had courier-delivered cupcakes or a canvas bag full of cornbread.

"Can I get some of that?" someone asked.

"Yeah man," Erik said, and tore off a generous piece. He shoved more moist cornbread in his mouth. His eyes went glassy as he splayed himself against the wall, a great goofy smile spreading across his face, and began to twirl a cupcake in his hand, peeling the foil wrap gently from the chocolate.

Erik said he felt dizzy, though one could tell from his weak smile that it was a pleasing, diaphanous drunk sugar-high kind of dizzy. It took him a moment to notice, when we skipped onto an elevator about to close, that the elevator was packed tight with Cisco and Cisco's five-man Hispanic entourage. Erik came to consciousness in an awkward silence as we together ascended the fourth, the sixth, the eighth floor. He stared at the floor and rubbed his hand over the back of his neck. One of Cisco's men leaned against the poster of Erik.

A small voice came from the back of the pack.

"Let's jump him!"

Everyone laughed.

Erik had stocked the refrigerator in his room with small turkey sandwiches. He would incorporate food slowly, permitting himself only one every hour, along with a smattering of Ruffles, though chips are not an accepted part of the prefight diet. He popped onto the bed and watched, for the first time in weeks, something other than The Food Channel.

"Ruffles?" Wes asked. He had arrived just in time for weigh-ins.

"Yeah, Ken says it's cool."

Ken was Erik's conditioning coach back in Cedar Rapids, and it seemed highly unlikely that he had made any actual judgment on the Ruffles.

Pettis swept into the room. Duke came in behind him.

"What's with the chips?" Duke asked.

"Anderson Silva eats two Big Macs before ev—"

"Calm down, you ain't gotta justify it," said Pettis.

Erik's manager walked in, followed by a large pony-tailed man carrying a leather bag.

"Doctor's here!" said the manager.

"Hey," said Erik, who was engrossed in another sandwich.

I thought perhaps the doctor had come for some sort of postweigh-in physical, but instead of examining Erik he pulled out a fluid-filled bag attached to a tube and scanned the room, lips pursed, for a place to hang it. He settled on the large piece of hotel art hanging above Erik's head, stood on his toes, and jolted it into position until the bag hung perilously from the corner of the frame.

"Can't find your vein," said the doctor as he stabbed Erik.

A minute later: "They're so small."

A minute later, to the manager, "Do we have any smaller needles?"

When the IV was finally in, the doctor gone, Erik watched *Everybody Loves Raymond* with rapt attention. His eyebrows kept rising, as if everything were slightly new to him. The colors. The fully internalized presence of other people. The way their voices travel through space. Erik's exposed abdominal muscles were disappearing under a blanket of skin. His transformation was that of a wilted houseplant newly watered, stiffening back into life, and like a houseplant in revival it was a change only slightly too slow to see. For the first time in days, he was following the back-and-forth of rapid-fire conversation. This episode of *Everybody Loves Raymond* was funny. It was the funniest thing he had ever seen. When he laughed the knobs reappeared in muscle, then receded back under the swell. He ripped off a piece of turkey club with his teeth.

"What happened with that girl?" Erik asked Wes during a commercial. Wes was playing with his phone on an armchair.

"Didn't work out," said Wes. "She was, you know, an older woman."

"How old?" I asked.

"Like, almost twenty-six."

Erik's phone rang, and he ignored it.

"When are we going to the Rio?" Wes asked.

Erik didn't look away from the screen. "I think that's a bad idea."

Erik's right arm lay palm-up on the bed, so as not to disturb the IV. In the window that ran the length of the room, evening was shading into night and lights were beginning to glow on the Strip.

"I read on the Internet," Erik said, "that people get food poisoning there."

•

Reporters wanted to talk to Erik. Not many, as Erik was relatively unknown—a less familiar presence than even Jesse Lennox or Josh Neer—but some. One of these reporters was a fighter herself, and in her Erik took great platonic interest, as if they shared something intimate I myself could never know. Erik introduced me as we stood beside the octagon of the lush Tapout gym. "She's a writer," he added.

She had a list of questions on a sheet of paper, and after every one Erik said "Good *question*" though they were by no means particularly distinguished lines of inquiry, and in any case would only lead to a writeup on an MMA website with which I was not familiar. The entire errand seemed to me unnecessary.

She reached the end of her list, and turned to me. "Who do you write for?" she asked.

I felt Erik's gaze upon me, as if I were being tested—as if, confronted by a "writer" whose intentions he understood, my presence in his life was suddenly inexplicable. There was a long, uncomfortable pause. I could hear a man grunting as he lifted weights in another room. Who did I write for? I had recently written a paper for one Richard Knowles, who had awarded that paper a "D" and threatened to fail me for the course.

"Well, it's complicated," I said, glancing at Erik, who looked somewhere between skeptical and annoyed by this answer. I panicked. "I write for the *Cedar Rapids Gazette.*"

Erik smiled in that bright-eyed, surprised way one smiles when one has solved a problem.

"So you're going to write about this fight for them?" she asked.

"Yes," I said, greatly displeased by this development, "I do plan to."

It was more than a little alarming that Erik would now expect a writeup in the sports section of his regional newspaper, but I put my hypothetical association with print journalism out of my mind as we dealt with a succession of actual reporters.

"I didn't have a job. I didn't have any way of making money," Erik told someone on the radio. "I just decided to train six or seven hours a day," he told someone from another MMA site. "Most people won't do that."

Erik did not particularly want to talk about his fluidity, his striking, his record; he wanted to talk about everything he had given up, all the possible lives he had rejected. He did not have a "back-out plan" he insisted over and over until I could see rowboats burning in his wake. Had he been able he would have told you from which particular sacrifice every piece of him emerged— the narrowest hinge of his hand, the curve of his neck, systole and diastole. How impressive Erik was before the microphone! Even when he could feel his stomach curdling and his eye-sheen shriveling his words were smooth and full. Often the question of from where Erik Koch had come—he was described to himself by interviewers as having "burst out of nowhere," which was an invitation to an origin story—involved a kind of generational inevitability. He was the "new breed" because he was well-rounded, and he was well-rounded because he hadn't trained as a wrestler or a kickboxer but as a mixed martial artist, and this was possible because he had come of age in a different world than that of his older opponents. Sometimes he had started training at ten, sometimes eleven, sometimes sixteen or seventeen, but always he was "just a kid" and always MMA was a thing he'd latched onto, hard and of his own accord. It had been there to pull from the air like oxygen and like oxygen his body just knew how to absorb it, break it down, become the thing he'd found. "My brother taught me," is not a story about sacrifice, which is perhaps why the brother remained an anonymous figure around which conversations danced.

In Cedar Rapids that evening, Keoni and Beau and Lonnie and a dozen other members of Team Hard Drive make their way to a viewing party at an establishment that sponsors Erik, known to the fighters as Cici's but formally and fittingly "Cici's Pizza Buffet." The fighters bring their kids, mittens hanging by strings from their sleeves, and let them loose to play arcade games in the back of the restaurant. The adults drink Coke out of tall plastic cups and ignore the fights before Erik's fight, making fun of the one guy they always make fun of and only going quiet when Keoni has something to say. The pictures flickering across the screen are familiar; they know the cast by name. There is the octagon, cerulean blue and crosshatched by red beams of light. There are the ring girls and the long camera shots that follow them around the ring; there is the kiss they blow to the camera as they twirl and sit back down. There are the referees the camera stops and acknowledges—Herb Dean, Big John McCarthy, Steve Mazzagatti—and the top tier ticketholders it humors, platinum-haired women in diamonds and glittering tanks on the arms of hairless, polished, elaborately tattooed men. There is Stephan Bonnar's boyishly jacked inflection carrying the viewers through each hit—oh and a straight right *drops* him; Michaels is *all over him* with some *vicious* ground and pound; he landed that left hook earlier; smiled and answered with a *laser* straight right hand, right down the middle; *armbar, it's on!* There is Bruce Buffer's voice, operatic in scope, hailing the arrival of each fighter into the sacred space with oceans-deep rich rolling swells of sound that rise gently and dip hard with the demands of the ritual welcome. This is the second time they will see Erik at the Palms, and the fourth time they will see him fight live on national television, but still when he pops onscreen it seems to Keoni as if his brother has walked onto the set of some old sitcom they'd watched together as kids, has disappeared from his bedroom and reemerged in this flat and glittering world.

Erik has his own warm-up room and Duke and Pettis are there, gently there, minimizing their presence as Erik hops and swings at imaginary opponents and as the fights tick by. Nothing is articulated here. There is a television in the warm-up room but no audio; hits happen soundlessly, chased by the low boom of the crowd outside. Duke slides cracked red mitts on his hands and stands in front of Erik, who thrusts his shins into them; *thwap*. Pettis sits on a metal bench and stares at the screen, worrying his knuckles, *crack crack*, sucking on the lace of his hoodie.

Erik's is the ninth of eleven fights tonight, which means he is a "contender" but not yet a "champion," and the pressure implied in this distinction is considerable. He is wearing white shorts that crink and whistle as he walks and although he looks hydrated and healthy it is hard to imagine this slight white figure—"Powder" people will call him from the stands; "he should get a tattoo of a tan," someone will tweet—conjuring the kind of power it takes to throw any man to the ground.

Everything is waiting. He waits for Pettis to put on some pads so he can punch them and he waits for the seventh fight to end and the eighth fight to end and he waits for the room-rocking thump-thump of his entrance music and waits for Duke and Pettis to gather behind him with his banner and waits for Pettis to slather Vaseline on his face and then he is in the cage, finally in the cage, only now he is hopping around and waiting for Cisco the Californian, who evidently has many more fans in Vegas than does Erik, and he waits for the cry of Cisco's crowd to move up through his feet to the tips of his fingernails and something is gathering and then finally Steve Mazzagatti, a man Erik has watched from a couch in Iowa referee fights for years and years, says "Let's get it on," and Erik begins to sway.

He and Cisco step forward and backward, forward and backward, rocking in hypnotic rhythm, a low kick here, a missed uppercut there, and Erik leans low and right and swings his left shin high into Cisco's head and the head whips out of rhythm and Cisco drops like a dead man and Erik lunges onto Cisco and Steve Mazzagatti jumps in between them because Erik Koch is the winner and the champion and millions of people are watching and the whole room is standing and grown men are moaning and as I look at my hands wet with my tears Erik flexes every muscle in his body—hands fisted, arms low—and screams.

Sean – Spring 2011

IN THE EARLY SPRING SEAN RODE HIS BIKE downriver, then away from the water, down busy thoroughfares, along sandy shoulders, atop cracked icy sidewalks, into the paved parking lot of his most recent place of employment, Chorus Girls. His was the only bike chained outside the strip club. "That some DUI shit?" a fellow bouncer asked. It was *not* a DUI, but quite the opposite, the vehicle of a man sobering up from a long intoxication, the ten-speed of a fighter back in training. Had that same bouncer been a practiced watcher of men, he might have noticed Sean's chin tapering, his cheeks tightening like loose canvas pulled across a frame. He might have noticed a waist taking shape under Sean's shirt.

For ten months I had awaited this physical transformation, but I had never lost faith in Sean's future; I assumed his divorce was, like most, a temporary destabilizing force, and I knew his weight to be particularly sensitive to his psychological equilibrium. He had lost twenty pounds in the Navy not because he was made to march but because of one single incident, in which he was ordered to pick up the body of a fellow soldier who had been run over by a tank. When he picked up the body it collapsed in half, and afterward every time he sat down to a meal he was overcome with nausea, such that when he returned he was 155 pounds. Beyond fear or boredom, nausea was the feeling he most associated with war, and he loathed the feeling so much I never worried he would reenlist.

It is one thing to spacetake for a fighter on the downswing, and another for a man in his prime; but to spacetake for a fighter reborn! You can have your undefeated Anderson Silvas, your José Aldos; I had a man burning so brightly with something that his very crust was melting away, as with a planet two positions too close to the sun. The rooms he walked into changed in character and affordances, became mere tools for his fighterly use. Through Sean's newly focused eyes the Big Shows were not a spectacle to be watched but the place where, any day now, he would be.

Of course his speech changed. The burning shot boastful words through his open mouth. "You have to do what you came here to do," he said instructively, sitting back at his kitchen table and scratching behind the ears of his new roommate's pitbull. "I'm not supposed to be anything else in this world but a fighter. When you have the chance to be the best in the world at something, and you don't do anything about it, it really eats at you." Sean leaned back, grew philosophic. "But then there is this other side of you that struggles to get its shit together. So to speak."

We were seated in his new apartment, three rooms just above the gym and owned by Pat Miletich himself. I had read about this apartment in books about Miletich: specifically, *Blood in the Cage* and the indispensable *No Holds Barred*. It was a space reserved for men who wanted to train morning, noon, and night. Some previous resident had ripped the door off the bathroom and it stayed tilted against the wall, in case women came over and needed someone to hold it there. Sean made the apartment half bedroom, half mat, and on the wall above the mat Sean and his new roommate Brandon hung a wipe board on which was scrawled a training regimen.

Sean's legs had always been skinny, but not until this period had I noticed the way his torso broadened so dramatically from the hips, such that a massive pair of shoulders sat atop a small square abdomen. This was the Sean of whom I had heard tell for years. "I used to take punches from Tim Sylvia all day long," he said over the whir of the blender. "I went two rounds with Jake Ellenberger. How many people can say that? Went two rounds with Jake Ellenberger *and* the night before me and Spencer were out drinking vodka cranberries. I could have been in the UFC by now. Easily. But I'm just so lazy. I'm the laziest professional athlete there is."

With every strip-club-bound bike trip Sean's endurance expanded, as did my faith in his future. Perhaps he would find in a sequence of wins the fortitude to ignore mewling distractions born of adolescent trysts, and we could continue our partnership throughout his thirties. I was aware of at least one MMA luminary who had staved off retirement until the age of forty-three, which theoretically left Sean and me another full decade to explore various relevant phenomena in one another's company.

Over this time I would compile a complete account of consciousness in a state of ecstasy, and Sean would ascend to fights just as large and legitimate as the one I had seen in November. What Miletich had once noted in Sean was not just a fighterly spirit but a quite remarkable competence, and an ability to absorb strikes well beyond that of many men already in the Big Shows.

In this mood of infinite possibility we set off for Des Moines, to a fight Sean was too honorable to decline and too small to win.

•

Do not believe for a moment that because I had been previously transported in a Vegas stadium among famous fighters I thought myself beyond your average Des Moines encounter. I was most happy in my own fighterly neighborhood, among men the world might not recognize but I surely did. And though I hesitate to say it, not wanting to seem corrupted by sentiment, I missed Sean when a thousand miles away from him. On the Saturday night when Sean was slated to fight a 6'2" 220-pound man, I spent almost the entire evening on the locker-room couch, at his side.

Consider if you will the view from the locker-room couch, the "before" and the "after," the mystery-laden reverse makeover to which we are not, on the couch, privy. Boys run out whole and hard and green, and ripen on the outside, come back to us with soft parts, bruised like fruit. Boys run out digits attached and come back digits dangling. Boys run out cushioned by cornermen and come back exposed to the bone. There is a doorless doorway and a white hall and beyond that, darkness, into which the imagination may project a Minotaur, a jungle, or infinite emptiness beckoning self-flagellation.

I well realize that it might seem, to the layperson, that to be couch-bound is a great disadvantage, walled off as the couch is from the spectacle, that all there is to see one sees by paying for a ticket close to the cage. But then why is it that getting close to the cage requires only two bracelets from the capable hands of the women in the parking lot, and getting back here requires three? The three-braceleted spectators can be anywhere they like, out by the promotional Monster Energy booth, for instance, or in the laps of the well-dressed ladies who purchased the pricey cage-side table, or among the rough-hewn common people out behind the ropes. But they were in the locker room, most of them, pressing up against one another, grunt-apologizing with every shift. A Hispanic man, minutes after a loss, sat backward in a chair and stared at the wall. We sent him through the door and he came back broken, an extra angle in his ring finger. His voluptuous brown wife rubbed his neck in sad, silent, consolatory circles.

Despite his nominal victory, Sean's February fight had failed me, and so naturally I worried. To calm myself, I fixated on the other fighters in the room. I settled upon a fighter named Pete; I focused on Pete's ominously long neck, his delicate unmangled nose. Pete's lanky arms and legs, I noted, looked many times more snappable than anything on Sean. This milky-skinned, unblemished man was pacing the room so hard his long blond bangs swung near to horizontal. His bony fingers twitched in their tape, as if to clutch at an invisible briefcase—as if to suggest a less painful way of life for Pete. "Peter Sampson!" spat a microphone from outside, and Pete jogged toward the same door that to us delivered a much-reduced Gomez. On the floor sat five cornermen, surrounded by fighter detritus: half-empty bottles of Gatorade, rolls of gauze, empty energy-bar wrappers with the foil undersides exposed, untouched cans of Monster Energy Drink. Someone's toddler, a boy the color of damp sand, ran in and out of the room screaming at full capacity.

Beside me on the couch Sean was dead asleep. Occasionally, people stopped by to marvel at this. "Does he always sleep before fights?" they asked. Is he meditating? Sick?

I supposed then that what made Sean so relaxed before the darkness of whatever lay outside the room, what helped to soothe in him the nerves that afflicted each of the other ten men in his exact predicament, what left him seeming, in his usual way, almost impiously immune to the gravity of the occasion, was his devotion to the encounter, and not the outcome. He would fail a test he could not pass, which would leave his sense of self solidly intact. Who could say how Sean might have performed against an opponent his own size? Consider the absurdity of fighting a man a foot taller and forty pounds heavier than yourself, and the probability of loss swiftly departs the fragile uncertainty of a decimal to arrive at the comforting bedrock of one.

This, at least, is what I told myself in the locker room. In retrospect it's quite obvious that Sean was not thinking of this encounter at all, but of an entirely different encounter that would follow not twenty-four hours after. In exchange for another sixty dollars, ever-entrepreneurial Alexis had agreed to let Sean spend a few minutes with the boy she claimed was his son. This fight was merely an obstacle, a toll he had to pay midway on the long drive between home in Davenport and a Best Western in Omaha. Given the imminence of that particular encounter, there was perhaps not a lot of fear left to waste on Chuck Grigsby.

"I'm trying to relax," Sean said in a brief moment of consciousness, "and these guys are getting me all amped up and shit." He searched through his duffel bag for a towel, threw it on his face, dropped back asleep.

"Does he want to hit some pads maybe?" asked someone else's cornerman, clearly worried about Sean. I shrugged sympathetically; I knew what it was to need small anxiety-quelling tasks.

Pete obligingly continued to serve as a distraction. He limped back in ten minutes after he left, pushed his way through a few men, and brought with him both a cigarette-slim blonde and a silence complete but for the crinkling of an energy bar wrapper. His left eye had so swelled around the brow that he looked half Neanderthal. There was no blood, just a grotesque sacrifice of symmetry. ("Oh, the blood!" preen the people who want to ban these encounters, which just goes to show you that they have no idea. Blood is a veil between you, the spectator, and the body postpenetration. Squeamish people should *pray* for blood.) No one in the room wanted to meet Pete's good eye so we stared at our hands, and Rick, a middle-aged backcountry-accented balding man, fairly tiptoed out the doorway when his name was called. It was his first-ever fight, this late in life, and I felt grateful not to be spacetaking for a rustic tyro.

Sean woke up, took out his phone, showed it to someone's cornerman.

"Cute," the cornerman said.

"Yeah," Sean said. "Looks just like me, right?"

We waited for Rick to return, and we heard him before we saw him, choked cries blossoming into sobs as he neared the door and entered elbows first, palms on his red cheeks. He had three spacetakers with him, a woman and two men, and the couch sagged under their collective weight. Rick lowered his hands to reveal his face, not only intact but untouched, with nary a souvenir bruise.

"It didn't hurt," he said to the silenced room. "It wasn't hurting."

The fight, we could all see without having seen any of it, was called on the basis of gross incompetence. Rick was not hurt because the ref, noting his flailing helplessness under another man's flurry of strikes, stopped the fight well before Rick was ready for it to end. These were the tears of a man who had resolved to fling himself off a bridge the moment the impulse struck him, had marshaled every psychic resource toward the end of that moment of escape, and had, when the will was most full in his breast, been yanked clean from his glorious climax.

"It didn't hurt," Rick said again.

"It's not broken. . . ," said Pete's girl to Pete, "I don't think it's broken," at which point the doctor finally appeared, and Rick's spacetakers began the unenviable task of piecing together a shattered fighter's ego. With three fighters down, the room had become half infirmary, half therapy session.

"If you ain't gettin' beat," said Rick's spacetaker, "you ain't fightin' anyone worth a damn."

"Most people wouldn't even go out there," said Pete's girl.

"What happened was," continued the spacetaker, "you punched him real hard at first, and that got him real mad, and—"

"Can you see any light out of that eye?" the doctor asked Pete. "Only black? You have to go the emergency room."

"—if you hadn't punched him so hard, he wouldn't o' won!"

A commendable consolatory effort by the spacetaker, this idea of a world in which you lose a fight because you hit too hard. While Rick considered the possibility, a man younger than Pete or Rick or Gomez—seventeen, if we're being optimistic— hopped in the floor space between all three of them. His was the fight just before Sean's. He was black, and small, and without a single cornerman, which was lamentable, because a single cornerman might have enthusiastically deflected the obvious for a boy who had thus far seen three men leave the room and three men return defeated, who knew that the main event would be between the very competent Josh "The Dentist" Neer who was not in his locker room and the incompetent Andre Kase who was, and who saw another fighter, three short fights from show time, dead asleep on the couch. Why a promoter would stack a card with one-sided fights, and why he would assign all the fighters on the less enviable side of their matchups to the same locker room, remains unclear, but with every subsequent loss new aspects of the room revealed themselves. There was, for instance, the private bathroom, the wall-to-wall carpeting, the room-length closet one cornerman was sitting in. There was the lightbulb-lined and diva-appropriate vanity, the spinny scalloped chair one usually finds attached to such a vanity, the massive mirror stationed before it. There was the couch. Somewhere on the premises lay another, presumably more masculine locker room, a locker room perhaps with lockers, and the men hidden within its walls were men who had begun to look very threatening indeed.

Sean dragged himself back to wakefulness. "Doesn't he look just like me?" Sean asked, shoving his cell phone at a fellow fighter. I had seen the picture and noted only a generic baby lacking any distinguishing characteristics. "My mom saw the picture," Sean said, "and was like, oh yeah. That's familiar."

Sean's fight was minutes away. Summoned, the kid slipped through the door.

In the prefight video, asked how he thought he would stack up against a fighter nearly a foot taller than himself, Sean said, "Well, I'll probably take a lot of punches to the face." I realize that such a statement will shock the sort of person who tends toward overuse of the word "wellness," and were Sean a little girl he'd spend a lot of time in the guidance counselor's office being counseled to take a templelike attitude toward himself. Stitch it up when it's torn, we're told, slather slippery creams on its surface, inspect for rot each body-destined vegetable because within every joy lurks potential menace. Pay anxious attention to the sheath, which is vulnerable to burn and aridity, which ought not be overstretched, which, when torn, spills forth in precisely the way no one around you wants to see. None will be more revered than the man who can stitch the shell back together, keep the insides in and the outsides out. And if at some point this all feels like hanging curtains in a jail cell, like replacing the buttons on a straitjacket, well, you might find yourself on a couch with a man who feels the same way. Still, it won't fit anyone's definition of healthy, wanting to break out of the cage that you are.

Sean pulled the towel off his face, stretched, pulled both hands into fists and then stretched the fingers straight. My breath quickened as I watched; how open he seemed, how ready to receive. As the kid returned with a bloody nose and a brown birthmark of a bruise and some galvanic current ran up my spine, Sean paced the hallway. He lifted the top of a large canister, peeked inside, walked to the other side of the room, tilted his head toward the ceiling. Sean had not given the DJ a song to play during his walk out, and so the DJ went with "Eye of the Tiger."

Sean let the first two stanzas pass, because who was in a hurry? Only the kind of man who needs a project would rush this moment rather than live inside of it. At the words "thrill of the fight" he made for the cage, a little shuffle of his feet, a blank expression on his face.

How they bellowed for their hometown behemoth! One could only pity them their simple chauvinism. They had yet to be converted; they did not know Sean.

It only took the larger man hovering in expectant silence over the smaller. In the seconds before Grigsby begins tearing into Sean I am already expanding into the flickering stadium, itself robbed of any illusions of permanence. Grigsby backs Sean against the cage, cocks his arm, and rips without mercy into Sean's cheek, his cratered nose, his forehead. Sean takes the punches with waking grace and pushes heavily forward into them, as if walking against a great wind, until he is within striking distance of Grigsby's massive head.

Sean swings and misses and Grigsby dances away, each step of his long legs taking him halfway across the cage. Again Sean works forward, absorbing a jab, an elbow, a kick in the side. He is a piece of matter being roughly sculpted at a safe distance from an audience held, by the spectacle, rapt, and with every knock of Grigsby's knuckles against his flesh, he is beginning to bring people over to his side. The moment he is close enough Sean throws a long loping upsweeping hook that lands loud on Grigsby's chin.

Grigsby's hand clicks past Sean's vaselined face like a greased gear churning through him; Sean turns with the punch. A graze across the skin stings, drags like a rock through gravel. Churn jab churn jab churn. Grigsby kicks a thick thigh and the thigh quivers; Sean pushes in and grazes Grigsby on the stomach with a jab as Grigsby glides away and the bell sounds. Sean is awake now, and thanks to him, so are we.

As the men approach another once again in the cage, a bleeding Sean smiles hugely and nods, waves his hands forward in that come-hither way: *Bring it on.* The crowd loves it. They love Sean. "Yes!" I hear the promoter say as Sean bounces back from yet another jab to the face, "Sean is my *favorite fighter.*" Though he loses almost every exchange, it's Sean we all watch, the man who has somehow sworn off protection of the self he was given.

Sean takes a kick to the right leg and hops around, then throws himself at the hopeless task of taking a huge man down. Grigsby shakes Sean off his legs like a dog throwing off water. Sean drives right back in, wrapping his arms against Grigsby's huge waist and pushing with all he has. Grigsby shakes him off and slams at a gash he has already made in Sean's face. Sean shakes his head theatrically, smiles. The crowd cheers. You're not supposed to be able to live here, at this pitch, for more than a moment. But Sean, again and again, finds a way to stretch that single moment of ecstatic bliss into minute upon minute of blood-borne release. He is escaping through the slice in his forehead, the knuckle-cuts, the rip down the line of his nose, and it is possible to believe, for fifteen short minutes, that we've found a way out.

By the third round Sean's body is flooded with lactic acid, and his shuffle has become lumbering and unsteady, but still he is standing, still amidst the burning of his lungs and the shivering of his bruised thighs he takes another jab to the eye, a knocking kick to the shinbone. Grigsby is uncut but covered in sweat and breathing hard. The bell sounds, the fight over, and a great cheer rises. The judges count up their ridiculous check marks and deem the man who absorbed fewer strikes and took fewer takedowns the winner. Grigsby's hand is raised, but only those slavishly committed to the written rules of MMA think the victory his.

I wished desperately, when I saw Sean's nose in the locker room, that I had the skill to stitch it up myself. His face bore the familiar price of a few minutes' liberation, a rotting house left untended and reluctantly reclaimed. He was so swollen that the true dimensions of his head were hard to discern. His left eye was nearly hidden behind a swollen purple cheek. The left side of his face was split vertically from brow to halfway up his forehead, and then horizontally right across the eyebrow. The side with the gash, which was also the side on which Sean's nose had permanently cratered, was swollen purple above the brow rather than below. "You need stitches," I said, and went to find the fight doctor, who was not easy to find, and dragged him back to the locker room, which was not easy to do. The doctor looked at Sean's gash but did not touch it.

"You need stitches," he said, hands on his hips.

"Can't you do them?" asked Sean.

"Well," said the doctor, "I'm not that kind of doctor."

We stared at him.

"I'm a psychologist," he said.

It would be hours before I would come down from my postfight elation, but Sean was quiet, even melancholy, as he awaited his $400. This loss had not had the enlivening effect, for him, of the loss in St. Louis. After the fights ended he planned to drive west alone, and I to go back to Iowa City to prepare for a midsemester examination, and so alone Sean headed to the hospital in search of that kind of doctor.

•

When Sean wakes up the next morning, on the promoter's couch, broken capillaries spider up his sore calves and thighs; his face is held together with black stitching, and he isn't certain whether his hand is broken or merely too sore to pull into a fist. He wobbles to his car, which is a rental, because his own is in the shop. Between Des Moines and Omaha the autovehicular excursionist will find 150 miles of newly planted cornfields, cow-and-horse-dotted grazing grounds, milling plants, and rotting barns. Upon occasion the drive will slow for a town: weathered welcome sign, church, school, the odd piece of menacing farming equipment parked by the road. No one is ever outside in such towns, but there is inevitably some evidence of civic vigor, such as an illumined plastic parrot in the window of a newish Mexican restaurant just before the town ends and fields reappear. A town with a Mexican restaurant is still a magnet for someone.

The Best Western is an isolated cube of a building on a flat piece of earth. The room smells like smoke from a time when smoking was allowed, and Sean waits on the king-sized bed, eyes on the ceiling. His face feels papery now, stiff with scabs that make themselves known every time he involves his eyebrows in an expression. Three o'clock, the time they had agreed to meet, comes and goes. He calls her twenty times. He peeks out the curtain into the parking lot, opens the drawer in the end table, fingers through the Bible. At four he is livid, at five he is simply depressed, and at six she walks in with her sister and her son.

"I had a fight with Kris," she says.

Sean's eyes don't leave Josiah, his elbows, the backs of his knees, the soft hollow of skin above the plastic line of his diaper. Josiah faces the door, nestled against his mother, his chin on her neck. A stripe of light from the window, half obscured by a heavy curtain, falls over the bed.

"You want to hold him?"

He forms a stiff cradle, shaking, and then Josiah is looking up at him from his own arms. Sean stands still as a rock, as if the slightest tremor would leave Josiah bruised.

"So perfect," he says, moving even his lips with a cautious gentleness, and he'll treat those words as incantation, repeating them over and over whenever he tells the story.

Alexis, amused, lifts Josiah like a sack of flour and lays him on the bed. Sean leans in but does not touch the baby with what now seem massive and callused and defiled hands. Josiah is four months old; just last week he discovered his ankles. The bed against his back, Sean's stitched-together forehead hovering, Josiah stares, transfixed, at his own feet. At the limit they sprout into five cylindrical toes, each slightly curved and creased but not yet articulated into three hard parts, and at the limit of each of these is the small round suggestion of a toenail. They're wrapped in white-and-pink mottled skin so new it's nearly translucent. The toes look like something made to live underwater, something to propel all the other parts to safe places. Sean leans in to graze Josiah with pursed lips, but Josiah doesn't notice. He isn't interested at the moment in Sean, or his mother, or his mother's sister. In the light of early evening, like a kid with his face pushed up against a picket fence, Josiah considers the very edge of the boundary someone else has drawn for him. He is awake.

Erik – Spring 2011

THE ERIK KOCH WHO EXISTED IN THE mysteriously named "Xbox" was not so good-looking as the man I knew; he was thicker about the nose, and possessed of a permanent snarl. Like the real Erik, he was fluid, but the middling portraitists commissioned to create "UFC Undisputed 3" managed only an excessively uniform fluidity that lacked the perfect cadence of human movement. Which is not to say that there was no resemblance; there was in fact enough resemblance to make watching one Erik play another Erik a rather ghostly thing to endure. One day in Wisconsin, many months from the time I want to tell you about here, I sat upon a dirty futon and watched a lackadaisical, sore-from-practice Erik Koch direct his hyperactive doppelgänger in the bloody undoing of José Aldo. The powers of virtual world-making had recorded Duke's voice, such that one could hear him shouting from the corner; they had found some generic techno music to play as virtual Erik walked to the virtual cage; and they had gotten Erik's prefight walk-out head-bop rather eerily right. Erik hit a button on the controller, and his digital double threw a punch; flesh-and-blood Erik moved a finger, and his doppelgänger kicked Aldo in the stomach.

Now this situation—a warm-blooded yawning daemon utterly controlling a figure made in his image—had some Cartesian implications, as you will have already surmised; for who was to say that some still greater game-player was not directing us; that flesh-and-blood Erik, not to mention flesh-and-blood Kit, were not in fact being played by some greater god being watched by a greater spacetaker on a more elevated, presumably cleaner, futon? It wasn't until later in our story that I saw Erik play himself, but I relate it here because the image of Erik Koch, outside his body, directing that body toward a competent violence, is the image that comes to mind when I recall the events of that spring.

What I saw in Erik's Vegas victory scream was less a fighter who loved the encounter than one who reveled in the rapt attentions of 2,000 heads, 4,000 eyes; and what I saw in Erik's win was a man knocking out another man because until he did he was forced to share the stage. "I hate losing," Erik had told me again and again, which I had taken to be the mere expression of a competitive spirit, but ever since Vegas when I think of those words I see a stadium full of heads turning away from Erik and toward someone not Erik. I hear the rip of it, the quick flick of an eye unpeeling itself from an object. With every fight Erik found a bigger audience, more heads, more eyes, and so the potential pain of their turning from him grew.

I redoubled my spacetaking efforts, though my aversion to Milwaukee remained in force, and so I had to play the part of patient, interested listener many miles away. I had at least bought some goodwill with a *Cedar Rapids Gazette* news article inelegantly headlined "Koch earns first KO in WEC" and employing all the clichés, colloquialisms, and redundant quotations I thought necessary to the task. "The solidly pro-Cisco crowd," I wrote in passable imitation of a journeyman sportswriter, "watched in horror at the Palms Casino as Koch finished the Californian, funneling two months of training into little more than a minute of relentless striking."

> After knocking Cisco flat with a high kick, Koch pounced. Cisco failed to defend himself against Koch's blows, and the match was stopped at 1:36.

> "That was perfect," the 22-year-old Koch said moments after his win. "That was a pretty good kick."

> "He followed the game plan to a T," added coach Duke Roufus. "The plan was to kick him in the head."

The word Erik used to describe the piece was "sick," which he intended as an expression of emphatic approval.

On the phone he was excitable, jumping from subject to subject with associative leaps I could not always follow, and I imagined him shadowboxing with the hand not holding the phone to his ear. He continued to offer admiring updates on the exciting life of his housemate Anthony Pettis, whose fame had grown ten-fold following an awe-inspiring fight in which he had run up the cage like some kind of Parkour stuntman and, before falling back to earth, kicked Ben Henderson in the head, knocking him out. The kick was played all over television and always played twice in a row; it was an eminently filmic moment. Pettis was technically the champion, yes, but he was even more universally known to casual fans as an acrobat of perfectly executed violence. He was really and truly famous. And I cannot say whether it was a desire to look more like brown-skinned Pettis, or because those afore-mentioned tweets about his paleness stung, but Erik soon began to provide unsolicited updates on his melanin levels. "I go tanning every single day," he told me over the phone. "I am addicted to it. Everyone knows me there, the owner Jeff, the girl at the front desk, everyone. Jeff says he is coming to my next fight."

I never asked about a next fight, knowing that the news would spill forth from Erik the moment it came to him, but it was what I hoped to hear every time I felt the trill of a call in my blazer pocket. I had by the time filled three notebooks with my observa-tions, and had begun to consider the tradition in which my work of phenomenology would fall. Too bold for conventional aca-demic minds and the nonsmoking, healthy-minded, hidebound thinkers therein, it would harken backward to comprehensive works of genius such as *Inner Experience* and *The World as Will and Representation*. The glorious heightening of the senses, I had come to believe, was only the first stage of an ecstatic moment, after which the feeling changed from that of a body made extraor-dinarily powerful to escape from that body altogether. It wasn't enough to say that one could see a flow of dancing atoms where others saw a static cage, or hear the squishy whisper of colliding cells where others heard only the dull thump of a landed strike. The categories of sight and sound no longer applied, for a mind in the throes of ecstasy had expanded outward, beyond these rough tools of perception, to greet the universe without the interference of anything so frail as an eye or an ear.

When the fight finally came, it came on the heels of news that would ensure a plenitude of watchers such as neither Erik nor I had yet seen. It was as if a team of benevolent deities were conspiring to create just the conditions necessary for my ecstatical experiments. I won't bore you with the administrative particulars, but before spring there had been Big Shows for lighter fighters and Big Shows for heavier ones. That spring the two promotions quite sensibly merged to form one monster promotion that would fill far bigger stadia. The bonuses would be larger, the sponsorships more lucrative, and the cagefighting reality show more prominent in public consciousness. And Erik Koch, said some shadowy figure at the helm of the newly behemothic promotion, should start preparing for a fight in Not-New-York.

Why Not-New-York, you ask? The statesmen of Albany had banished MMA from New York's considerable jurisdiction, and so promoters edged right up to the line, in Newark, not ten miles from Manhattan. There in Jersey, though no law prohibited our presence, the public was not particularly educated in our chosen variety of ecstatic encounter; each taxi driver I encountered in that outermost borough of the world's greatest city asked me for what I had come and then, with no prompting whatsoever, condemned the enterprise. "We haven't advanced since the Colosseum!" said one, though it was rather my impression that the prisoners of war and unfortunate Caspian tiger thrown together into the Colosseum were not there by choice, nor that any man (or Caspian tiger) in the Colosseum might escape certain dismemberment by the gentlest tap of his hand (or paw), but far be it from me to challenge the well-wrought histories of Newark cabbies, fine storytellers all, and in their Italian patrimony more closely tied to any bloodthirsty Roman emperor than I. In any case, when we arrived in Newark we found the weekend was dominated by another activity; we saw crowds swelling round the stadium for that eminently peaceful enterprise, professional hockey.

The hotel where Erik, Pettis, Duke, and I stayed was a fine vertical Hilton, top-of-the-line, and doubled as a train station to the city. You could walk from the hotel elevators, through a couple of double doors, past a Subway and a Starbucks and some delis that serve lunches in clear plastic boxes that close with a snap, to the train. Down below the Hilton was all dead space—great wide streets, a "riverwalk" on which no one had ever actually walked, discarded styrofoam cups stuck in untended grass. Were you to stand in that grass you'd see empty space and then great vertical masses of concrete huddled for no obvious reason other than every structure longs for proximity to the train station, and thus to Manhattan.

The Hilton barely had a lobby; it was just elevators and guards who kept people off the elevators. But in that small space not fewer than twenty shadows huddled with programs to be signed. Every time a man descended from the Hilton, the twenty pulled out their phones and searched for his face among a gallery of fighter photos. Though not fighting in Jersey, Pettis was recognized and asked for autographs ("badass kick, man, seriously"), whereas Erik and I would glide through sadly unmolested. "Perhaps," I said, "they do not recognize you with your tan." Erik, rather agitated by the entire Eastern milieu, did not respond.

To understand the discomfort of Erik in Not-New-York one has to be able to see how much more alien Jersey is to a young man from Iowa than even Vegas. Vegas is a bigger Branson, Midwestern-transplant-packed, made merely of flashier versions of Davenport casinos Erik knew well. But Newark. Erik had never heard men who, standing at the deli counter, stress every syllable of every word—"*You gettin' a sandwich? What kinda meat?*"—had never seen mentally ill homeless people conversing with themselves on the sidewalk, had never been in a public bathroom and left it without urinating because a man proffering a bag of something made him unsure of how to proceed. And all of this while he was near-to-starving with his eye bones bulging and his knee-hinges poking out of his stick-legs.

"I could never live here," he said to me in the Hilton lobby, as men stared at him, then at their phones, then at him, and as a couple of very large officials wheeled out of the hotel a scale on a cart, a sign hanging off it that read, "This scale is official. Do not _____ it up." It is unquestionable that all this unwarranted stimulation, all this odd novelty, contributed to Erik's distraction and eventually the misstep that would confirm so many of my fears about his constitution.

Coach Duke, on the other hand, had no problem adjusting. The day before the weigh-ins Erik and I sat in the hotel room as Duke wandered from subject to subject like a coked-up life coach. There was a silence for a while as he showered, but the minute he emerged from the shower the silence was broken.

"Can't I shower so fast?" he said. "I had five brothers." Then a moment later, "This is such a mess. I wore two different shoes this morning, I brought so many pairs of sneakers. I'm going to clean this up, I always clean when I'm nervous. I'm way more nervous than Erik right now."

Perhaps it was Duke's stream-of-consciousness narration that allowed him and Erik to be so openly intimate. "Love you coach," Erik tweeted at least once a week. "Love all my fighters," Duke tweeted back, and then always some inspirational nostrum about the rewards that redound to the hardworking. Erik relaxed into his coach's warm presence. But even Duke wouldn't know what exactly happened that evening; he would be cloaked in ignorance nearly as long as I would.

That afternoon Duke and Erik and Pettis were training in a Hilton conference room the organizers had filled, for the week, with mats. Duke ran Erik through some striking maneuvers, holding bright red pads for Erik to slam with side-kicks and jabs.

"Niiice," Duke kept saying, "doin' some work tonight, doin' some work tonight."

Erik was visibly weak with hunger, and Duke stopped him after a short while. Duke turned to Pettis, who had a fight coming up in three months against a particularly squirrelly fighter named Clay Guida. Guida was a bouncy, raggedy, long-haired

Tasmanian devil of a man who barreled into each punch, getting deep inside his opponent's range and then striking with a wild hook that looked sloppy but seemed to knock out enough people to warrant respect.

"Move like Guida," Duke told Erik, intending to demonstrate for Pettis how best to catch him. So Erik jerked back and forth in a manic Guida-like manner. Duke faced Erik and matched his swaying motion for a moment, then turned back to Pettis. "So it just takes a quick jab," he said, and jerked his right hand in a tight quick motion meant to catch a moving target. Duke had not realized that Erik was still directly in front of him, swaying. And so Duke, a 6'4" 220-pound champion kickboxer jabbed 145-pound Erik in the head. For the first time in his life, Erik staggered backward as if tripped.

"Whoa whoa whoa," said Pettis.

"Oh no, sorry," said Duke.

"You aright bro?" asked Pettis.

Erik smiled as he steadied himself against the wall, which gave Duke and Pettis permission to laugh. It was not terribly uncommon to punch someone slightly too hard in practice, to "get one's bell rung," to accidentally unleash one's power in a setting meant for gentle play. "I'm OK, I'm OK," he said, laughing. "Whoops!"

With this assurance, Duke and Pettis continued to practice for another fifteen minutes while Erik watched, and then Erik went back to his hotel room to make lists of foods he would enjoy the following evening. He made weight at 145.5, caught a glimpse of his opponent—a Brazilian named Raphael Assunção—and returned to his room, where Wes, having just arrived, waited with a massive order of sandwiches. There too were Cliff and DJ, two Hard Drive friends who had, in the end, refused to take sides in the Kochs' fraternal feud.

Of everyone assembled, only I had ventured to New York City, and that was years before I had become Iowan. We together left the hotel, its Starbucks and deli and nail salon now closed, and headed toward the train platform, where the wait served as further evidence that Iowa was cradle to a superior civilization.

"Is it ever coming?" asked Cliff.

"Are we on the right side?" asked Wes. "I don't think we're on the right side."

"Maybe we're too late," said DJ.

"I could never live here," said Erik.

We arrived at the greatest city on earth and commenced our principle New York activity, which was staring. In Times Square Erik and Wes and Cliff and DJ cocked their heads to take in the scrolling marquees, the flashing light-lined block-sized billboard for *Mamma Mia!*, the Toshiba sign rising up from a bulbous sea of yellow cabs. To see New York City for the first time in the dark is to be liberated from any limiting sense of scale; one sees only lights and no edges, as if the night sky had lowered and arrayed itself about you. In this inverted bowl of light we walked the sidewalks with no particular destination. We stopped on some stairs to watch a lady wearing a knitted red cap chatter to herself: "Venus system," she said over and over as Wes looked to Erik in alarm. We waited for Cliff as he went into a McDonald's bathroom, then ran back out because "someone was drying his dick off with the hand dryer." We stared at a massive rat running circles around a dumpster. We watched, on a bit of concrete beside Penn Station, a small white plastic-bag-toting man being shoved by a larger black man, an altercation Erik called a "bum fight."

I suppose to the shuffling natives, their hands in their pockets, their heads down, we seemed unmannered gawkers from some rude, probably militia-ridden sinkhole. And surely there are spectacles toward which one should not turn, such as the curious interstitial moans of a disabled wheelchair-bound conversationalist. But surely too there is more evil done by the refusal to look at the least pleasant link in a causal chain, by the willingness to note the reposeful voting citizenry but not the democratically elected tyrant, the politician declaring righteous war at his podium but not the soldier who comes back in halves. I was proud to be among men who looked not only up at the majestic flashing lights but down at the women slumped in alleys, who treated each part of the spectacle with equal fascination. Experienced travelers tend to avoid places they call "touristy," but one of the many lessons fighters have taught me is that if you want to see a place unknown to the world, the truly untraveled anteroom of any city, go to the most touristed place in your vicinity, and look down.

"Fuck your mother!" said the white homeless man.

"He didn't pay his bar tab!" the other man said to us, then thought better of it and walked away.

"I'm glad I didn't have to get involved," said Erik as we followed him down Ninth Avenue to an Italian restaurant where he bought, in his munificence, a pasta dinner for every spacetaker.

"So much poverty here, so much when we were driving through New Jersey. I've been all over now, been to Vegas, been to Canada, been here, and I still want to spend the rest of my life in Cedar Rapids."

"This is what a Caesar salad is?" said Cliff. "It's just lettuce with mayonnaise on it."

"You know what I'm gonna buy if I win," said Erik. "A hybrid. You save so much on gas money!"

What Erik did not tell anyone that night was how, as he first looked up at the kaleidoscopic radiance of Times Square, he felt confused about where he was; about how he could not focus for long on a single point. We didn't notice him swerving on the sidewalk, losing, for a brief moment, his balance. As we stared at a woman vomiting on New Jersey transit on our ride back to the hotel, we did not see Erik holding onto his seat as if there were some risk of it crumbling underneath him.

Back at the hotel, Erik told Pettis, and only Pettis, that he was disoriented and dizzy, and that it had started with Duke's jab.

"That sounds like the kind of thing," said Pettis, "where you go to sleep and don't wake up."

Faced with this most ominous prognosis, Erik was really and truly terrified. He took Pettis to mean that if he were knocked out the following day, at the fight, he would very likely die. But were he to tell Duke of his disorientation, the fight would certainly be canceled, the months of training and self-starvation all for naught, the eminent men who controlled the Big Shows ill-disposed toward him for ruining a fight but hours before it was slated to transpire. Erik thus elected to take his chances and tell no one else; and so Duke and I would watch the next night unfold in utter ignorance.

•

At the thrillingly dense, meticulously organized city that was the Prudential Center, I had the best seat I'd ever had—better than my seat in the bubble, better than my seat in St. Louis, because the men who ran the Big Shows were profoundly impressed by my association with the *Cedar Rapids Gazette*. I looked up from that press box to see people seated on every side of me, floor to ceiling in four sections, between the sections scrolling marquees—Jon "Bones" Jones—and above all that cameras that swerved on black tracks bolted to the ceiling, and everywhere laser lights weaving about our heads, Jumbotrons hitched to the wall. There were 19,000 of us seated there in Newark, waiting for the first fighter to be announced, the first fight, and on top of the cacophony of our voices the promoters had chosen to blast a genre of music I believe is called "party rock," such that one could not be heard without shouting. In the press box chubby white men tapped on laptops, and in the front row a legendary fighter named Chuck Liddell shouted something to his attractive wife.

The reason these 19,000 had come to gather here was not to see Erik, but to see Shogun, Erik's hero and the man Lonnie claimed could beat Jesus. In the night's final and most important fight, twenty-eight-year-old Shogun would fight twenty-three-year-old Jon Jones for the light heavyweight title. In the night's first and least important fight, Erik would face Raphael Assunção;

and even among those two, Erik was deemed the least important, and would walk out first. Only the final six fights would be broadcast on Pay-Per-View; his bout would not be televised. Thus it was that in the bar the previous evening the night's least important fighter had walked up to the most celebrated and had told him, through Shogun's ever-present translator, that watching Shogun as a kid was part of what made him want to fight in the first place. Shogun smiled and nodded politely and Erik returned to his table to not eat or drink while Duke had a Coke.

Erik had lost control of his body, existed outside of it as if he were merely playing himself on the Xbox, and now a whole machine had sprung into motion, beginning with the bridge-burning injury of his brother, driving toward this enormously choreographed spectacle, and concluding, quite likely, with a beating from a black belt. To leave would mean to return to Cedar Rapids, but the Cedar Rapids he knew was gone, had disappeared the moment his brother hit the mat.

In the locker room, Erik held out his hands, Duke laced up his gloves, and they sang in unison Eminem's "Soldier": "Even if my collarbones crush or crumble / I will never slip or stumble." Erik thought that perhaps if he consciously tried to regain synchronicity between his brain and his body, some missing piece would click back into place. When he heard his song he bolted out with a defiant bounce, shaking his arms as he strode toward the cage between Duke and Pettis, bopping his head to the music.

He stopped before the cage, took off one sock, handed it to Pettis, took off the other sock, handed it to Pettis. Duke tilted water into his mouth, handed him his mouthguard. The ref checked his hands. Duke vaselined Erik's cheeks, and for a moment Erik stood perfectly still, eyes closed, as Duke rubbed two greased thumbs over his cheekbones. Brown-orange complected, head shaved, Erik was a completely different creature than he had been in Vegas. Instead of looking ill in a recognizable way, he looked simply other, glowing brown-orange under the lights, shadows over his sunken eyes, under his pecs and neck, under each tiny ripple of stomach. He accepted a hug from Duke, a hug from Pettis, and stepped through the cage door to a bright, white, sterile cage. He had never fought first before, never seen a cage so clean.

Raphael Assunção walked out, singing along to his entrance music. He was four inches shorter than Erik, with broad muscles unlike anything on Erik's body. He had a flat brown fighter's nose, a wide brow, dark stubble about his mouth.

"Are you ready?" the ref shouted to Erik. Erik, looking grim, gave a thumbs up. "Are you ready?" the ref shouted to Assunção, and he nodded. "Let's fight," said the ref, clapped, backed himself toward the cage.

"Here we go!" said the TV color man.

Erik runs in and leans low on his legs, almost squatting—the stance of a man preparing to be pulled down, afraid to be knocked off balance by an opponent five inches shorter than himself. And yet even in this awkward fearful hunch Erik moves so fast he is hard to see, arms up and down, hands fisted then palms open, a step here and a step there—to Assunção's every motion, three in response. Erik kicks high with the kick that had downed Cisco but Assunção just throws an arm in front of his face, blocks it.

The TV color man compares Erik to Anthony Pettis—"long and lean, that reach"—as Erik carefully hops toward Assunção, and Assunção carefully hops away. Assunção stops his slow backward walk, swings, misses, and backs away more. They are falling into a partnered pattern, rarely touching, forward and back. "He's got that right hand loaded," the color man says of Assunção, and it's true, Assunção is just waiting for the moment to lunge that right hand into Erik's face, knock him to the ground. Assunção throws a high kick, and Erik pops away with a single deft jump, so smooth it seems Erik knew where Assunção was headed long before he threw. Assunção swings, misses, and Erik does not retaliate.

"Come on guys," shouts someone from the crowd, "this is a contact sport!"

"Just throw!" shouts Duke from behind the cage.

Erik is afraid of losing focus; the fight is a minute and a half in; he feels that he must end the fight or he'll simply fall. But he hasn't yet found a range, and there is that loaded right hand. A normal fight for Erik is a moment of total absorption, but with the newfound cloudiness, the way it throws him off, he must somehow keep track of his own body in addition to Assunção's. It is as if Erik is standing outside himself, reminding his body to do what it is told. It's all so unstable, the body's obedience so subject to chance, that Erik is desperate for a way out.

Assunção lands a light kick to the shin, as if checking to make sure Erik is solid matter. Erik hits back with a left but Assunção dodges it. Erik finally lands a loud thwap of a kick to Assunção's chest; the sound resonates through the silent stadium.

"Set it up!" says Duke.

Assunção jabs with his left, misses, and charges, swings hard with that loaded right. Erik sees him coming. As Assunção runs toward him Erik throws a light left hook, barely visible. His fist hits the soft spot behind Assunção's ear with all the strength of his cocked arm, but also the force of Assunção's own charge; it appears as if Assunção has run full speed into Erik's clenched hand. It is a moment in which Erik hardly moves; his arm only slightly extends past his own body, a movement almost impossible to see, and so there is a confused silence as Assunção hits the ground, his head with a thud, his flaccid arms hitting the canvas above his head a millisecond later. A realization passes, the silence breaks. Nineteen thousand people scream.

"It's all over!" shouts the color man. "Just. Like. That!"

This moment lasts for days. We can only open our mouths in a united wordless moan. We are each of us simple tools of perception, free of the cloudying intellect, allowed a thinking of the body only accessible when men like Erik can, for a single solitary second, lead us outside ourselves. He has torn a small hole in consciousness. It is already closing.

"Wow," says the color man. "Wow. Perfect."

Erik collapses onto his knees, lifts his hands to his shaved head, looks up in tears of gratitude at the fact that he is still alive. He places his head on the mat, kowtowing, jumps up, fist bumps Bruce Buffer, who doesn't break pace as the ref raises Erik's hand: "Referee Kevin Mulhall has stopped this contest at two minutes thirty two seconds in the very first round, declaring the winner, by knockout, Erik 'New Breed' Koch." The color man hops onto the canvas with a mic, which Erik grabs so as to pump up the crowd: "What'd you guys think, was that a good opener?" And the crowd launches into its scream once again.

But now he is shooed off the stage for bigger, more important fighters. We watch the other fights as we come down, reenter ourselves, reacquaint ourselves with the limiting walls of perception. We wait for Shogun to defend his title as the best light heavyweight in the world. In his last fight, against Lyoto Machida, he was glorious. But Shogun is twenty-eight and we realize, as we watch him pummeled, kicked, ground into the mat, and finally slumping against the cage like a tired drunk as a younger man knees him in the face, that Shogun has grown prematurely old. The ref steps mercifully in. The fight is so unexpectedly quick that the Pay-Per-View gods have time to fill; there is room to televise an extra fight. And so a million people, after they see Shogun fall, watch Erik watching himself knock a man to the ground.

Summer 2011

IN APRIL, WHILE TAKING A PHILOSOPHY OF Aesthetics class with the Director of Graduate Studies, I felt motivated to write an assigned paper. The topic was open, and so I chose Schopenhauer's (correct) belief that in contemplating great art, we suspend the clouding lens of the rational intellect, and perceive purely what the world provides. I related this, as you might guess, to my year of observation, and appended to my insightful meditation seventy pages of uncollected thoughts about the heightening of perceptual capacities I experienced in the presence of fighters.

Some weeks later I received an email from the Director of Graduate Studies saying that he had read my paper, which he took to be an "excessively literal take on Schopenhauer, who had been talking about artistry, not athletic contests." There was so much wrong with this assessment that it was hard to summon an apposite response. Did he suppose all artists were bescarved Frenchmen bearing palettes? *I* was being literal?

"I am convening a panel of faculty," this misguided dispatch continued, "to discuss whether, given your three incompletes and two failing grades over the previous three semesters, you are progressing satisfactorily toward your degree. You will, as stated in the handbook, be given the opportunity to justify your continued presence in the program before the panel."

This I had not expected. Of course serious philosophical inquiry required sacrifices in the straitened realm of academic apple-polishing, but I assumed that the faculty were all in sympathy with my ambition. I had dared to make the unknowable show itself, and I was in my investigations resurrecting old works of philosophy thought irrelevant by their contemporary critics. Then and there, at my laptop, in my Iowa City kitchen, beside a bobbing wooden cat that read "Welcome" which I had picked up at a charming local thrift store, I began building my case. But even as I ticked off my justifications, I knew what they would turn my project into, these small scholastics with their ceaseless referencing of better men would, if they even allowed my explorations as a subject of dissertation, demand a dull tome with the tiniest flicker of insight buried underneath 800 pages of exegeses of other men's work. Instead of being celebrated as a pioneer of modern phenomenology, I would merely be a footnote in the future study of Schopenhauer, whom, without my prodding, no one would study in the future.

"I am sorry that you have so badly misread my work," I wrote to the Director of Graduate Studies. "I voluntarily withdraw from the graduate program." I found that I could not press *send*, so I reread my paper for courage. "A preference for questionable and terrifying things," Nietzsche said, "is a symptom of strength." I sent the email.

With this I felt a kind of unpleasant unmooring from my academic home, but on the other hand, Erik had never before seemed so solid a subject of philosophical inquiry. I would not have mentioned it to Sean, who was subject to jealousy on this one dimension, but post-Jersey Erik Koch was the eighth-ranked featherweight in the world. His financial problems were no more, for his knockout carried with it the honor of "fight of the night," which involved, on top of the payout and sponsorships, a $70,000 check. He bought a car and a nicer television and let the rest come to him without effort. He was now an object of veneration on which fashionable corporate entities lavished their swag. Never again would a TV color man stumble over his name; now they would speak casually of Erik's powerful striking, his role as "the next generation," as if these were particulars of Erik's quintessence any spectator already knew. And because I was kept, like Duke, in a dark pall of unknowing, I could watch this flowering with unadulterated joy.

I might never have left academic philosophy had Erik mentioned the possibility of a concussion, but even if I knew Erik to be injured, I would not have known that a concussion could persist through months and months of training. That all those diminutive axons, sheared from the force of the blow, too often failed to pass whatever message they were charged with passing, and so left Erik confused, anxious, unable, very often, to follow the winding thread of a complex conversation. That less blood was coursing through the damaged part of his brain, and each compromised axon failing to recharge itself. Had he still been ensconced in Cedar Rapids, packed into the circle in Rocky's living room, rewinding the same film and reciting it in a giggling chorus, Erik would, of course, have had many confidants with whom to share his suffering. In Milwaukee he kept his dysfunction from Duke, from his parents, from his spacetakers. He could not discern whether his anxiety, which kept him up at night with great knots in his stomach, was born of any injury itself, or of the fear that he might have such an injury.

Every night, when the anxiety grew worst, he thought about telling Duke that something was wrong. But then he was offered a fight, and there was, again, every reason not to expose himself as a site of corporeal unraveling. I was even further from the truth than was Duke, because this was a time in which Erik began, upon occasion, to fail to return my calls. He had local spacetakers now; I took this development with the dignity of a professional. I would see him in New Orleans, for his September fight, and then would reclaim my rightful place at the head of his pack.

Erik's neglect left me more time to be with Sean, where I was, after all, most happy, though too often being with Sean during this period involved being in the presence of Sean's roommate, a 5'2" muscled logorrheic ball of nervous energy, owner of the aforementioned pitbull. He never stopped talking, not even as he and Sean were rolling, most of what he had to say being intended to impress the listener with his mastery of many subjects. He was simultaneously pursuing a career as a fighter, writing a jiu-jitsu instruction manual, attempting to obtain his master's in economics, and raising two young sons who lived with their mother. In the bathroom with no door on it were many prescription amphetamines with his name on them. If asked to invent from whole cloth an anti-Sean I could not have done any better than Brandon, who spilled forth with such an excess of energy that it was causing problems with his schoolwork. ("I have trouble focusing," he explained in his deep drawl. "I'm too imaginatory.") This was the fighter and roommate and the fellow spacetaker who was ushering Sean toward his comeback. Like two Mormons sent to mission, the pair kept one another clean—no naps, no Reubens, and let us roll again.

Unlike a Mormon, Brandon tended to spill forth with disturbing stories about his past, when he was a stuntman for films in Hollywood.

"I used to sell horse testosterone," he told us once, looking up from an economics textbook.

"To who?"

"Fighters. I'd buy horse testosterone from the Feed n' Seed, then sell them individually to people to inject. It's the same stuff, you know? But way cheaper for horses."

Brandon was in general disagreeable, and regularly told me that I was lucky Dopo—who never failed to kiss me upon my ascent into the apartment—did not tear me to pieces. And yet I was grateful for the way Brandon kept Sean focused on fighting, for Sean had a fight two months away, against someone his own size, and Brandon would keep him practicing so he could stay active for three long, transportive rounds. It would be the first evenly matched encounter in which I saw Sean fit, trim, that unbreakable box of a body over two slim legs.

Often Sean and I would walk around after he had trained for the day and find a grassy knoll on which to lay ourselves out and watch the river fowl rise and fall with the current. Should he win this next fight with a knockout, and a few more after that, it was perfectly likely that someone would call him up to the Big Shows, where I could be of great service to him as someone now deeply familiar with that organization and its glamorous ephemera. Other men in his weight class would take the fact that he had never been knocked out as a challenge. He would be revered for the hardness of his skull, an unteachable advantage possessed by some of the most beloved fighters. Perhaps, when Sean finally made it, other fighters would come to recognize me as a small but crucial part of his resurrection.

"You know my friend John in Knoxville," asked Sean, "the one I talk about all the time?"

In our hundreds of hours together I had never heard Sean talk about a friend from Tennessee, or if I had, I had not been listening.

"Yes," I lied.

"He died last week. From an overdose. OxyContin or something. He was my best friend as a kid. We did everything together, got into so much trouble."

I was shocked by this, and wanted to know more about the details of his demise, but with talk of his friend's passing Sean turned again to what he called his "legacy," which was a euphemism for Josiah. Sean had recently seen Josiah for the second time. Alexis was visiting a friend in Davenport, and with a few hours notice she told Sean he could spend a few hours playing with the boy in return for sixty dollars.

"She took him to the doctor and the doctor couldn't believe how strong he was, how strong his fist was," Sean told me on our knoll. He had brought a candy bar, which seemed strange given his recent devotion to diet and exercise, given the way I could follow the curve of his cheekbone from mouth to ear.

Though not invited to the meetings between Alexis and Sean, I did see pictures—more pictures than I wished to see. That spring Josiah sprouted all the distinguishing characteristics that would transform the former suggestion of humanness into a statement of full-fledged childhood. A suggestible person might have made an argument for a resemblance to Sean—the round face, the ruddiness—but this world is full of round-faced, ruddy babies, and these qualities are insufficient to determine genetic affinity.

Periodically Alexis asked how much Sean made.

"Then after I tell her," Sean explained, "she says, 'Oh, it wouldn't be worth it. I won't get much.'"

Alexis's reasoning held that it would not be worth granting him legal rights because, given his paltry, erratic income, the government would demand very little in regular payments. I turned away, plucked bunches of grass from the knoll. Alexis was striving to push Sean into a suit, a nine-to-five, precisely the kind of routine it was necessary to avoid were he to remain a fighter. A year into the project, we did not have time for such distractions. Sean was thirty-three. In the fall, I too would be in my third decade. Moments of ecstatic experience were so few and far between that I knew I would require many more years to compile my study. Five might have been enough, should Sean start to fight more frequently, but this was now my life's work, and I was more than ready to devote ten. I had no life to which I might otherwise return.

"He's my son," said Sean, quietly, as we lay back to back and stared up at some cloud cover. "Do you know what that means?"

I sighed, audibly this time. Sean had already called government employees in Nebraska, and government employees in Iowa, asking for the right to pay child support, because paying child support would give him the legal right to see Josiah with some regularity. But none of the government employees seemed to know what to do with a man who wished to pay rather than avoid child support. Get the birth certificate, someone finally said, and when we have legal documentation of your status as Josiah's father, we will proceed.

On the knoll that day Sean showed me another grainy picture of the boy, but it was entirely different from the others I had seen, because Sean himself was in it. The baby was in his arms, mouth open in the midst of emitting some infant sound, and Sean was staring at him with his head cocked and a smile wider than I had ever seen on him. His eyes were closed, as if he had given himself over to something. Someone with a less precise vocabulary might look at that picture and say that Sean was ecstatic. I felt a tightening in my chest.

Sean was waiting for some reaction, and so, searching for an appropriate sentiment, I pronounced him "healthy-looking." I heard no more of Josiah for a few weeks, until one day Sean got a slim envelope with a Nebraska postmark. It was Josiah's birth certificate. Josiah Tiberio, it said, born to Alexis Tiberio, it said, and under that, listed as the father, someone named Kris. As far as Nebraska was concerned, the issue was resolved. Alexis said this Kris was the father; the state would take it no further. I took Nebraska's decision to be definitive. What could one do? Sean didn't even know where Alexis lived. He would have no choice but to return to the gym.

"I'll have to hire a private investigator," Sean said.

The correspondence between Sean and Alexis plunged to new and disturbing lows.

"She is a terrible person," he said one day, slabbing mayonnaise on some cold cuts in his kitchen. "Look at this."

He walked over to his computer, sandwich in the other hand, a mouthful of meat in between each reading. Alexis communicated in her characteristic debased phonetic patois, which Sean sounded out for my benefit as we hovered over his screen. It was the first time I had actually seen her correspondence, rather than had it related to me.

> Give up u lost. Hes our baby. Ur no1 sean. Sean who? Lol!
> —Lexy n kris—!

"See how ignorant she is?" he said. There was a dab of mayonnaise on Sean's mouth. Sean's replies were in sentences, with occasional punctuation.

> I can honestly say that you are beautiful on the outside but, inside, you are weak, shallow, and very ignorant. Josiah is a gift.
> —Sean

He is very much so. He is a gift 4rm u tht u wil nvr
b able to enjoy.
—Lexy n kris—!

You don't make sense you are like a crazy person.
—Sean

Fag
—Lexy n kris—!

Sean made another sandwich, which he finished with a sigh.
I thought of him back in the Navy, overcome by disgust and nausea, having carried that crushed slop of a corpse and then carrying the memory in such a way that tainted every meal. This
was his worst memory of the war because it denied him his most
accessible comfort. I went to visit him a week later, to find him
five pounds heavier, and two weeks later, to find him ten.

Erik – September 2011

HOW OBVIOUS HIS IMPAIRMENT SEEMS in retrospect! Why, in retrospect, I can fairly see those neurons failing to connect, little zaps of white energy fizzling out before they touch. But my ignorance went levels deep: I did not know about the punch; I did not know what longterm symptoms which a concussion was capable of manifesting; and even if I had, I could always, with the self-delusion of an ecstasy-seeking optimist, attribute irritability to nervousness (though this was not characteristic of Erik) and absentmindedness to the extended effects of starvation (though this, too, was inconsistent with prior experience).

I thought little of the fact that when I arrived at Erik's New Orleans hotel room, notebook in hand, he was not there at the appointment time. An hour later Erik and Wes and his four Milwaukee-based spacetakers arrived to find me sitting in the hallway.

"Oh," said Erik. "Hi."

"I thought we were meeting at four?" I felt the protective eyes of his other spacetakers upon me.

"We were? Guess I forgot."

There were several nonconcussive, unpleasant explanations for this lack of courtesy. I had arrived late in the weekend because I had not wanted to leave Sean; perhaps Erik's other spacetakers had told him to turn on me due to my divided loyalties. Perhaps Erik wanted to rid himself of every vestige of his pre-Milwaukee life, though the presence of Wes agitated against that particular conclusion. Or perhaps—and I thought of this as I gazed at the young bright faces of Erik's other spacetakers—I had passed some threshold of agedness that rendered me unwelcome. Fewer than two months from a momentous birthday, I was especially sensitive to this consideration, and wondered whether I seemed to these men more a misfit elder than a fun-loving comrade. Perhaps the power of invisibility, which I took myself to have when among Erik and his friends, atrophied, like everything else, with time. I thought of Pettis's vulgar uncle, and the unseemliness of his tagging along with a group of much younger men.

In the hotel room, on a table beside the bed, was an instructive list Erik had made for those already present: "Whole Foods—Biggie 11:30; Jimmy John's—Brent 12:00" and so on. Erik had remade his social life, such that what had been a team of equals was now a coterie of eager underlings.

Normally at this stage, having weighed in, rehydrated, and incorporated any number of sandwiches, Erik would be shadowboxing and chattering animatedly about the fight. He would want me to know what he thought of his opponent, or what he might buy with the money should he win. But he said next to nothing as the pack of us left the hotel and penetrated the city. Sweaty bands of tourists, blue beads around their necks and beers in hand, crowded the sidewalks and slowed traffic. A driver, surely intoxicated, backed onto the curb in front of the Marriott. "Fuck that curb!" a stranger shouted.

"Is that seerp?" a raggedy black man asked us, gesturing toward a red gallon jug of Pedialyte in Erik's hands. Erik didn't seem to hear; he kept walking.

"He means syrup—cough syrup and 7UP—what Lil' Wayne drinks," translated Biggie, the only black spacetaker and the youngest. Biggie was chubby cheeked and almost as excited about eating as was Erik.

"Really, cough syrup?" said someone.

"Seerp!" said Biggie. We tried the sound on our tongues. Erik led us to the French Quarter. Women in lingerie slunk in doorways, under neon signs that sucked the light from their skin and replaced it with blue pallor. We all stared, except for Rick Glenn, a married twenty-two-year-old from central Iowa. Earlier they had tricked Rick Glenn into coming with them to a strip club on Bourbon Street. "I didn't know it was *this* kind of place," he had said, grimacing at the floor with his hands in his pockets. These were not men like Anthony Pettis; they were all possessed of a certain innocence.

On one side of Erik was the curb; on the other, Biggie. I wished to engage Erik in conversation; perhaps because I wanted some assurance that everything was as normal between us. So I sidled between them and suggested that a vice-ridden city like New Orleans, so uninvested in the ecstasy-denying impulses of civil order, was an ideal place to stage a fight. But it was Biggie who responded, to say that there was vice in Iowa, too, and if you showed up in the wrong place in Waterloo, you could be killed. He said it like he wanted to believe it.

The Italian restaurant Erik had lusted after, the one where they hand-pull the pasta, was on a quieter corner of the French Quarter. He walked in with the jug by his side, in a jersey and jeans, with six spacetakers in T-shirts behind him. Every man in the restaurant had a jacket on; most were seated near a fire-place away from the street. The maître d' looked at Erik. "Are we allowed in here?" Glenn said from the back of the pack.

I suspected that we should redirect our party to the nearest Jimmy John's, but we were led without comment to a large table by the window. The Pedialyte made a loud thunk as Erik plopped it on the table, beside a vase with a wine list tilted against it.

"They got goat on the menu," said Biggie.

"What's rabbit taste like?" asked Grant.

"Squid ink!" said Rick.

"What's arugula?" asked Grant.

The waiter explained what bruschetta was, and then he explained about arugula. The squid ink cavatelli, he said, was not as briny as might be expected.

"What's in the jug?" he asked.

"Pedialyte."

"He's a fighter," said Biggie. "He's fighting tomorrow."

"Oh!" said the waiter. "Like MMA? Oh, wow. I have a friend who fights sometimes, I mean not that serious, but he is really into it, goes every week, but he knows a lot of chokes and—"

"Oh yeah?" said Erik, politely but without looking up from the menu. He ordered bruschetta, orecchiette, spaghetti, soup. "For now," he said.

"Tomorrow, you're fighting?" the waiter asked.

When the food came—Rick's jet-black squid ink pasta was a shock to him—the owner of the restaurant, a middle-aged man in a suit, came too. He shook Erik's hand and thanked him for coming to his restaurant. "Tomorrow we will watch and say we saw you!" he said, very nearly bowing, while the waiter rattled off a list of bar recommendations to Grant, and agreed, with Biggie, that bruschetta was a strange word.

Erik was staring into space, his fingers tight around the handle of the plastic jug of Pedialyte.

"What?" he said, lost yet again, unable to keep up with the multiple conversations being held across the table.

"The strip club," said Grant, catching Erik up, "Rick wants to go."

"I hate strip clubs," said Erik. "I want frozen yogurt. Why is everyone taking so long?"

Erik had the check in front of him, but he seemed to have drifted off, deep in a lonely thought none of us could reach. Had there ever been a time for him to admit to his dysfunction, it was certainly not now—now, when we six spacetakers had journeyed 1,000 miles south of Iowa in hope of release, when 7,000 fans were en route to this gothic swamp, when 1.8 million Americans had made their Saturday night plans and their Saturday night plans involved watching Erik Koch fight. When Erik's eyes flickered back to attention, and he saw the bill before him, he simply put his hand in his pocket and drew out his wallet as if everything were normal.

The next afternoon I made my way to the venue alone. By September of 2011 my project had endured precisely a year, and the anniversary brought with it certain concerns about the speed of my progress. By nature opportunities for the observation of ecstatic experience were few and fleeting; each required months of preparation that might, in the end, come to nothing, as I had dejectedly discovered while ensconced in the bubble. I had no intention of rushing a work that would be of such lasting importance to the study of consciousness, but it was dispiriting to reflect upon the fact that in over a year of observation I had accumulated only five moments of heightened sensation on which to expound. And having recently abandoned my program, struck out as a sole roving scholar without any institution at my back, I longed for a moment of reassurance from the universe I was chronicling.

I approved of that flat water-side arena, the way it held us all on the same softly tilted plane instead of shooting up into steep terraced walls. We looked, pressed together at such a uniform height, like a crowd that might with small provocation incite ourselves to riot. For that reason I rejected the cageside seat labeled "*Cedar Rapids Gazette*" for a cheap seat in the rafters. If there were some possibility of an ecstasy-driven uprising, I did not want to be isolated among bespectacled sports journalists.

There would be four televised fights that evening of which Erik's was the second, but most of those watching his fight would be far more familiar with his opponent. In 2011 Jonathan Brookins was already a television phenomenon. Over twelve seasons of *The*

Ultimate Fighter, the insulting, undignified reality show in which producers forced a dozen martial artists into a tight living space, took away solitary entertainments that might detract from social drama, and kept the lights on twenty-four hours a day, Brookins was the first to vocally bemoan the lack of books. He was the first to express a longing for his local library, the first to appear in a yogic headstand before his fight, and the first to describe his time in the house as "a journey of self-discovery." When finally it seemed like Brookins might win the show, he was seized with a horror that he might lose his humility. "I hope only to be worthy of the word humble," he said. "I'm praying every day, 'Lord, don't let this thing go to my head. Let me go home, ride my bike; let me go to the library.'"

I cannot say whether Brookins was albino, though his black features and alabaster-blond complexion suggested melanin deficiency and a "caveman" quality to which others alluded. Unlike Erik, who would grab any microphone in the vicinity, Brookins grew nervous and fidget-prone on camera. "I'd rather be focusing on bigger questions of the universe," he said, quite admirably I thought, halfway through the show's duration. He won the season, was granted a loyal following, and found himself, but a year later, fighting the rather less famous Erik Koch, which he said was a great honor. Thus it was that Erik found himself with the problem of nurturing enmity for the world's most cordial opponent.

"I hate how *nice* he is," Erik had said in the hotel room that afternoon.

"He looks like a caveman," offered Wes.

"At weigh-ins he was like, 'It's an honor to fight you.' Yeah, well," Erik said, as if repeating something he'd heard somewhere, "it'll be an honor to knock you out. I'll be the bad guy if I have to be."

As the pre-Erik fights flew by that evening I endured the conversation of my neighbor, who knew not the slightest thing about the spectacle pouring forth. He had won the tickets, he told me, through a contest, which he called a "sweepstakes," and as he said this I noticed that a quarter of the crowd was wearing the same T-shirt as this man—they were all sweepstakes winners swept in by a beer company as if this sacred encounter were a Carnival Cruise to be enjoyed by the common tourist. The worst sort of desecration comes not by the hate-filled vandal but by the oblivious pleasure seeker; think only of the way the sublime majesty of the sea is sadly wasted on actual cruise enthusiasts. The blue-shirted had come not to heighten their perceptual capacities, find escape, but to dull even further each already attenuated sense.

When my charge burst into the arena all the listless languor of the previous evening was gone. He danced toward the cage slapping the sweating hands of dancing fans, mouth open, each step a jump, each hand-slap a definitive smack, each scream unworded as if he were too present to require the cold distancing mechanism of a language. He must have been terrified of drifting off in the middle of the encounter, forgetting where he was, losing the thread on which was strung each fighterly moment, but there was nothing even the most intelligent observer would have noticed in his demeanor to suggest fear or uncertainty. Brookins waited, patient and polite and soon to be penetrated. The laser lights shifted like roaming eyes and the ring girls touched their hair and the cameras slid on tracks with the glorious simultaneity of a proper spectacle.

Brookins was even taller than was Erik. How this is possible at 145 pounds I could not figure; it would seem that a man so long of limb would exert more gravitational pull, unless he were made of some superior substance, some hard and light frame on which to hang his flesh. But still I was not afraid, even as the uneducated man beside me left for more free beer, even as the ref put his hands together in a prayerful gesture of respect before the octagon, paused, and waved his flat palm as if to chop in two the air between the fighters.

With his blond hair pulled into cornrows, Brookins' ears were unpleasantly visible; he looked nothing like lithe Erik, who had in his being the satisfying consonance of a marble sculpture carved from a single slab. Brookins crossed the cage with a long lumbering stride to rush his vastly more graceful opponent, slamming Erik against the cage. From where I sat I saw only Erik's back, white diamonds of flesh outlined in black wire. He wrapped his arms around Erik's waist and pulled and pulled and grimaced, pulling still more, but could not pull hard enough to yank him to the mat. "What's happening?" asked the man at my side, and I ignored him, for if he could not see that Brookins was afraid to fight standing up, there was really no hope of my helping him through this brief encounter.

But how odd Brookins' persistence appeared to the seasoned watcher of fights; how inelegant this hard dull adamancy in a pursuit meant for the playfully supple. He did not grow playful or more interesting, but he grew tired; so instead of trying to pull Erik to the ground, he stood tall and hugged Erik tight against the cage. Erik focused his strength on breathing inside Brookins' arms, forcing his chest to rise and fall against the crushing pressure of Brookins' hug. Neither of them could strike, as Brookins' arms were wrapped around Erik and Erik's arms were pinned against his sides. Brookins' chest slid an inch across Erik's chest; he leaned into Erik with the full force of his weight, shoved his shoulder into Erik's windpipe. Again he tried to drag Erik to the ground. One of 7,000 people coughed. Ten seconds passed, twenty seconds. I felt embarrassed, as I am sure the whole crowd did, at Brookins' animal persistence, his refusal to surrender to the fluidity of the fight.

"Fight!" someone screamed from the cheap seats. Erik slid his right arm from under the clinch; Brookins lifted his left arm to wrap Erik back up in the hug. Erik slid his arm out and Brookins wrapped him up again—a slow labored weaving of limbs, two men swimming into one another. Locked in the hug, Erik thrashed and writhed, throwing his shoulders and hips at Brookins in an attempt to break free. Another cough from the crowd. "Elbows," someone shouted. Sweepstakes winners got up in search of beer while on television announcers struggled to fill the air with chatter. The camera stayed unchanging on this still of two men trapped. The audience waited for Brookins to untie himself and give them the show for which they had come.

At the ring of the bell I began to breathe deeply as I had been instructed to by the woman of Korean descent. The man beside me looked at me, concerned, but really he ought to have been concerned for himself, for he would always be trapped in his body, and I had a way out upon occasion, though perhaps, it was dawning upon me with a growing sense of disappointment, not this occasion.

At the dawn of the second round Brookins rushed Erik once again. He tried to drag Erik to the canvas, just as he had before. He pulled on one of Erik's legs, then the other leg, then the ankle of that leg. In all of his other fights Brookins had been able to yank the other man to the floor and submit him, but Erik would not go down. Brookins went, once again, to his plan B, which was to play human straitjacket. Erik spun to his right, and the caveman spun, and Erik spun, and they landed right where they started, clinched, with no air between their two chests. Erik hipped and pushed and kicked and spun and finally, finally he was free, with inches of space between his body and Brookins.

Broken free, the fight was an open, dangerous thing; in the space between Erik and Brookins lay all the possibility for terror, all hope of pain and penetration. The moment Erik finally spun out in the great glorious empty center of the cage I breathed deep and let loose a supportive scream, for now the fight might begin; and just as I shouted Erik unfurled his balletic limbs, stretched his right arm long into a lunging jab. There was a gasp from the crowd, then a quick breath in; for no satisfying solidity met Erik's fist as he swept past. Brookins was fast, perhaps as fast as Erik, and though Brookins could not throw a punch he could duck Erik's punches with the flickering speed of a puckish sprite.

Erik shook his head and shoulders like a kenneled dog stretching upon its emergence back into the world. This was his opportunity to unleash himself on a lesser man. Instead of unleashing, he tapped Brookins with a few tepid shin-kicks, as if daintily dipping his toes in icy water. Brookins rushed Erik and they were again against the cage, Brookins hugging Erik, both men cobwebbed into a dull and ordinary stillness. The opportunity was lost. The round ended. I closed my eyes, breathed heavily. I was cold in that arena but a sweat had broken out over me; drops of water popped onto my neck and slid down my shirt.

"Someone doesn't want to fight," I heard Duke say. He meant Brookins, but Erik too was withholding. He ought to have rushed Brookins just as Brookins rushed him, not cautious shin-taps but a vicious slew of strikes, not this halting static hug but a fluid writhing roll. The Erik I craved would slide out of a clinch like an eel in a fist, shed the skein of self-conscious worry and unravel before us. If not for himself, then for us. For me.

At the advent of the third round Brookins stood in the center of the cage and let himself be hit. Erik seemed to be waiting for something, his feet free once again, dancing around Brookins as if trying to solve a problem—a careful kick to the shin, a safe, quick jab. Brookins' cornrows had fallen out into thick stalks of blond hair, dreads really, and when Erik finally landed the perfect shot to Brookins' face the dreads fanned golden like spread feathers behind his head. I tried to feel myself dispersing, the chair broken into a billion atoms, the illusions of temporal space ripped from consciousness. But all I felt was the effort of trying. This, then, was the fight's most beautiful moment and it was only that—beautiful.

"What are they doing now," asked the man, clearly bored. "Hugging?"

"Failing," I snapped without looking at him, "they're failing."

Brookins rushed Erik, hugged him. The crowd booed. On television the announcer read an advertisement for a new sitcom.

"Who won?" asked the man, and I came back to consciousness of his presence with no small embarrassment. The world thought us cretins, children warped into perversity by the abandonment of a careless god, bloodthirsty thugs with no sense at all of the sacred; and for all this man and his fellow sweepstakes winners would ever know, we were exactly that. Another opportunity had passed me by, and it would be months before Sean or Erik had another fight.

"I don't know," I told the man, turning away. Bruce Buffer inhaled deeply and exhaled a string of numerals—30–27, 30–27, 29–28—by unanimous decision, *Erik "New Breed" Koch*. Erik squinted his eyes, frowned, and fell to the ground in tears.

At the press conference following the evening's final fight, Erik was asked a question about his lachrymose postfight display. "I'm an emotional fighter, man, and this fight was for me, for some of my demons," he said. "Yeah, I cry. Real men cry too."

"This is what happens when you go on a journey of self-discovery," Jonathan Brookins said. "You don't fight that well."

I was by this time fairly desperate for a drink. There are many lesser ways to forget oneself, and a shot of whiskey is among them. Which is not to imply that I considered Erik and his entourage ideal company for an obliterating binge. I would be better off going to my old university library and selecting random graduate students from their respective carrels.

"He's a UFC fighter!" Biggie said as we approached the doors of the club at which the official after-party would take place, and the bouncer rushed ten people—all of us touching to show that we were really just extensions of Erik—into the club without a cover.

Now as I say, if you seek regular partners with which to consume emboldening amounts of alcohol, with which to scout and pursue single women hoping to be scouted and pursued, with which to unleash musical displays of physical competence ("In the dance," says Nietzsche, "the greatest strength remains potential"), professional fighters are not your best option. Firstly, their tolerance for drink is horrendous. They won't drink, and when they will, a few shots have their knees buckling in a dispiriting and unfamiliar division of mind and body. They cannot dance, certainly. They do, in their defense, attract women—unless the fighter you have chosen is Erik Koch, and then, it seemed to me late that night, he would actively seek to repel them. Picture Erik at the official after-party, alone in the corner, checking his texts, dancing with his phone, bopping his head as his thumb brushes across the single square of light, bright in the dark bar. There are women dancing around him, attractive women whom one supposes would not be averse to attention from a rising UFC star, but Erik would not cross the chasm. Self-denial may become a kind of sickness. Perhaps Erik was no longer capable of giving himself any satisfaction that did not relate to a victorious encounter.

Erik swayed alone, all light and youth, veins like taut rope running down his muscled arms, bright blue eyes, skin so perfectly unlined he looked even younger than twenty-two. I remembered then why I had chosen him. Here was health itself, a perfect machine right off the line.

"Where now?" Erik said.

"Let's go back to the French Quarter," I said.

"I can't walk everywhere with my ankle fucked up," Erik snapped at me, and the other five grew quiet. I looked straight at him, shocked—this, his first impolitic words to me in our year of acquaintance.

I turned away sharply, toward light heavyweight Ryan Bader, who was gathering women into his massive wingspan and smiling at the pigtailed official UFC photographer. Bader, at maybe 220 pounds, and Joseph Benavidez, 135 and 5'4" on a good day, brushed themselves against the same blonde with a sparkly T-shirt and three different shades of blue eyeshadow. I wanted to know nothing of Erik's sexual proclivities, but perhaps fighters, who cannot love lest they lose themselves, require a release that looks something like the blonde. It is one thing to maintain the kind of space from other people that makes a fight possible, and quite another to exile yourself completely. Watching victorious Erik thumb through his phone that night, I thought I had never seen a man so alone.

We got in the taxi, but it could only ferry us so far into the French Quarter, so Erik would have to walk. His ankle was flaring up and he lurched with zombielike stiffness; Biggie made fun of him. Having gained twenty pounds since last night, he'd traded the menacing shadows around his skull for a newfound softness around the eyes and cheeks, but even as he grew healthily fatter the bruises under his eyes were growing darker. A teenage girl in heels and an "Ask Me to Bayou a Bud Light" T-shirt stumbled into him, nearly knocking him into Biggie. The group of men she was with rushed past us; due to Erik's ankle we moved more slowly than the rest of Bourbon Street, and crowds spilled past us in both directions. A slow crowd of our own coalesced; suddenly Duke had arrived, and Duke's wife, to whom Duke introduced me as "a great writer for the *Cedar Rapids Gazette*." Anthony Pettis was there, and all the many spacetakers who took their positions behind him, and everyone was eating by-the-slice pizza in cold fluorescent light. "Brookins is tough," Erik said, perhaps because complimenting Brookins' chin gave him a way to talk about the pain. "Everywhere I hit him hurts. My hands hurt, my elbows hurt, my knees hurt. Something in my ankle is definitely cracked."

The night had only grown more humid; every reveler was covered in a sweaty sheen now, gone electric blue in the neon. A girl in a wedding veil with a Corona in her hand and six friends packed tight around her jostled past us. Erik's eyelids were half closed; he was just following the crowd now, into a bar where when you ask for a beer they hand you three, and Erik was given six shots of vodka, plus some tonic, in an oversized white plastic cup.

"I'm going to go hit on some bitches," Erik said when the cup was empty, not without determination.

But when he lurched back toward us he just said that it was time to go to another bar and plunged everyone back into the wash of limbs, back through a door, slow up some stairs, onto a trellised balcony. At this bar a block down Bourbon, waitresses wore pins: "Ask me about my tooters: $3." From the balcony we watched cops on horses clop between the masses. One of us dropped a ring of beads; a middle-aged woman picked them off the ground without looking up, placed them around her neck, and walked on. Someone had just washed the stones in front of the bar; they glistened blue. Elbows on the wrought iron, Erik stared at the top of a lighted sign, where a dirty white bra lay abandoned in the long limbo between porch and street. It was 2:00 AM, 3:00 AM, no one knew anymore. Grant was approaching a shot in a test tube lodged between the breasts of a waitress. A tooter, $3. Biggie was still inside, leaning close to another waitress with a larger goal in mind. "Look," he was saying, "I'm leaving tomorrow. I'll probably never see you again. One night. What do you say?"

She had orders to take, and was gone.

A four-foot black porky waitress in black lingerie, all breasts and thighs and no waist, grabbed Erik by the collar and shoved him into a chair she had placed in the middle of the bar. She jumped on him, pressing her bare round thighs into his bony legs, hooking her ankles behind the chair back and bopping up and down as if riding a bucking pony. She jumped off, went prone on the floor, thrusting up her round buttocks in a kind of erotic worship. The bar went quiet. Pettis, who had arranged this encounter, was positioned a few feet from the action and quite casually holding a flipcam. Erik sat up, looked around with a frozen smile. The waitress stood up and shook her buttocks inches from his face. Erik glanced at the camera. He raised his hand a few uncertain inches and began to spank not her ass, but the air just in front of her ass, as if he might simultaneously please Pettis by the apparent licentiousness of the spank and waft her, like a barely extant airborne particle, up over the balcony and down to the street below.

Sean – October 2011

LET US AGREE THAT IT IS A MISTAKE to attribute any human behavior to a single cause, and yet I cannot help but note that mere weeks after Sean found his name conspicuously absent from the birth certificate, his cheekbones disappeared back into the soft mound of his face, his waist receded into a blur of excess torso, he stopped the visits to Chicago, and the daily regimen lost its motivating power. He had agreed to fight in Des Moines at 185 but it was 205 pounds he carried the week prior to the encounter, and so he had twenty pounds to lose in a matter of days, which he managed though not without considerable sacrifice. He lost almost all of it in forty-eight hours, jogging in rubber, sweating in a sauna, soaking in a salt bath. His body was running on a drastically reduced amount of liquid, the heart pumping doubly hard to recirculate its diminished pool; the vessels narrowed to maintain, shall we say, the force that through the red fuse drives a fighter.

He still failed to make weight, arriving in Des Moines three pounds over, but his opponent elected not to quibble over a few pounds, and late that evening all seemed to be well. Feeling fine, Sean drank his weight in Gatorade.

I don't know how it is, but fighters so often seem to suffer most *not* when they are most deprived, but when, finally free to return to normal, their strained bodies are given exactly what is most needed. Six hours later, the lining of his stomach began to call attention to itself, and swirling waves of something deep in his torso began to swell. What foul mist ran up his pipes sought some purchase it could not yet find. He gagged and willed it outward until finally he vomited and felt for the moment cured; but then having found egress the sickness surged, and surged, and surged, and by dawn on the day of his fight he was vomiting so profusely the situation seemed, even to our relatively unflappable subject, somewhat alarming.

Sean asked the cornerman with which he'd come, a dapper Miletich-trained heavyweight named Sherman, for help. Neither was possessed of a map, or a smartphone, or a GPS, and so they simply drove around the Des Moines suburb in search of a hospital. When they finally found one, Sean hobbled in, vomiting on the sidewalk, only to be told that he had arrived at a nursing home. He got back in the car. They found a hospital, and a doctor willing to diagnose Sean.

I knew nothing of this until I arrived at the fight. "Well," said Sean when I finally saw him in the very same locker room he had left to lose to Grigsby, "my kidneys kind of failed this morning."

Here I registered a tingling in the tips of my fingers, a quickening of breath. For me it had ever been a source of wonderment

the way in Sean cracks and fissures and tears are simply swallowed backward into seamlessness. That in lieu of a locatable
break, the whole oily system might cease to run was not something I'd had occasion to consider.

"But you're still fighting tonight?" I.asked, worried, and
guilty—for when I was most needed, I had been back in Iowa
City, nursing a cold a hardier spacetaker might have ignored.

"Yeah, fine now."

Fine here take to mean only that none of his organs were at
that moment in abeyance. As Sean related this story I began to
note the sallowness in his cheeks, which I had at first thought
merely to be the result of weight loss; I began to note the yel-
lowness of his pallor, which I had thought merely the dressing
room fluorescence; and I saw the heaviness with which he lifted
his chest. This was something new to the world: Sean breathing
against a slow, creeping, unlocatable pain. He was nauseated. He
hadn't eaten in three days. Where the hospital techs had tried to
stick IVs in Sean's narrowed veins, his wrists were stippled with
pricks. Among the many bits of advice the doctor had offered—
do not attempt to lose ten percent of your body weight in two
days, for example—was the suggestion that Sean avoid fighting
that evening.

"It took forever for anyone to see me," Sean said of the hospital. He and I were sitting on the couch, across from a fighter getting his hand wrapped and Brandon, who was, as usual, pacing. "I
was like doubled over and the nurses were just walking by. They
made eye contact and kept doing what they were doing. Crazy."

"Here's what you gotta do," said Brandon. "Next time, you

walk in there, you say you have chest pains. Then they see you right away."

"Yeah," said Justin, the fighter getting his hand wrapped, "you have to grab your chest."

"That's some cauliflower ear," Justin said to Sean.

"Yeah," said Sean, touching his ear, "I haven't seen many like it." Sean stretched his legs, sighed. "Except in Japan. In Japan you see guys whose both ears are like this."

Sean curled into the couch crease, hands against his stomach, legs fetal, face pressed into the armrest. After a few slow minutes watching him furl up among nervous fighters, some nameless sensation welling under my lungs, I realized that I was afraid of what might happen to him in the cage. I thought to advise him against fighting at all, but thoughts of my project, not a month after New Orleans had come to nothing, stopped me. And so I plunged myself into the project of a priori spacetaking, trying to anticipate his needs. Perhaps he would awake hungry and think to eat an energy bar, I thought, not displeased with the idea of leaving the locker room for a few moments. I had no desire to learn more about proper emergency-room strategy.

Outside, past the curtain, the stage, the locker room bouncer, the place was packed. It was just a warehouse by day, parked next to a megachurch in a Des Moines suburb that seemed to have no real streets, only wide highways with car dealerships popping up from the flatland, and the kind of uninterrupted sky that makes the streetlights seem too close to the ground. I slipped past some guards, some drunk spectators, and outside into a warm October evening. Across the parking lot, on the church sign—Christian

Life Worship Center—no worship times, only a smiley face oriented changelessly toward the stream of passing cars. The trees in view were saplings, shepherded into being, staked against the wind and ringed with haloes of mulch. A half-lit convenience store cast a red glow on its corner of the parking lot.

Back in the arena, on my way to Sean with a pocketful of energy bars, I ran into Brandon and his majestic girlfriend. Sammy was a zaftig self-assured college student and part-time stripper, a gorgeous virago who commanded so much attention that I found myself doubly invisible beside her. She and Brandon had taken some front row seats I can't imagine they had paid for. "I'm realizing that there is a lot Sean doesn't know," Brandon said to Sammy. "A lot he doesn't know. Eating healthy isn't the same as eating like a professional fighter. Like, for instance, you'd think fruit would be good for you. But it's full of sugar and it holds water like a motherfucker." It wasn't clear whether Sammy was listening; Brandon turned from her to the fight. "Kidney shutting down," Brandon said, letting the wind whistle through the gap in his teeth. "Man."

When Brandon and I returned to Sean, he looked skeptically at the assortment of bars, then chose one, tore it open, and nibbled, which is not, you will notice, a verb I have heretofore associated with Sean. Justin returned to the room stoop-shouldered and ushered in the kind of silence to which our room was accustomed. Sean's fight was minutes away. Brandon and Sherman and I were standing now, hovering, Sherman and I in our worried silent way, Brandon in his manic-but-helpful manner.

"You have a bucket, Sean?" Brandon asks.

"No."

"OK, that's OK, you have a towel?"

"No."

Sean pushed himself off the couch and walked around slowly. He handed me the bar, half-uneaten, and shook his head.

"No bucket, no towel, you a warrior, Sean! That's OK, that's OK, I tell you what—you get real wet and I'll just take my shirt off and give you that, OK? What are you walking out to?"

"Um," said Sean, "I think Metallica."

"Way to be original, Sean, way to be original."

Sean pulled on a shirt with a pink fist and a big pink ribbon picture on the front. "We won't stop 'till breast cancer gets slept" the shirt said.

"Breast cancer research is your sponsor?" I asked.

Sean looked down at the shirt. "I don't know, somebody said he'd pay me fifty dollars to wear it."

Sean pushed away from us, strolled in and out of the room, his eyes far away, bobbing his head as if listening to music the rest of us could not hear. He was frowning, the lines on his forehead as deep as I'd ever seen them. He lifted the lid of a dumpsterlike container placed in the hallway right outside the locker room, peered inside, replaced it, walked in the room, walked out of the room. He wasn't breathing so much as sighing repeatedly. He waited for the first bars of "Enter Sandman" to pop on and walked out, little Brandon scurrying with long-legged Sherman strolling in his wake.

Teddy Worthington has the same red glow as Sean, that Scots-Irish tinge that so readily yields to bruise-blue. His eyes are small below a large forehead—that, at least, is fighterly about him—but his neck is so long, and the red scruff about his chin so sparse as to seem unwillingly sprouted, like the awkward first mustache hairs of a boy hoping too hard for adolescence, that he cannot wear comfortably an air of intimidation.

At the bell Ted rushes pale, tired Sean, unleashes all his lanky limbs upon Sean's huddled form. He lands a hard kick to Sean's torso not far from where I suspect a failed kidney is trying to recover, and rains down so many punches Sean shields his face like a child. He catches Sean on the chin, and Sean doesn't roll, just absorbs; he lands a body shot where the kick hits, under the ribs. Sean rides out this red whirlwind, hands up, legs planted.

That is when I notice something in my peripheral vision—a brunette right outside the cage, standing over a seated blonde and pointing, screaming, poised in runner's stance such that the deep gravelly rush of words bellows from her torso and out of her mouth in a stick-straight line of invective. Her voice rises incredibly above the din of the stadium, to the astonishment of everyone on that side of the cage. It is Sammy, defending her right to the seat I suspect she stole, and when I look back at the cage Sean has tripped Ted and is mounting him from the back, all Ted's limbs splayed out on the cage floor like a squashed spider, and Ted is trying to squirrel out but Sean keeps catching him and pressing him back into the cage floor. In the moment all eyes turned to Sammy, the octagon had arrived. Sammy knew this. She stopped and turned from her victim, looked to the cage, and screamed a command.

"YOU HAVE FUN, SEAN!"

On the opposite side of the fence Sean pops up from Ted's chest, shouts with a force equal to Sammy's one single monosyllabic sound. "WOO!"

Sean is facing Ted's back now and searching for a submission, looking to lace both his legs through Ted's and one arm round Ted's neck, but slithery squashed Ted never stops moving under Sean's weight, wriggles this way and that, slides his leg outside of Sean as soon as Sean catches one. Sean thinks this is funny. "Why don't you get up?" he whispers in Ted's ear, playing big brother to Ted's infantile immobility. "Come on, get up." Ted cannot get up. Ted turns, and Sean turns with him; Ted kicks out a leg, and Sean hooks it back in. To watch the ease with which he corrals Ted's body is to know that not a trace of his sickness has followed him into the cage, that his body has suspended its calls for help and rest and granted him this much respite from nausea-laced fatigue.

The round ends with Sean still flat against Ted, Sean's legs laced through Ted's in such a way as to render Ted totally immobile. At the start of round two Ted, finally erect, jabs Sean in the face a few times and flails until Sean throws him down and holds him, once again, against the floor. They're facing one another now, their necks touching, and I can see the top of Ted's torso where a wash of blood is smeared across his delicate collarbone. He huffs under Sean's weight, wriggles, breathes, wriggles. Sean needs merely to inch his body forward to undo all the work of Ted's effortful wriggling, which he does, and Ted closes his eyes in frustration as round two ends.

In the ring between rounds little Brandon and big Sherman hover over bucket-seated Sean, begging him, no doubt, to finish the thing before another organ fails. When the bell rings Sean allows Teddy to throw a few jabs, then lunges for Ted's legs and pins him to the floor. He's found yet another way to render Ted immobile; legs astraddle Ted's slim waist, Sean sits atop him as Ted tries to kick himself into a better position, which at this point would be any position at all. Ted is wide open and unable to move. Sean should be slamming him with punches, laying in, putting all his weight behind great heavy sledgehammer jabs. It is what the crowd, growing restless, very much wants. But Sean knows himself to be so much stronger than Teddy, and the fight has taken so definitively the shape of an adipose bully going after a bespectacled underdeveloped loner, Sean can't summon the will to do more than stay firmly mounted. Boos rise up from all sides of the cage. Later Sean will say he lacks the "killer instinct" required to put a downed man to sleep, though I suspect that he simply doesn't want to be outside the cage, where his focus, adrenaline-sharp, will melt back into that sad couch-bound malaise. Instead Sean lets Ted squirm out, traps him, lets him squirm out again. When the bell rings and Sherman and Brandon jump back into the ring to high-five Sean, who has undoubtedly just won.

"You just laid on him 'cause you're fat!" screams a lady cageside.

Sean looks at her. She's not small herself. "This lady just called *me* fat?" he says to Sherman.

He saunters over to Teddy. "Hey man good fight," he says, touching Ted's back.

"Get the fuck off of me!" says Ted, to which Sean cops a wide-eyed look of extreme surprise, then chuckles.

"Well," says the ref to the crowd, "that wasn't the most exciting fight."

The decision comes back and the ref reads: "The winner by unanimous decision, Sean Huffman!"

Sherman raises Sean's hand and the whole place boos, so Sean puts a hand on the ref's microphone.

"Hey," he says, "I won that fight fair and square."

The ref has his hand on the microphone, and he is tugging it gently back in his own direction.

"I'd like to dedicate this fight to my friend John," Sean says, "whose life was way too short."

The ref pulls back the mic; there are more fights, and no time, and he is out of the cage smiling and slapping hands and being manhandled by everyone in the crowded path from cage to locker room. He looks happy, even glowing, but now I fear a trick of adrenaline has us seeing a victorious form that will, like a hologram, appear from another angle only spent. I would rather have seen his face torn and bulbous, as it had been last time we left this arena—a slice to be stitched back together—than known of some dark curdled part calling out from deep beneath his ribs.

Sean watched the rest of the fights, and I watched him recede gently back to his former fatigue. He dipped lower and lower into the couch, growing imperceptibly smaller like a balloon left over from a child's birthday party, until finally Sherman said it was time to go to Sean's postfight celebration. Sammy had decided that we'd go to her favorite Des Moines bar. Sherman drove a beat-up sedan.

"Where are we going?" I asked as we turned onto the highway.

"Some gay bar," said Sherman.

Sean laughed. Then reconsidered. "No but seriously, I love gay people."

"Gay people are really fun," said Sherman.

"Gay bars are so clean," said Sean.

Sherman walked ahead of us in the bar parking lot, where Brandon and Sammy waited. I had not met many heavyweights, and it was hard not to leer at Sherman's physique, his huge sharp cheekbones, his thick hands, endless ivory nailbeds. He stood a full foot taller than Brandon.

"Sherman is huge," I said to Sean.

"Sherman?" he said slowly, coming back to me. "Are you kidding? He's lost a ton of weight."

"Why?" I asked.

Sean shook his head.

"Why?" I asked again, persistence being integral to good scholarship.

"Rectal cancer," said Sean.

The bar was called Kung Fu Tap and Taco, and though it was in a wealthier section of West Des Moines, the clientele seemed to be primarily grizzled gray-bearded bikers. Sean sat quietly, not listening to Sammy recount her altercation with the woman whose seat she stole, and stared past all of us. He sipped a Coke, then shuddered and sighed as a wave of something foul passed through his body. A diffuse pain burned in his lower back and he could not forget himself as Sammy was forgetting herself, now sweeping her long brown hair back to better imitate the blonde's irate boyfriend. This party was not for Sean at all; it was another thing he had to endure.

No one in that bar was as conscious of his body as Sean was: the juices of his stomach rebelling, his kidneys blaring a long loud ache that made him lean back in his chair and stare at the ceiling. The rest of us could drink and forget, having drawn our high from Sean without the tiniest of disturbances to the wet skin along the soft of our eyes.

"I'm thirty-three," Sean said, picking the label off his Coke bottle and I wondered but did not ask how many fights he'd had now—sixty? a hundred? Instead I said, "Randy Couture still fought at thirty-three. He fought at forty." This was the standard call and response, the Couture-did-it palaver every spacetaker feeds every post-thirty doubt-ridden fighter, and it was so uninspired a thing to say Sean just raised his eyebrows and turned away.

"I've still never been knocked out," Sean said to the wall.

"What do you think it would take?" I asked.

"Maybe the first time I get knocked out, I just die," Sean said, and laughed. And even as I watched Sean suffering in his breast-cancer T-shirt, sipping on his Coke, I was worrying about when the next fight would be, when he'd heal up, how long I'd have to wait before he abandoned himself once again.

Sean – Fall/Winter 2011

"Do you watch all the debates?" Sean asked me at The Paddlewheel as I shifted in my seat. From a high-perched television a heavily made-up woman I did not care to watch spoke of ephemeral political maneuverings I did not care to fathom. "I can't believe it. It's like watching *Jersey Shore*. Like a bunch of babies arguing over something that happened in high school."

I nodded.

"I mean those people are gonna be sitting in the office that decides a lotta shit."

"What was that?" I asked, and he repeated the sentiment with the kind of gentle patience a person such as myself never could have summoned, for it wasn't the first instance in which I had required redundancy, nor even the second. All the while Sean was talking that night I was sliding a finger over the surface of my phone, hoping for some word from Erik, so that I sometimes lost the thread of Sean's thoughtful diatribe. Though I cannot attribute my neglect fully to distraction; in fact I was having some trouble hearing in the weeks after Sean's Des Moines fight. Sometimes when he and his friends would talk their words would melt into the din of the crowd and I would sit back in my stiff-backed chair, alone. It was as if I were being sealed in.

"Want to smoke?" Sean asked, and we walked the cold block to his apartment, through the unmarked door at the back of the gym, up the narrow stairwell. When we were fully lit, seated across a dining room table with Dopo at my feet, Sean threw his head back and stared at the ceiling. His palms lay flat on the table, as if to steady it. "I've missed a Father's Day, Halloween," said Sean in a kind of whine, "and now Christmas. She stole that from me."

I slid to unlock, tapped the picture of the envelope, swiped down the length of the screen to refresh. Having not received a message forty-five seconds ago, I did not expect to receive one then, but something about the very motion, the cold imposition of glass against the warm pad of the finger, kept me from having to stand and pace.

"What do you think of Ron Paul?" Sean asked.

Most of what I knew about Ron Paul I had learned from Keoni, who had recently become such an enthusiast that he papered the gym with pro-Paul signs and dropped the words "gold standard" into casual conversation with fellow fighters. Perhaps, I thought for the eighth or ninth time that December afternoon, I should ask Keoni why Erik had stopped responding to my phone calls and text messages and emails and notes through various social networks, but I came to the same conclusion I had in my previous phone-bound reveries: To ask Keoni about Erik was like asking a priest about joining the parish next door, an oblique challenge to the quality of one's product, a notice that one was shopping for something more sating. It would not be well received, and even if it were Keoni would say that he'd be the last person to know about his deranged brother's whereabouts, a position he would state with a kind of pride, as if knowing would be weakness. It was Keoni's belief that Erik would rend any relationship at any moment at will for no particular reason, as he had ended relationships with Jared and Rocky and himself, and the person who did not expect this to happen deserved all the condescension with which Keoni treated memories of his younger, naive, Erik-soft self.

"I don't know," I said. "Why?"

"Just been thinking about him."

"You've been thinking about Ron Paul?" I said.

Sean shrugged.

"Seems like a good guy."

I would rather have talked politics, certainly, than progeny. In the winter of 2012 Alexis had moved from Omaha to Moline, a city inferior but adjacent to the fighterly city of Davenport, where she had a stepfather evidently willing to provide shelter and monetary support. Sean knew nothing of the move until she called, prevailing upon him to help her move a couch her stepfather said he could not possibly lift without another man's assistance.

Sean left his apartment immediately; he left the door unlocked and rode his bike along busy streets the few miles to her house. It was November, and filthy, stubborn patches of snow lined an icy sidewalk not particularly friendly to bikers. He weaved in and out of the streets, where sidewalks and traffic permitted, and arrived finally at an undistinguished rectangular white box of a house in a neighborhood of such houses. He ditched the bike in the yard and jumped onto the porch, rang the bell. When she didn't answer he walked over to a window, peered in, and knocked on the siding.

Alexis finally came to the door, Josiah on her hip. She met his eyes and backed up, wordless, to let him in. Josiah shifted ever so slightly toward him and away from his mother, a few inches of encouraging movement in which Sean would later take great solace.

Alexis led Sean through the small house, over some garbage bags and between piles of dented cardboard boxes. "We could live here together," Sean thought, though he had come to despise Alexis, and this was not, in the end, her house.

"I'm going out," she said, placing Josiah on her bed. She was fully made up, her eyes lined black and her black hair blown unnaturally straight, as if in reference to the linear and insincere life she wanted to impose on Sean. "Can you watch him and build his crib?"

Sean nearly cried then, so strong was the force of his gratitude. And he intended to build the crib, right after he played with Josiah, felt the boy's tiny hands squeeze his once-broken finger, asked him all sorts of questions—"Who's your favorite fighter?"—and answered for him—"Daddy? OK good choice." Sean lay with his back on the floor and the baby on his stomach. He placed his thick hands around Josiah's tiny body and lifted him straight into the air, blew air from his mouth in a manner intended to mimic an airplane, and lowered him back down. Sean's was a broad, warm chest, and Josiah seemed happy to lie there rising and falling with Sean's breath. The baby fell asleep, and from that moment Sean was as good as paralyzed. He remained completely motionless for two full hours, pinned by his progeny to the floor.

With the sound of gravel crunching, a car door slam, Sean considered running. But still he did not move. "You didn't build the crib?" she asked, setting down some plastic bags, tripping over a box and steadying herself against a wall. She snatched Josiah from Sean's chest. "Get the fuck out of here," she said.

"You kidnapped him," said Sean from the ground. "I should take him home."

Alexis pulled her phone out of her pocket, dialed 9-1-1, and held the screen up in Sean's direction. Sean stood up, walked slowly to the door—backward, so he could still see Josiah as he walked—and left. It had grown colder and darker, and he fell off his bike twice on the ride back to his apartment.

"I saw the lawyer," Sean told me shortly after the episode. I was prepared for this, but it remained a disturbing image—Sean, gnarled-eared, smash-nosed, in the presence of a skirt-suited middle-aged lawyer, as if an altar boy had wormed his way into a brothel, having been wrongly informed that therein lay true salvation.

We needn't dwell on this grotesque descent step by ungodly step. A man with expenses has need of a job. A man with a job has need of an ordered existence—a pleather-bound planner, tax preparation, automatic bill-pay, if it came to that. I could see it all coming, the slide into the world of human arrangement. It wasn't a week later that Sean told me he had found a position at Pizza

Ranch, a well-known establishment that pushed a bread-and-cheese product on Iowa's populace. Sean, the man I had watched give himself over to chaos and be repeatedly penetrated by another man's fist, would prepare, every morning, forty trays of chicken. He would chop vegetables. He would pour mayonnaise into neat rows of porcelain cups. There was a schedule on the wall with his name on it, as if Sean were just another laborer, no different from other people who toil from nine to five because they're no better at confronting the terrible immensity of the world than is anyone else.

The lawyer's job was to force Alexis into a DNA test, such that Sean might be determined Josiah's father and thereby extract some right to see him rather than pursue his correct vocation, which was giving himself over to the universe in the course of a violent contest. It took, in the way of lawyerly contrivances, many months.

"Need $50 fr food," Alexis texted one afternoon.

"Let me see him," Sean said.

Alexis indicated a park at which they would conduct the transaction. Sean arrived early, as was not at all characteristic of him, and waited on a swing, its chains thick and rusted, under the shadow of a water tower. Sean, having never been able to play with his son in such a context, planned to sit his son on that swing and push him very gently, back and forth. Across the street, patches of snow dotted the otherwise tidy lawns of semiprosperous Iowans.

When Alexis pulled into the parking lot Sean ran up to her minivan. Through the back window he could see Josiah strapped into a plastic baby contraption itself strapped to the minivan seat. Alexis rolled down the window.

"Where is the money?" she asked.

Sean ignored her. He pressed his face into the window and took in the image of his strapped-in son. Josiah stared back.

"Here's twenty-five dollars now," he said, handing her some crushed bills from the pocket of his jeans, "I'll give you twenty-five when we're done playing."

Alexis took the twenty-five dollars, rolled up the window, and drove away. Sean ran after the van a bit, then sat down on the pavement, thinking perhaps that she would come back. After fifteen minutes passed, he left.

"There's something wrong with her," Sean told me afterward, "something not right."

I hated this story in a nonsensical way that somehow made me feel implicated, as if Alexis and I were on the same side, in league, both of us using Sean for what we wanted and then watching him crumble from the rearview mirror. But of course my wishes were aligned with his interest in living a worthwhile existence, while Alexis merely sought to extract small amounts of cash.

From the table I stared fixedly at the blue mat that took up half of Sean and Brandon's apartment, which was clean and uncluttered in contrast with the rest of the place. It looked unused in a way that worried me.

"When are you leaving for Christmas?" I asked.

"I can't go home. I need the gas money to pay the lawyer," he said.

With that I turned again to my phone. I had dispatched six, seven text messages to Erik that day. I sent another one: "I will purchase airplane tickets to Vegas presently."

Not two months hence he was to face a Louisianan named Poirier at Mandalay Bay, and obviously we were to face this challenge together, fighter and spacetaker. Yet I had heard nothing of travel arrangements, as if my presence were not crucial to the coming contest.

Now it is not unheard of for a fighter to drop a spacetaker just as brutally as Nietzsche turned on Schopenhauer; indeed some may say that it is his right, but I consider the arrangement more democratic than tyrannical, soluble only under mutual agreement. Certainly we had had no quarrel that I could recall, no reason that I ought to be traded in for another—someone who would be attracted to Erik's new celebrity, but would know nothing of his past. Had I not, a year and a half back, perched myself on a wooden bench in a ramshackle gym and been therein baptized in the sweat of a dozen men? Had I not taken space beside a violent bum in Manhattan, a closed buffet in Las Vegas, a fat shimmying stripper in New Orleans? Indeed, given that he had never lost a fight at which I was present, I thought I could make a strong case for being a kind of luck-bestowing phylactery, an animate amulet without which Erik would be vulnerable to injury. For even if you are not given to superstition, your subconscious may be, and who was to say that Erik would not, at the last moment, look with panic upon the empty cageside seat where I would properly be? "You are making a mistake!" I wished to wail into my phone, but to display such raw need would surely put me among those who, like Jared and Rocky, had been summarily abandoned. Erik did not like to feel thusly obligated to people who had provided prior services; his history with Keoni told us this much.

Fifteen minutes later it became clear that there would be no answer to this query, either, and I found that I wished to be alone. I gathered my scarf and jacket and, grabbing both sides of his enormous head, bid Dopo a merry Christmas.

"Why would he simply cease all communication?" I asked Sean as I left, knowing this to be an act of dereliction, the speaking of one fighter while spacetaking for another.

"Because he's an asshole," said Sean, inverting a green plastic lighter into yet another packed bowl. "Maybe he's injured. Maybe he has an STD."

I sat in my freezing car for a few moments. I was, truth be told, a little afraid to drive. Having left Sean's house this intoxicated once before, I had experienced a rather unpleasant sensation on the long drive home; gliding along the highway, I began to meditate on how easy it would be to drift unknowing off the side, and so drove all the way back to my domicile clutching the wheel that I might not, in a moment of inattention, slip clean off the road. I thought it better, this time, to sit in my car and wait for sobriety.

Cold air blew from the vents. I slid to unlock, tapped the picture of the envelope.

All I saw for a moment, were symbols on glass.

GOOGLE ALERT — erik koch

For some reason I thought that I ought to go back upstairs, find Sean, but before I could fully consider this course of action I lowered my hovering finger.

"Fast-rising featherweight Erik Koch suffered an undisclosed injury during training camp that has forced him out of a highly anticipated bout with fellow contender Dustin Poirier, UFC announced Tuesday."

Why does it seem that my fears are forever ill-directed, that what pessimism lies in my nature leads to no true prophecy? How is it that I am always prepared for the very misfortunes I am spared? Know that the reaching tendrils of the analytical mind, even as they wrap themselves round a million problematical abstractions, leave a universe of calamity untouched. The world has infinite ways to wrong us. I feared that I would lose Sean to age, and now, incredibly, risked losing him to the animal mundanity of procreation. I lay awake December nights preparing for the delicate navigation of Erik's emotional state, some finical politicking through the prickly kingdom that was Erik's ego. All day in Sean's apartment I had prepared judicious and rational arguments I hoped would win my way back into Erik's favor. But this—this was a natural disaster immune to maneuvering. Do not ask me, then, what catastrophe will reduce this sorry Earth to dust. I will be the one staring at the skies speaking of asteroidal collision as below my feet the world splits open to swallow us whole.

Erik – February 2012

THE WINTER OF 2012 WAS NOT KIND to the spacetakers of notable fighters, who were forced to watch, with uncommon frequency, their charges fall to the new fragility of once-unbreakable forms. One heavyweight dislocated his thumb and another halved his humerus and a third was sliced into by surgeons who wished to stop two bits of backbone from pressing into his spine. Jon Jones overstretched an elbow and Shogun dislocated his clavicle such that an odd knob would forever protrude from the spot where neck met shoulder. Into each of the spaces absented by these fighters a healthy man stepped, as Ricardo Lamas stepped into the spot vacated by injured Erik. The title of the event for which Erik was to fight was "St. Pierre vs. Diaz" until some tissue in St. Pierre's knee was inconveniently rent a month previous to the show, and three separate welterweights also scheduled to fight were torn or snapped or crushed in some way none of them chose to specify. Two weeks before the fight Ricardo Lamas was suddenly downed by an injury of secret provenance, and so Erik's replacement required replacing.

The growing uncertainty of my position became every day more evident, but I found considerable comfort rehearsing, in my head-space, the details of a plan to find Erik. I did not know his latest address, but I had conducted some research into the activities of his spacetakers, and discovered that Biggie would be fighting in a Harley-Davidson store transformed, for the occasion, into a fight venue. Where his teammate was fighting etiquette demanded that Erik be, and so I would wend my way through the Harleys and present myself to my fighter. He must have been embarrassed about a long-standing injury, I reasoned, and thus avoiding me out of shame; he would be only happy to see how willingly, how selflessly, I resumed my spacetakerly capacities beside an injured man. I waited in Iowa through January—for in January I had no leads as to Erik's whereabouts, despite thorough monitoring of any social media on which such clues might appear—and in February, on the night of Biggie's fight, drove north toward Wisconsin.

I have spoken before of my disapproval of those who return to the places of their birth, the home-visit's tendency to entrap us in the false contingencies of our making, and it is not my intention to restate these sentiments anew. I was oppressed by memory the moment I crossed into Wisconsin and provoked by each age-stained waterslide that extended over the highway. (Though Wisconsinites are thought by the world to worship cheese products, it is in fact cranberries and waterparks they find inexplicably captivating.) My place of birth is Baraboo, Wisconsin, and though I would not under any circumstance traverse the Baraboo boundary, I decided that I would, given my state of agitation, indulge myself in the one pleasure that the state affords. South of my origin-place upon a seventy-foot-column of rock sits a mansion, built by an eccentric long dead, whose compulsive need to collect led him to fill the place with monstrosities of every kind—a roomful of carousels, an orchestra of self-playing string instruments, a hallway stacked with calliopes, any number of guns encased in glass, and—my favorite—a dimly lit room floor-to-ceiling with hundreds—or more probably thousands—of discarded porcelain dolls, some in bassinets, others tilted against grandfather clocks, most sitting at attention as if it were perpetually time for tea. The room felt animate with something not human, some sense not aural or optical but infused in the empty gaze of ten dozen glass eyes.

I came often as a child and in that room felt very slightly transported to a place that was not Baraboo. Perhaps it was only the eccentric's madness that attracted me. He had not been adequately tutored in wellness, it appeared. And if circumstance made it such that I had to return to Wisconsin, I would at least allow myself a moment's pleasure alone with the dolls' quiet gaze. I could conceive of this attraction more clearly now, after so many months in the company of ecstasy-seeking men. In my best mid-fight moments I too had been reduced to this, a pair of eyes, a body diminished into the pure act of perceiving.

The house is fronted by some winged cast-iron creatures, whimsically reptilian, who climb about flower pots that in February hold but blackened stalks of long-dead vegetation. I pulled past the pots at midmorning. The grounds were dusted with snow, the trees surrounding the house spindly-bare to the last twig, such that the house's Pagodan aspect—the owner had been inspired by a trip to the East—was unusually evident. I tugged at the great furry hood of my parka and worked against the wind, up the ramp of a long wrap-around deck, to the gift shop, where I intended to purchase a ticket from a woman with wire-rimmed glasses who, operating under the humorous misconception that my interest in the dolls was born of girlish enthusiasm for feminine playthings, sold me such tickets in my youth. I arrived at the door, wrapping my gloved fingers around the handle, breathing though a scarf wrapped around my mouth. It was all the same—the House on the Rock keychains in the revolving case, the thimbles and commemorative spoons in orderly display.

"Hello," an elderly woman said. I lifted my hand to remove my hood, but stopped short as I watched her replace the tape in the cash register. Her hands were blue-veined, raisin-skinned, the knuckles too large and the fingers sickly thin. The skin on her cheeks hung low, and a capillary had broken loose under one eye. Where the skin had thinned to crepe it was also stained dark with subcutaneous blood. Were it not for the glasses, and the way she squinted over them to fool with the mechanical register contraption, I would have not realized her to be the woman I knew, grown monstrously old. It had been but seven years. She fished through the register with her hideous twiglike fingers; and then, when I did not respond, only standing there with my hand on my still-secure hood, she looked straight at me. I did not look at her but at the ruined skin under her eye. "Can I help you?"

Without a word I walked back across the snow-dusted deck, across the parking lot, where shakingly with benumbed gloved fingers I fished the key from my pocket. I blasted the heat, turned up the radio, but did not move. My thoughts turned to Shogun, now suffering from a dislocated clavicle, and the moment Erik and I watched him fall during that fight in New Jersey: Shogun's telephone-pole legs buckling twice under him as he took punches to the face, leaning into the fence like a sobbing drunk as he absorbs the blows, until he takes that final strike, crumples altogether. I thought of Erik in the days of Hard Drive, the wet morning I watched him fling weights straight across a damp field, the way Erik shrugged and smiled and sprung after the perfect throw to retrieve the weight, throw again. For the first time this memory felt like a crisis averted. He might have dislocated his shoulder. He might have trotted right into a depression in the sopping soil, twisted his ankle.

Still in the car, leaning into the heat, I wanted to go home, to Iowa. To Sean—Sean, whose torn meniscus and snapped phalanges all hardened back into the same miraculous substance, like iron melted and cooled to a slightly different shape. And then, of course, I remembered the yellow pallor of a man with two kidneys in open revolt, and I remembered, too, Josiah.

I cannot account for this hysteric episode and know not why I include it; only I feel that it has something to do with my folly. A fully formed person ought not to relive formative experience. One has nothing to say to it. How could I respond but with a shocked silence? I stared at the melting ice, even the stone reptiles red-flecked with age, and as grief overcame fear

I resolved to go to the Harley dealership, much as a man bereft of hope finds it most easy to face a firing squad. Perhaps Erik would not be there, but I was increasingly unsure that I had anything to go back to, in any case.

The venue was so packed that I had to park at an adjacent McDonald's and walk against the wind, breathing through my scarf. Inside the Harley dealership there were no Harleys. There was a regulation octagon surrounded by metal folding chairs, many of them straining under the weight of their Wisconsinite cranberry-stuffed occupants. The place was full, with a line out the door I avoided by simply cutting through and pretending not to hear when a line-waiter shouted at me. I sat in my cageside seat, which I was forced to purchase at no small expense, as if I were but a spectator again—and perused the crowd in a systematic clockwise manner. Erik would be a minor celebrity here, and I assumed that if I found him it would be in the center of an admiring pack of young fighters. I did see Duke, sporting a fisherman's cap that made him look like a 220-pound middle-aged newsboy and hauling a red bucket of items to the cage behind a fighter I did not recognize. And I saw Sean's cancer-stricken friend Sherman, in Milwaukee to corner a Miletich fighter, standing against a wall looking dapper in a turtleneck. On the brick above where Sherman stood someone had painted a picture of the twin towers next to the ship bombed during Pearl Harbor; both were under the words "Never Forget."

I saw no sign of Erik, and I tried not to consider how little space we together filled, how much larger the world beyond it, how many other places Erik might be—a hospital, perhaps, or an asylum for those driven mad by homesickness, or, for that matter, home. But I felt better the moment I saw Biggie standing before the cage, the crowds milling about in a break between the fights. He had lost perhaps forty pounds since New Orleans; young muscles made themselves known down the side of his abdomen, and the fluorescent lights reflected off his high cheekbones in a way that set his whole face aglow. Tall and ripped and jolly, he looked as if he might crush any of us, and do so with a smile.

There was a break between the fights, and the promoter jumped into the center of the cage.

"You guys having fun?" he asked. "Because I've got a surprise for you." A couple in square glasses one might associate with a certain modern *soi-disant* "creative" bourgeois subset of any city—were they lost?—shuffled out of my line of sight. And right beside Biggie, next to the cage, my gaze settled on a man, shadowboxing as he spoke, who moved with a grace given to only a few men on this earth.

I hopped right over a packed row of metal chairs, slid through a canoodling couple, shunted aside a child, and planted myself in between Erik and Biggie. In the cage ten feet away the promoter was talking about whatever that surprise was—some special guest, a VIP—but I was focused on the man I had come to see. Erik looked at me. My heart pounded; I felt the cage at my back. He scrunched his eyebrows into a look of exaggerated confusion. And—how my heart sings to recount it!—he broke wide into a bright smile.

"And here he is, WEC veteran, future champion, UFC featherweight Erik Koch!" said the promoter. But I heard nothing;

knew not that I had dashed into the middle of a spectacle in progress.

"Erik!" I cried, and—grown emotionally disinhibited, perhaps, by my recent encounter with the aged gatekeeper—I hugged him. I had eyes for only my charge, and a mind filled with our future together.

Everyone was backing away; the promoter was staring at us. We were surrounded by fans—seated, standing, in the balconies—and every one of them turned to stare at Erik and the spacetaker wrapped round him. Only after I saw their heads turned toward us did I feel that stare penetrate me from all directions, and realize that I had intercepted his ceremonious walk to the cage. Erik gently unwrapped my hands from his torso and walked around me. Duke was staring at us, uncomprehending, Biggie had a scowl upon his face, and I felt a hot blush come upon my cheeks. Erik walked through the gate and hopped lightly into the octagon.

"Tell us about your plans," said the promoter, "and tell us about your injury."

Erik clutched the mic and lifted it high, pacing the octagon with practiced swagger.

"You know I've had some setbacks, had to take some time off, happens to everybody. But I'm here to say that I'm one-hundred percent healthy!" said Erik. "I'm trying to get the winner of Hioki versus Palaszewski. You guys wanna see that?"

They did want to see that.

My moment of embarrassment had already transformed into a glow of pride. The entire room saw that I was his, and he mine.

"You scared the hell out of me!" Erik said as he descended from the octagon. And he led me to the locker room chattering, a fighter with a little less space to be taken.

•

Thus began a happy reunion, and my joyful introduction to Erik's Milwaukee milieu. Erik, having won over $100,000 in New Orleans, was unburdened of the borrowing he had so struggled under when we first met. And yet his new residence was a single-story brick structure next to many other identical structures that gave the distinct impression of public housing. He no longer lived with Pettis, who had since fathered a child, but with the considerably less intense Biggie. The morning after the fight I let myself in through a thin door that closed behind me with a hollow thunk I found singularly unconvincing. I closed it twice to see if it wouldn't make a more satisfying sound.

As I fiddled with the door Erik jumped up to greet me, and though at no point since our reunion had he mentioned his absence, the ignored texts and voicemails and email, he animatedly reenacted the circumstances of his concussion. There in his kitchenette beside an empty fridge and a rack full of various supplemental powders, he dodged and weaved as Duke had when demonstrating the proper approach to Pettis. "And wham!"—he staggered backward—"I moved into it! I felt fine, went back to the hotel room, didn't think much of it, but I kept spacing out. And the lights in Times Square! I felt like I was swaying the whole time!"

Strange this, the retroactive attribution of internal states onto memories I thought fully formed. I remember that inverted bowl of light, the words *Mamma Mia!* sliding across the horizon, the cabs. I remember Erik, alone with us, walking a few feet before the group, and a few feet behind, and watching a homeless man argue with someone over a bar tab. What I had interpreted as a kind of thoughtful prefight quiet was a man terrified by the sticky slow way his thoughts seemed to move.

"I didn't feel right after the fights," he told me in Milwaukee, "not after the Assunção fight, not after the Brookins fight. I knew I had a concussion. I knew it. But I couldn't admit it to myself, you know, I didn't want to cancel the fights, I didn't want to be an injured fighter."

Back in December, Erik found himself trapped in an accelerating thought-spiral: anxieties piling upon anxieties, the symptomatic paranoia of a concussed brain circling around the legitimately terrifying potential of a concussion. He pictured Duke's disappointment, the smug satisfaction of Rocky and Jared, his father's heartbreak. He drove places and arrived with no recollection of having gotten into the car. He refused to go out, and so had more and more time to be alone with the memory of Pettis telling him he might "not wake up." Instead of going to practice one day he went, by himself, to a local clinic. And the doctor confirmed what Erik already knew to be true, which rendered the Poirier fight an impossibility. The doctor prescribed six weeks away from the gym.

"It's the worst. The worst," he said. "I couldn't do anything. I haven't not trained since I was sixteen years old. I wanted to hit something so bad. I couldn't do anything, I just watched TV. You know what I watched? I watched *The Walking Dead*. Have you seen that show? With the zombies? Someone told me about it and I was like no I don't think so—zombies?—but now it's all I watch. Oh, and *Breaking Bad* too."

"Anyway," said Erik, moving in for a shadow jab, "my six weeks are over." He jumped side to side in the space afforded by his hallway. "And I feel fucking phenomenal!"

Erik needed only wait for the UFC to assign him a fight. I lazed a bit on his dirty futon, watched him play himself on the video game. I asked him to show me the city, his city, all the places he had lived, the old gym, the new gym. We got in his new car, already garbage strewn, and together drove to the apartment he had shared with Pettis. "Such a good song," Erik said to most songs that came on the radio, bopping his head, dancing as he drove. I attempted to sing along, though I rarely knew the words.

"There was a stabbing here," Erik said. And then, "I'm gonna make a stop at the tanning place. It'll only take a sec."

"You use this one, right?" the woman at the desk said, handing him some lotion. He came in and out as if he owned the place. There was an article about him pinned to a piece of corkboard.

He showed me Duke's gym—"Nice, right?"—its endless mats, flat-screen TVs, clean rows of standing bags. Nothing was frayed, everything newly painted. There was a juice bar at the front of the gym, a wall-length mirror at the back. There were neat cubbyholes in which to place shoes, comfortable stuffed chairs from which parents watched their kids practice, five well-caged sections in which simultaneous practices might take place. There was a coherent color scheme, and a women's locker room, and a check-in desk. There were free pens bearing the name of the gym.

I picked up a pen, rubbed my finger along the circular Roufusport logo, which involved a stylized R and a sketch of some Grecian laurels. More than two years ago I had walked into a gym called Valhalla, and the heat had hit me so hard I felt a moment's panic. I'd watched six pairs of men writhe in silence on the floor, deep in the thought that it takes to piece seven, eight positions together until the other body opens itself for attack. Above me bits of ceiling had flapped down; the window fogged. It felt like a cult. It felt like something you had to break your brother's shoulder to leave. And so while I watched Erik's teammates arrive, suit up—"You're coming to my fight, right, Erik?" asked Sergio Pettis, Anthony's little brother—I marveled at Erik's ability to slough off that life. I returned the pen to the front desk, beside some waivers for new customers. Roufusport was a place one could, with little regret and no hard feelings, abandon.

The rest of the team arrived and plastered themselves in padding. In gloves and leg pads and arm pads and a mouthguard and headgear Erik reminded me of a plaything, some plastic figurine stuck in its stiff place until a child changed the posture. All the grace was gone; there was only blunt force, strikes that could not penetrate. Into this strange mix of trammeled men Duke, a head taller than everyone else, entered with no pads at all, and turned it all into a game. As they went at one another in pairs Duke taunted them, shoving one, crowding another, sneaking up on someone and lightly bopping his head. If someone swept at Duke he would double over as if very hurt, then laugh. He took

Erik from Pettis, pushed Erik's face, caught Erik's leg, laughed. I cringed, fearful that Erik would fall backward, twist a knee, or perhaps catch himself in the wrong way, break a ring finger. Because this was practice, and Erik could not hit with full force, he made full-force sounds. "Bop-bop," he said as he tapped Duke. "Ah-ah-ah," was Duke's punch-sound, so when they went at one another it was a curiously musical "Bop-ah Bop-ah." "Knee knee knee!" Duke said, then absorbed the knees. "Now, high again."

Duke backed off and watched the rest spar. "Doin' some work tonight, doin' some work tonight. Oh! You guys are dirty over there. Gotta little Puerto-Rican-on-Mexican violence today. Don't worry, you'll get Koch back, we're equal opportunity abusers. Just try everything. You don't practice it you don't perform it." He had an endless string of phrases he'd picked up somewhere, thoughtless words that dripped from his mouth all through that two-hour practice. Nothing seemed meant to stick. I was in a world of Erik's creation.

That afternoon I left feeling that the world had been restored, though knowing also that it was unalterably cracked, for concussions are not reabsorbed unaccountably; they compound in ugly layers of wound. Erik and I resumed our normal correspondence. "Grinding nonstop," he replied in response to nearly every inquiry I made of him. I knew him to be every day growing stronger in this, his twenty-third year. I lay in bed at night picturing Erik thrown back into the swell, all his perfect plenitude, the pressure of that virile abundance, the way it would overbrim its boundaries at some unknown date and time. I could only wait, the energy all gathered and dammed up in my limbs, for the moment of release I now knew to be coming.

A month after my visit, the promoters of the Big Shows decided that it was time for José Aldo to defend his belt once again; he would do so in Calgary, Canada—Canada being the country with the most fight fans per capita, a circumstance I think responsible for its people's uncommon civility in other matters— or in the heart of his home country, Rio de Janeiro. The promoters approached the Japanese fighter Hatsu Hioki. But Hioki, to their surprise, declined to fight José Aldo, presumably because he knew he would lose as the previous fourteen of Aldo's opponents had lost before him. The other highest-ranked featherweights, the Korean Chan Sung Jung and the Midwestern Dustin Poirier, were scheduled to fight one another. There was Chad Mendes, but Chad Mendes had been the last to fight José Aldo, and he had lost so badly no one thought he deserved a rematch. The top four featherweights who were not José Aldo were therefore not available to fight José Aldo. That left the sixth, but few fans had heard of the sixth, and no one thought he had a chance of winning, and people would complain that it was a waste of a fight.

"Aldo?" I texted Erik on the drive back from Sean's apartment, half-joking, bored at a red light.

"Fighting for the title, my friend," was the message Erik sent, after he had finished speaking to his stunned manager, after he had processed enough to effect an air of nonchalance, after he had sunk to his knees in that small hallway and screamed. I stared at my phone; other cars behind me were beeping, but it was a long moment before I returned my foot to the gas. If I had sometimes doubted the wisdom of devoting two years of my life to Erik Koch, I did not doubt it then.

Sean – March 2012

IN MARCH SEAN FELT COMPELLED TO VISIT a sickly
Sherman at the University of Iowa Hospital. I accompanied him
with no small reluctance, for while I have no particular fear of
medical institutions, I do feel an aversion to bodies in the act of
betrayal. I could have waited outside the hospital, of course, but
I thought it necessary to stand sentry and shield my charge from
emotions that might interfere with his next encounter. In the half
of the room that was Sherman's, between a window and a curtain, he lay on a pillow in the shape of a panda bear. Tattoos circled his arms like skeins of black yarn. In my adolescence I had
seen cancer eat away at an elderly acquaintance such that, by her
final days, she wasted down to the size of a child, diminutive and
wizened like an amulet. But still-muscled Sherman was so tightly
woven that the disease could not easily eat him down to bone. He
was lodged in space in a way the old lady had never been, and
cancer could only diminish him with deliberation, reveal to us
his sinew, feed slow on his fibrous biceps.

Sean, healthy and overfed, half-sat on Sherman's bed, and together they flipped through pictures of fights they'd helped one another through. "This was in West Hollywood," Sherman said, and laughed. "This was when you walked outside in jeans and a tight white T-shirt and couldn't understand why so many men were staring at you."

"Got any hot nurses?" Sean asked, looking around as if he might come upon one hiding in the curtains. I sat nervously in a chair in the corner, flipping through a women's magazine, marveling at Sean's ability to talk to a dying man without changing his cadence, his intonation, his subject matter. He addressed Sherman with all the unpitying nonchalance owed the living.

"Maybe I'll get my nursing license," Sean said, and thought for a moment. "But not to be a regular nurse. To be like a nurse with mountain rescue."

He walked around the bed to where a bag of fluid hung beside Sherman. "What's this," he asked, "some kind of space food?"

"Well," I said, standing, "I am sure Sherman needs to rest. And Sean needs to train." I hadn't known I was saying it until I said it; for how out of turn this was, a spacetaker determining that her charge ought to leave. But Sean only shrugged, saying goodbye to Sherman for what was certainly the last time, and followed me out toward the parking lot, brightly lit in the glare of the cold March afternoon.

"I can't train tonight," Sean mumbled as we walked. "I have to work." This was the period in which Sean was doing time at Pizza Ranch, shoveling money at his family lawyer, reading up on court procedure. I was accustomed to his unfortunate engagement with the ordinary world of work, but something in his tone had changed. The job had become as routine as the construction gig he had long ago abandoned for its threat of conformist constancy, and yet he never spoke of quitting.

"Why don't you call in sick and train instead?" I asked, shielding my eyes from the sun as I looked at him. "They can find someone else."

"I don't think so," said Sean, his arms crossed. He had only a hoodie against the cold.

"I see," I said as we approached a staircase. We walked up a flight in silence, though I was quite certain he could hear anger in the way my boots hit the concrete.

"Do you think you might be taking a break from fighting?" I asked at the top, as we turned toward the car. "I mean, to work all the time?"

I was ahead of Sean, but I noticed when the sound of his footsteps halted. I turned to see him locked in place.

"Uh, what? I'm not even *close* to being done with that." He rolled his eyes and his gaze landed on me. "Not even *close.*"

I had before this moment seen Sean roll his eyes many times, most often while talking about promoters or politicians or poseurs of the sort given to swarm any fighter, but I had not yet seen them rolled at *me.*

"I got years left," he said lightly, and opened the car door. He looked at his hands as I pulled out, and fiddled with the radio. He slipped back into his usual aura of serenity, but something had passed between us.

•

I took this outburst to be a promise, a promise made to a space-taker who had spent two years of her life diminishing the space in his wake, who had watched more than one surgical needle slalom through the skin above his eyes, who had sat on his mattress on a Monday and stared out the frosted window to the snowy scraggly sideyard of a run-down house.

"Yeah," I said, "you have a lot of time left."

I so wanted to believe in our parking lot covenant, though I realized even then that Sean would never give up on Josiah. Perhaps, I reasoned, I had been wrong that a man who chooses attachment of any kind cannot abandon himself fully to the fight. Or perhaps other men had to choose, but Sean, unbreak-able Sean, might if he so willed transcend the bounds of possi-bility. I had to accept the mechanics of Sean's world, in which we were always on the brink of tragedy until, miraculously, the world arranged itself in our favor. This was a world in which an oppo-nent you can't overcome loses a fight for himself by elbowing you in the spine while staring at the judges, a world in which two of your body's major organs fail in the morning and work well enough by evening that you emerge from an encounter victori-ous, a world in which you give, by chance, your ludicrously out-dated bloodwork to the doctor at the very moment when he is too distracted to notice. This is a world in which not a single person on the staff of the Sheraton hotel notices that you have been pos-ing as a guest with sauna privileges for a full two years. I had con-structed for myself a rule that successful fighters had to live a life shorn of complex relationships, but perhaps Sean was not sub-ject to this rule, as he seemed to be exempt from so many others.

In the very last days of my acquaintance with Sean Huffman, his mundane magic appeared to be working. We squeezed into a sedan with Brandon and Brandon's sons Logan, eight, and Voyan, ten, many hours behind schedule on our way to Louisville (a city no one associates with martial artistry, and yet the only city in which Sean could find a fight), where an exhausted promoter weighed Sean and found him to be an astounding fourteen pounds overweight. It was Sean's very lateness that served him, for by the time we showed up everyone but the promoter was gone, and he was leaning dead-eyed over a single table in the bar of a Ramada hotel. When he found, around midnight, that one half of his main event happened to be egregiously overweight—neither Brandon nor I had ever seen the like of it—he lacked both the will to find a replacement and the witnesses to force him to adhere to procedure. Picking his scale up off the bar floor with the stooping, bone-weary air of a much-weathered washerwoman, he shook his head and sauntered out.

Together, a little stunned, we walked the narrow carpeted halls of the Ramada, resting our gaze on groups of fighters who had come for the same event, weighed in on time before we could get a look at them. A very tall adolescent strolled toward us, shoulders back, a slow-as-molasses walk, head to toe in branded fight clothes. He didn't move left or right but waited for Brandon and Sean and the boys and me to sidle past him, which we did, whereupon Sean and Brandon met eyes and burst out laughing, amused by the ill-executed machismo of his gait. "Dude," said Sean once the fighter was out of earshot, "you have *got* to stop that. You are *not* that tough."

Two more packs of young men slid past us. As they walked by, Brandon's boys stared up far above their heads.

"Who fights out of Louisville?" Brandon asked Sean. "Have you *ever* heard of a fighter out of Louisville?"

"Never," said Sean, as another pack of men spilled from a room a few yards down the hall. I thought first that they were some high school athletic team, soccer players perhaps, come to Louisville to compete, but when they came nearer I saw that they were all decked out in the same expensive fightwear. They too were aspiring fighters, even younger than the others we'd seen, their faces even less lined. They lacked the thick shells of Sean and Brandon. It was as if they were sheathed of a different substance, something gauzy and porous, and donned the fightwear to make up for a papery carapace. I stared at them and fast-forwarded ten years, adding a smashed nose here, a forehead scar there, many pairs of cauliflower ear. But I could see by their builds—tall and thin and long-necked—that they would never last long enough to look like the men by my side.

"Where have you been?" asked the promoter the next day, when Sean and I arrived late to the arena. "You were almost disqualified by the commission." Sean had wanted to smoke up before the fight, and so he indulged in the Ramada parking lot as Brandon texted him frantically and I tried my best to hurry him along. Sean shrugged and filled out his paperwork. Where it asked for an emergency contact, Sean wrote "911."

"Sean Huffman?" came a voice from the other side of the room. "Drug test."

I turned to the wall to hide my reaction. There had been no random drug tests in Iowa. They were not required in Minnesota,

Missouri, or Indiana. None of us had thought to check Kentucky. It was all for nothing then; the long cold months of waiting, the seven-hour drive between two minors, the seemingly miraculous way Sean sidestepped the weight requirement.

"One second," Sean said, and thumbed through his paperwork as if he might therein find something. Brandon leaned against the wall and slid down it.

The state official was armed with pieces of paper capable of detecting THC, and he would stand over Sean as Sean urinated in a small plastic cup. Brandon and Sean did not have the cash to get us back to Davenport; they had spent every last dollar to get us here, and for that reason Brandon had told Voyan and Logan they couldn't have dinner until Sean fought. The promoter was watching us.

Sean continued flipping through his paperwork.

"Sean Huffman," the voice said again. Sean sauntered into the bathroom as if nothing were wrong. He unzipped his pants in slow motion and stood before the urinal as the official turned his back.

"I can't pee," Sean said after a moment. "Can I just go grab a drink? I have a drink in the locker room."

"Hurry up!" said the official, annoyed.

Sean walked casually out of the bathroom and very fast down the conference center hall. He left the conference center and walked into the adjacent Ramada, down the hall and to his room. He reached into the shower for a trial-sized shampoo bottle and jerked its creamy contents into the sink. He poured a delicate amount of Snapple Iced Tea, which he happened to have on hand, into the bottle. He ran his fingers under the tap, waited for the water to warm, and let some of it fall into the shampoo bottle, thereby bringing the mixture to a temperature befitting a bodily fluid. He put the cap on, shook the bottle, and stuck it in the waistband of his shorts, where a different kind of man might have slid a gun. He ran to the end of the Ramada, walked back into the arena, and entered the bathroom.

"Ready now? Had enough?" asked the official.

Sean walked up to the urinal, squaring his broad back at such an angle as to best mask his hands from the gaze of the official, and tipped the contents of the shampoo bottle into the cup.

"Thanks, man," Sean said as he handed the man his ersatz urine, "I appreciate what you do."

The man ignored Sean, stuck a piece of paper into the cup, and minutes later Sean popped out of the bathroom with that tight smile on his face.

"Holy shit," said Brandon. He gave Sean a look of wide-eyed admiration, such as I had never seen pass between them. The boys smiled open-mouthed, impressed because they had perhaps never seen their father so impressed. I jumped from the floor, beside myself, and hugged him.

"Got through years of the Navy doing that," Sean shrugged.

There was a feeling of protection Sean's companionship conferred, but it wasn't simply because on the street other men stepped out of his way. There were few entrapments from which Sean could not, in his lassitudal manner, in his mundane magic, emerge unscathed. What hope I felt in that smile. For it bespoke of the old Sean, the man so confident, so impervious to anxiety, that every encounter is but another form of play. *This* was the meaning of our parking lot covenant; this the man who woke when waking became necessary. Fourteen pounds overweight, high as he had ever been, Sean pulled on his gloves. It seemed that even death and age could not come for Sean, that he would elude them with his lazy last-minute grace.

I wish I could stop here.

•

Above the cage hung a chandelier; in the back of the room a tux-edoed man sold Bacardi Cokes from atop a white tablecloth. Sean was the main event, and so Brandon, the boys, and I had hours in which to take in the spectacle.

The fights before us were rural in nature, their artistry naive, their participants innocent of contact with athletes. This was folk-fighting, and possessed of its own charms if taken on its own terms. As I procured a drink a tall teenager, slammed to the ground by a fat middle-aged man, sprung up and wriggled his way onto the thick man's back. The conference room seemed apt, then. These people knew not how to throw a fight, and the setting was integral to their innocence, like one of those folk artists known for the haunting quality of her quilting. I watched fight after fight and forgot the time.

Sean let his song linger and sauntered in slow, less high-fiving Logan and Voyan than letting his hand hit theirs. He ascended to the cage, shirtless, to no fanfare beyond ours. I took my place between a mustachioed man in flannel and a woman in heels.

Sean's opponent was John Troyer, native Louisvillian, heavily bearded and a head taller than Sean. As he made his entrance the lights dimmed; the tuxedoed man put down his ice tongs, stood at attention with his hands crossed.

The two men faced one another under the chandelier. Sean's flesh hung over his shorts, but Troyer too had extra padding in his gut and back. The ring girl circled and the ref karate-chopped and no one said a word as Sean and Troyer circled one another, feinted, jumped back. Sean landed a kick to which there was no response. He jabbed and lunged toward Troyer, clinching him, one arm under Troyer's arm, the other arm around Troyer's leg. Sean slammed Troyer against the fence and reached for the cage to steady himself.

"Quit grabbin' the fence, big boy!" screamed the man in flannel.

Sean dragged Troyer down but Troyer popped up again, still against the fence with Sean's arms around him.

"He's already tired," shouted the man, "Too many pancakes!"

Troyer, his back red, freed himself and hopped toward the center of the cage, where Sean met him. Troyer let fly knees, jabs, slobberknocking swings, an ugly whorl from which Sean simply backed away like a kid tiptoeing from the water's tidal edge. Troyer pursued him and backed him against the fence where Sean, trapped, endured another flurry—knees, jabs, more knees. The crowd screamed as Sean took it to the face and stomach, unblinking. A surge of gratitude coursed through us. The man in flannel had no more words, only the same shrieks of pleasure the bartender and the woman in heels and the boys shared. Sean's form was sharp in the light; I did not need my glasses to see him turn from the knee Troyer aimed at his side.

Sean danced away unbothered and Troyer followed him, striking still. He held Sean's shoulders in place and kneed him in the chest, once with the left, once with the right. Sean escaped to the center of the cage, where with a room-shaking tremor Troyer kicked him in the head and pulled him to the ground. Under Troyer Sean writhed, first on his side, then on his stomach, successfully slipping out and freeing himself. He clutched Troyer's arm, trying to straighten and wrap his legs around it and press the elbow in a direction Troyer did not wish it to go. As they squirmed on the ground, Troyer, feeling his arm isolated and vulnerable, was reduced to a panicked wormlike squirming under Sean. Sean, on top, dominant, had turned the fight around.

"Spin out!" screamed the man in flannel, his voice cracking with worry. "Why's everyone so quiet? This is a fuckin' fight."

Sean, face to face with Troyer, slid one leg between both of Troyer's knees and jabbed.

"It's gotta be the end of the round, right?" said the man. And so it was. A chorus of helpless murmurs acknowledged that Sean had won the round.

The ring girl, a middle-aged woman in a black bikini, circumnavigated a cage in which stood two very tired men. At the bell Troyer swung and missed and Sean slammed him in the face. Sean slammed again and hopped back playfully, spreading both of his arms long and straight, wide open, a split-second victory dance even as he huffed hard. Troyer charged, jab from the left, jab from the right, knee, coming at Sean with energy drawn from some second secreted store. Sean lunged for a takedown, but it was slow and tired rather than the explosive leap it needed to be, and it was Troyer who ended up on top, Sean with his back on the ground, knees bent and spread wide. Troyer set one foot on the canvas, one knee on Sean's chest. With every jab to the face and body Sean's body trembled; his knees shook, his feet planted. The moment grew long.

Sean knows what to do from this entanglement, as do I, as does Brandon, as do Brandon's boys. He knows what he owes us. He ought to wrap his legs round Troyer's and thrust his hips outward and knock him off balance, which would be easy, because Troyer's jiu-jitsu is primitive and unstable. He ought to draw his elbows in and move his head to the left and escape so as to extend the encounter and plunge us finally into the reverie for which we had come. The ref bent toward Sean, told him he had to move or the fight would be over. Sean shifted with a defiant dolorousness, as if to make himself more comfortable as he failed to fight back. Troyer flipped him over like a doll, wrapped his body round Sean's side, and jabbed some more. There was no roll to Sean, no snap to his response; there was no exchange. Sean pulled himself into fetal position, forearms shielding his face from the blows. It was the instinctual, self-preserving posture of a victim of violence. It was the posture of a man who had something to lose. I looked away, overcome with disappointment, and so did not see Troyer snake his arm around Sean's neck to end the fight.

The referee jumped in between the two and the room cheered and when the cheering was over, the ref ready to announce the winner, Troyer and the ref stood quite erect while Sean remained prone on the mat, eyes closed, huffing hard. Brandon charged into the cage.

"Are you OK?" he asked, over and over. Sean moaned. He lumbered to all fours like a patched-together monstrosity come to life. He placed one foot on the ground, and then the other, and waited for Troyer to be announced the winner, whereupon he walked out of the octagon, and we followed him, his dejected entourage, to the locker room, where he ducked under the table and lay down flat on the ground with his eyes closed. He had not spoken a word since the fight. This was the image that would come to me, months later, when Sean texted to tell me that a DNA test had determined Josiah his. This was what he had chosen—fetal in a cage, supine beneath a table, closed to the world as any ordinary man.

Voyan and Logan stared. There might have been those who thought him hurt, but I knew better, and I suppose I had known for a long time. I would not accuse Sean of giving up, exactly. I would say that he had remained divided for so long that something had given up on him.

"Is there water?" Sean said, head tilted up, looking at me. There was a water bottle a few yards away. I stared back at Sean without moving. For what had I to do with him, and he with me?

The promoter's assistant dropped an envelope full of cash on Sean's stomach. Sean fumbled with the envelope and grabbed some of the money, then went limp again. Three twenties stuck to his sweaty chest. Occasionally other fighters would walk over to peer at him, but they were young, and they did not know what it was they had seen.

Erik – Summer 2012

It had always been Erik. Here was I, desperate to escape from the limits of perception laid upon me by some rather ungenerous maker; and here was he, delicately dismantling the emotional machinery that kept him from the glory of abandon. Wherever in my heart had once lain the need for a community of scholars, it was dead; wherever in his lay the need for friends and family, he'd killed it. I no longer thought it coincidence that Erik Koch won every fight at which I was present. Together we were undoing ourselves, moment by moment, impulse by impulse, in order to achieve a more perfect dissolution. I mourned with force that made me ill all the time I had wasted in another city, on another fighter. Sean had chosen attachment over transcendence. He was anomalous noise in the data set that was Erik.

Take everything before this point as my search, often misguided and distracted and confused by the very sensory input from which I long to escape, for an ecstasy-worthy object.

One must always have an object, as anyone interested in non-knowledge understands—a sunset, a mountain, a public execution—before one can dissolve into unknowing. "Be entered ocularly," Georges Bataille advised, and the object itself will dissipate, and you will be freed for a moment from the illusions of stasis in which you are kept like a petal pressed into a dull book. I had my object now. He had taken me there twice, and I would wait patiently to be taken again.

After the canceled bout with Poirier, six weeks of motionless zombie-watching, and a year of concussed uncertainty, Erik accepted his Calgary-bound destiny with the calm of a man stepping into the single future he thought for himself fitting. Duke would remark to me upon this strange new mildness, the way Erik seemed cleansed of whatever demons had heretofore haunted every practice and all the hours in between. It was as if he had been nervous right up until he was asked to be struck by the reigning champion before tens of millions of people across the Americas and Japan and Australia, at which point he had stopped worrying, having finally been given his due.

This cosmic justice brought with it four thirty-something men lugging big cameras, come from the UFC to Cedar Rapids in order to film the "featherweight challenger." They asked for a narrative, a three-minute tale to tell in the lead-up to the fight, some story of obstacles overcome with which to regale uneducated Pay-Per-View watchers desperate to be invested. "Walk up those steps," they instructed Erik in front of his parents' house. "Walk down them. No, more slowly. OK now fast." This was a farcical attempt to make the wrong kind of theater out of a sublime spectacle, rather like trying to sell a literary masterpiece based on the fact that it was "now a major motion picture." But Erik's eyes were bright, his smile quick even when the men with their clunky cameras and clunkier attempts to extract a storyline asked him, once again, to walk slowly up the steps.

They sat Erik in a chair surrounded by lights in a setup that looked very much like the preamble to a brutal interrogation, and within the course of the interview we all watched, startled, as Erik employed the past tense to describe his conflict with Keoni.

"I've had a lot of hard times with my brother Keoni, a lot of arguments, brother stuff, it's inevitable," he said, shrugging as he spoke. "It was hard for me to be grateful. I just looked up to him so much. But he is how I got to where I am. I don't look at it as just, 'I am awesome, it's all me.' Without my brother I would not be here."

It became obvious to the men from the UFC that they would have to interview Keoni, and so they went to his house. Keoni agreed, though it was news to him that he and his brother had been through their rough patch and emerged even more loving in adulthood than they had been as small children. He was not one to be swept into a narrative with which he did not agree.

"We can do it right here," he said, and positioned himself on his couch, elbows on knees, beneath an upside-down American flag hanging in protest on the wall.

"Uh, do you think you can turn that flag right-side up?" asked the interviewer, placing his palm on the back of his head as if to look very casual, as if to say, might we move that potted plant to the left? This was not the kind of conflict he had come to manufacture.

"Absolutely not," said Keoni, clearly pleased that they had asked.

There was an awkward standstill, the man's hand still on his head, making nervous eye contact with another man behind a camera.

"Where else can we film?" asked the first man. So they went instead to the new gym Keoni had bought, a clean one-room space with fresh mats and gleaming chains and Ron Paul 2012 stickers pasted across the particle board on which hung the class schedule. Erik came too. When the men requested footage of the two fighters sparring, Erik and Keoni danced in the light of the single window. Two cameras bore down on them, a boom mic above their heads, one brother the milk-white he had always been, the other an alien orange to which he had turned. They sparred for so long that they forgot their audience and fell into fraternal rhythm. Erik was quicker than he had been when they had last sparred, and Keoni physically stronger than ever before, but there was for each the recognition of an odd echo of themselves in one another, the same flick of the head, the same hop back.

When the men with cameras left for Vegas, Erik asked his brother if he might come back to the gym. "Yes," said Keoni, who thought his brother mentally disturbed and thus incapable of true reconciliation, and who also thought the appearance of the world's second-most-important featherweight salutary to his aspirational business. None among us would have predicted that throughout the entire practice, where gathered Cliff and DJ and Lonnie and Jared and others, Erik would be extraordinarily helpful, an exemplary teacher, a peerless font of latent kinesthetic knowledge made articulate. A new kid, a long-necked skinny wrestler from the local high school, could not tighten a choke; Erik lay face up and invited the kid to crawl on top of him. "Put your hand on my forehead," he said, and the kid did. "Sink your hips down—no, not—yeah, there. More, hit the floor with your hips. Awesome!" said Erik, choking now, and the kid, horrified and elated to be choking the featherweight challenger, let go and spread his palms as if to drop a hot pan. At the end of the practice Keoni gathered his team in the center of the mat, where they made a pile of their palms. "Let's all take a moment to thank New Breed," he said sincerely, "the next featherweight champion of the UFC."

Erik asked Keoni—who had not been invited to any of Erik's fights in the two years I had known them—to corner him in Calgary. Keoni said yes in a manner both magnanimous and dismissive. Again he did not credit Erik's maturity, but blamed mental illness as described and enumerated on the Internet.

I followed Erik back to Milwaukee, unafraid, certain that the state could not warp me so long as I stayed within Erik's increasingly alien aura. I wanted to be two feet behind him, sitting cross-legged on his futon as he directed his Xbox avatar to victory over José Aldo. I wanted to sing with him in the car, hold his lotion in the tanning salon, eat what fast food he could not and leave the wrapper wafting in his direction.

I drove up weeks later, in July. It hadn't rained in so long that someone on the radio was always mourning the dying corn, and I drove past brown fields to Erik's brick-and-pavement neighborhood, where the sidewalks would burn bare feet and the dirt, so long unwatered, would not remain grounded but floated up and dusted your ankles.

I stepped through his flimsy door and into some air that had decidedly not been conditioned, and at his very presence felt a surge of being from my ribs to my knuckles. We stood in his kitchen as he combined some sort of white dust with water and downed the mix. The entire contents of his kitchenette, which he shared with Biggie, involved powder-filled canisters and capsules carelessly collected on metal racks. This diet, advised by a nutritionist to power Erik through six daily hours of physical exertion, appeared shorn of pleasure, but there was a box of grain on the counter, and Erik was in a place where he could talk about quinoa and celery with a rapturous glee.

"We have power now," he said. "We didn't last week because I forgot to pay the bill."

In the living room beside the wall-sized television lay a stack of four large boxes, each containing a luxury rim for a wheel of Erik's new car. On three walls hung official posters from fights Erik had won, all of them autographed. I was running my fingers down a stack of Xbox games as tall as myself when I caught sight of his right elbow, swollen, pyramidally grotesque, a bulbous anthill where had been the clean hinge of an arm. When he straightened his arm, the anthill remained, as if the elbow had become detached from the bones it connected.

"What," I said, shocked out of my usual habits of delicacy in articulation, "is that?"

"Bursitis," he said. "They can't drain it because it's infected."

There are in all of us small sacs of yolklike fluid keeping our joints well greased, and they are not made for constant pad-slamming against a sparring partner. Under the pressure of his current, pre-Aldo regime, the tiny vesicles neglected to stay invisible under the skin of his elbow and tumefied instead to their unsightly size. He thought no more of it than he thought of the usual muscle cramps, took it to be part of practice. Wash your sweat-soaked clothes, ingest your breakfast powders, drain the swollen sacs in your elbow if you can, and take antibiotics if you cannot. I took his lead, stared at the anthill, willed myself to accept it as part of his healthily evolving form.

That the featherweight challenger of the world lived in a cardboard-and-brick hovel would have surprised the various journalists who now harassed Erik daily for interviews, but I understood the hovel to be part of Erik's sacrificial genius, his retreat from the comforts of conformism and intimacy. Erik's life had been reduced to a grinding and dull formula. He had rid himself entirely of the lubricious glamour of Pettis's life, and of Pettis himself, such that the only time I saw Erik engage with a woman was when he asked the girl who worked at the tanning salon for more lotion. This was a life that required no thought beyond the ability to juggle a five-practice-per day schedule. It was an existence, in its ability to ignore every aim but one, of which Arnold Schwarzenegger would have approved.

"Want to watch *DodgeBall*?" Erik asked me that night, as we sat on separate futons in his living room.

"OK," I said, "I've never seen it."

"You never seen *DodgeBall*?" he said, and turned up both palms and cocked his head, as if exasperated, as if to call my spacetakerly credentials into question. He slid in the DVD, and we lay prone on our futons, elbows on the beds and hands on the chins, laughing at the slapstick antics of then-ascendant American comedians. And although at some moments that summer I might have missed Sean, thought longingly of the quiet way I could exist in his presence, I felt now that Erik and I were both merging and destined somewhere dark and brave, a realm Sean hadn't the sacrificial will to penetrate.

"My life is so boring!" Erik said good-naturedly the next morning, as we made our way to the second practice of the day, a strength-training regimen at an elite gym.

Inside an aluminum warehouse we found a number of stations and at them people toiling alone at whatever bizarre game a trainer had set them. A pert girl in a ponytail skipped down the length of some AstroTurf. Behind some old machines—everything here seemed to work on gears and pulleys—a man stood underneath some monkey bars and lifted his body parallel to them, over and over. Everything done was done repeatedly, as if the participants were robots running on simple programs, fit for this task and no other.

I watched Erik swing kettle bells, the tendons on his slim arm popping like wires, bigger than they had been that day in the wet field in Cedar Rapids. With the bell at its height he turned left as if to accept a dancing partner, then back to set the bell down as one might a glass vase. He held himself parallel to the ground in a forearm pushup. Staring at Erik's body board-straight, T-shirt riding up to reveal two hard hills rising from the deep valley of his spine, small tattooed biceps peeking from sleeves, lithe legs tensed and locked without the merest shiver of weakness, the trainer cocked his head. He placed a thirty-pound circular weight on Erik's board-straight back. Erik grimaced, sweat dripping from his brow, his torso now tremoring ever so slightly under the weight.

"This is fun, right, Erik?" asked the trainer.

"Brightens my day!" he said, only partly in sarcasm, and mouthed the words to the pop song then blasting from the primitive sound system. "Ninety-nine problems," he huffed, "and a bitch ain't one." I stood not two feet from his form and sang along with him to signal solidarity as he endured the lactic discomfort now visible in his eyes. The trainer looked up at me, surprised. I was determined that we become a single unit, harmonized for perfect abandon. "I got the rap patrol," we therefore sang, "on the gat patrol."

When we got around to the sand pit, Erik jogged to the edge of the pit and continued to run, on air now, legs spread and torso turned slightly, until he slid vertically into the sand. He popped up and trotted back to the piece of duct tape that served as a starting line. Over and over he jumped, each time a little farther, each time popping up as if he were a self-winding mechanism energized by his own movement. It was José Aldo's style to weaken kick by kick and chop a man down, but even Aldo, trained on the soccer field, would not catch an Erik who could jump and hover so. It was Aldo's style to stun with speed, but there were some, and I was among them, who thought perhaps he was about to meet the man who existed within the same compressed time frame as himself. Something of this fight would be lost to us with every blink.

After training, Erik massaged his muscles on the futon, moaned as a deep muscular pain revealed itself, and left for a five-mile run. There was an hour's recovery and then a water-and-powder lunch, at which point he headed to Duke's gym for stand-up, whereupon the entire team would attempt to tire him for two hours. This was his training camp schedule, the most brutal he had ever known, and he had been at it for three months.

The class of men who regularly desecrate sacred encounters in the form of what is called "sports writing" had latched onto Erik like halfwit harriers happening upon a housecat. He was "unworthy of a title shot," said adipose malcontents keyboard-pecking from the comfort of their mothers' basements; he had "skipped the line" and his "unimpressive victory" over Brookins was no evidence of true talent. These were men too lazy to even attain the status of shadow, and if they had the will to see what I now saw daily, even they, with their limited capacities, could have seen that my charge moved with an otherworldly grace and speed. Some men seemed to take Erik's ascendance as a personal insult, and thought it necessary to repeatedly remind their readers that they had barely heard of this upstart, as if their ignorance were some kind of virtue. There would have been even more of this anti-Koch palaver were it not for the fact that the MMA press corps was kept busy by another phenomenon—the curse that had befallen the Calgary fight card. The event was supposed to feature Thiago Silva, who withdrew with a back injury, and Rodrigo Nogueira, who pulled out with an arm injury, and then Michael Bisping, who tore his meniscus. No card had ever been so quickly shorn of its star power.

Time is a fighter's enemy, and all the classic time-passers available to you and me—drinking, eating, drug-taking—are not available to the fighting class. Due to his painful six weeks without training, Erik had grown expert at letting the minutes tick by. Two months from the fight he filled the gaps between practice and tanning with video games, talk of food, and a succession of movies. He watched *DodgeBall* over and over again. He and Biggie lay on their futons, calves and cores aching, and Biggie recited recipes, down to the ingredients in a salad dressing, they could both imaginatively savor. Erik rarely spoke of the fight but he always knew precisely how many days were left until he could unleash. It was the countdown that got him through the moments while his trainer added weights onto his shaking back, the countdown that quieted his grumbling stomach, the countdown that brought him back to Duke's when his legs were wobbly from the last practice.

On June 9 Erik's phone rang from across the room, and having just come back from Duke's, his legs afire, his abdominal muscles so sore they interrupted his pangs of hunger with waves of nausea, he considered not picking it up. On the third ring he hoisted himself with a quiet moan. It was his manager. José Aldo was injured. Something about a crashed motorcycle in Copacabana. For three months he had pushed himself to the point of pain to be ready for a fight extinguished in a moment's misstep on a beach 5,000 miles away. The fight would be postponed indefinitely. Erik went to his room, closed the door. Were I one to employ the dead language of therapists, I would say that he "isolated," but I will simply note that for ten days he felt so despondent he didn't see the need to fill the space in his wake.

I supposed an earlier version of myself might have been quite as devastated as he, but it was only in the service of emotional tact that I wore a concerned frown throughout this period. For wasn't José Aldo, supposedly invincible, hobbled by an infected ankle? Thiago Silva a bruised spine; Rodrigo Nogueira a ripped elbow; Michael Bisping a frayed meniscus? How tired and worn all of these men seemed to me, aging, parts chipping off them like the decrepit flaps of Hard Drive's quondam ceiling, like the crumbling curb outside Erik's window! They had not figured out what Erik, young and lithe and increasingly not of this world, had figured out. They had not diminished themselves into something too simple to break.

My certainty had no echo in Erik's psyche. There were too many voices tearing him down, and too many decisions lay subject to the whims of suited men in Vegas, who thought not about justice or sacral encounters but about tickets sold and customers reached. "Just because he was scheduled for a title shot doesn't mean he deserves it," read one piece that popped up in my inbox. The implication being that when Aldo fought again it ought to be against someone else; that Erik was just given the shot because everyone else was indisposed, and by the time Aldo was healthy someone else would be free.

Erik took few calls and avoided even Biggie, growing dangerously close to an un-Schwarzeneggerian pose of self-pity. He did not miss a practice, but with the countdown reset he had nothing to work toward, and so the boredom ceased to be charming or productive. Through the month of July it still had not rained and Erik still had no idea whether he had a title shot, but he had to practice as if he might, in the next few months, be fighting Aldo in some unknown city at some unknown date. He heard rumors: Aldo would be fighting Hioki in Sydney; Aldo would be fighting Erik in Las Vegas; Aldo would be ready next month; Aldo needed surgery and would not be ready for six months. One day Erik drove to the Cheesecake Factory, alone, to eat a steak in secret.

Ten days after Aldo pulled out, Milwaukee was declared to be in an "extreme drought." It was 105 degrees. After his second practice of the day Erik stood in his kitchen, closed his eyes, and pictured the cupcakes he would eat after his next fight, whenever that might be. His phone rang; it was his manager. "You're still fighting Aldo," he said. "Where?" asked Erik.

Rio

LIKE SOME WARLORD ATOP THE STONY mountain of Corcovado hovers a concrete Christ, one hundred feet tall, and whereas the tourists who do not even reach to the top of his toes see below them ocean and favela and forest, Brasileños see fences, boundaries, demesnes divvied up among the city's most right-thinking residents. Mere years ago, before the martial arts were mixed, the blocks belonged to fighters, each neighborhood apportioned to the practitioners of a particular discipline. *Here* may pass the jiu-jitsu artists; *here* practitioners of luta livre; here the boxers, the capoeirans, the Muay Thai boys, and a fighter who crosses the boundaries upon which Cristo glares is apt to end badly. Middle-class gi'ed-up jiu-jitsu boys on the dirt-poor favela-edged luta livre blocks could not but return with broken bones. Poor luta livrans who stepped over into jiu-jitsu territory might return home stripped of every piece of clothing in which they had come. It is in the nature of Rio, where painted lines are bleached out by sun and sand, for substance to spill over, and so there will be jiu-jitsu artists who spill into the lands controlled by the luta livre, and luta livrans who spill into the land controlled by jiu-jitsu artists, and thusly many great fights occurred in the days before Big Shows, before Miletich, before a Gracie ever thought to take the religion north. A knowing Brasileño will walk you along the beach—along Flamengo or Pipi or Barra—and point out the site where a Gracie fought a Wallid, right there in the sand, where two men now stand on either side of a volleyball net. At the end of our last century the civilizing authorities attempted to stage orderly indoor battles between the jiu-jitsu artists and the luta livrans, as if to settle once and for all which was the great-est fighting art; but the audience rose up, bled onto the stage, and with drawn knives rioted. The staged encounters were banned. To ban anything at all in Rio de Janeiro is to pretend, during those gray fog-enshrouded mornings when he goes entirely missing, that the concrete Christ will not reappear come the sun. And so in our advanced age they are again legal.

Had the art of fighting been elsewhere born it would be merely a pastime, a "sport" for the cruel and easily amused, men with the diversionary instincts of bored housecats. Fighting had to be born in the one place where ecstasy remained the organiz-ing principle, the seedful incipience of all life. The French sup-pressed Carnival in the sixteenth century and the Italians in the seventeenth and so on across a continent newly sanitized. Where, I ask you, does the maenadic instinct still persist? My beloved Iowa is white as wool except for a pocket of black called Waterloo. Where, I ask you, has pure lust overcome every low instinct of race and tribe to produce the most roilsome gallimaufry of glorious miscegenation? Where does even a bikinied nine-year-old, frolicking on the beach, one leg caked with sand where a receding tide pulled her into the shore, show us with the slow aimless swing of her arms an openness to the universe we never see on a New Yorker? Where on earth is the body more a thing to be used—pushed and penetrated—than worried over? What city can the insidious cult of wellness never pacify? "You exoticize!" say the bescarved scholars, the "internal review boards," and to my guilt I will quite happily plead, for there is one single place on this sorry planet free from the ordinary, and upon my life I will not pretend that its people are like you and me.

There is a form of anticipation that feels quite akin to fear. When I thought of Rio—and I thought always of Rio—my stomach turned and the smallest fine hairs on my diminutive wrists stood at attention. I knew not what the fight would do to me, how far it would throw me off the course of the healthy-minded, whether I would ever be able to return to life among them. I did not care. I pictured 50,000 Brazilians pressed into the stadium beside me, 100,000 eyes flickering, black cameras on tracks receding. I imagined all of us together reduced to the ocular root, simply receiving with the mute innocence of porcelain dolls sloppily collected, until something spilled over and we were together ripped from time. I wanted the hours to pass more quickly. I wanted Erik to call once an hour. I wanted the premonition that something world-ending would happen—injury, change of heart, natural disaster—to quiet its persistent tapping against my breast. I wanted, I wanted, I wanted. I drove to Milwaukee. I drove back.

Before Erik could take me and Keoni and Duke to Rio he had to go alone, as the UFC would have him commune with Brazilian journalists for a day-long publicity tour. In a better world we might have come along, but to the ignorant media a fighter always appears a Randian individualist, crafted by nothing but his own steel will. To the editors of *Jornal do Brasil* Erik has no need of a friendly spacetaker with whom to pass slow Sundays, no coach to structure each long practice, a practice he possibly does not require, so extraneous to him are other people. And yet how small and alone he was, planted behind a white desk fingering the mic in front of him, fielding questions with, in place of an entourage, a massive cardboard picture of himself at his back. And how pressed in upon he felt by Rio—a metropolis that did not much resemble his favorite city, Cedar Rapids, or his second favorite, Calgary. It was too much, he thought, the way the city's busiest streets seemed mere alleyways between apartment buildings, narrow corridors in which half the city was squeezed at once, and the traffic took no order he could understand. A motorbike cut in front of his car, and the driver jammed the brakes, throwing him toward the back of the driver's seat. Pedestrians dropped in between the lines of traffic casually, which Erik would only have attempted if in possession of a deathwish, and the whole neighborhood was so strung with powerlines—around each apartment, terrace, and sign—that it seemed as if the whole place had been tied to the spinning earth like a deer to the back of a pickup.

Had I been there I would have told him that he was in Flamengo, an area once controlled by luta livre fighters; that in Flamengo the jiu-jitsuing Gracies had been humiliated by a livran named Duarte, who ripped a Gracie's clothes off and sent him home naked; that the Gracies had followed up on this with violent reprisals until a kindly boxing coach in a far-off favela brought both sides together, and encouraged the martial arts to mix. I would have told Erik that he needn't take sides, could not take sides, because he is a child of that mix, loyal to not one art but all of them. This is something Keoni understands, and what Keoni meant when he named Erik "New Breed," though he would not have known then that the New Breed would return to the Old World.

At the press conference to which he was brought, a Brazilian journalist asked Erik how he felt about fighting in Rio. The question was translated back into English. Erik just said he would "tell his grandchildren about it," and the answer was translated back into Portuguese. José Aldo, seated beside him, answered the same question with a smiling fluidity while Erik leaned forward on the table and stared at his hands. Most questions went to José, who had defeated six title challengers over the past four years, who had hobbled them with kicks developed in his years as a soccer player and overwhelmed them with the speed of his strikes. José the celebrity was pasted across billboards selling watches, thrown into TV spots hawking cars. No fighter in all of the United States is as famous in that country as José is in Brazil, which is just one more piece of evidence pointing to Brazil's superiority.

Before sunset Erik was brought to the deck of a hotel overlooking the ocean. Someone shoved a straw-stabbed coconut into his hand. He would not remember where he was; he would later identify it as "that hotel near the beach" in a city made of shoreline; but this is the moment when a flicker of understanding would pass through him. To his right countless ramshackle houses rose up a mountain topped in green forest; below him thousands of half-naked bodies converged and separated on the beach, like bacteria under a microscope; from the far side of the deck he watched two lines of traffic merge haphazardly and fork off past the edge of his vision. The last rays of the sun melted into the ocean in a way that rendered the horizon invisible. There was sky and ocean and a vast blur between. If he and I were ever to cast off our illusions of solidity it would surely be here, in this loud wet place where the very atmosphere defied the eye's attempt at hard lines.

Erik returned with forty-five days until the fight, and whereas he had hour upon hour of self-inflicted physical punishment with which to bide the time, I had nothing but my own feverish planning. I filled the days by tinkering with a twelve-and-a-half-page itinerary detailing every spot I would visit. There was the bit of beach where Duarte and Gracie had met and the boxing gym where they had made peace and the place where a Japanese businessman first introduced his jiu-jitsu to a couple of curious Brazilian children. I would leave a week before the fight, as would Erik, and return I knew not when. It seemed presumptuous to purchase a round-trip ticket because I did not know when the person I would be when I woke from the fight's spell would want to return. Better to let her make the decision, thought I, and changed the itinerary's structural iconography from asterisks to bullet points. I thought often of the chance of riot and hoped, with only a tinge of fear, for the violence to overbrim its borders and spill onto those of us privileged enough to watch.

On two occasions—two moments of weakness under the enormous and growing burden of anticipation—I took out my suitcase and therein placed a roll of socks. Then thinking better of it, the fight still being two months out, I replaced the socks in my sock drawer and slid the suitcase back under the bed. "It's ages away," I said to myself, "anything could happen," figuring that I could make time go faster by pretending the fight was in the far distant future. I did not return Sean's calls. I did not have to return Erik's calls, because I invariably picked up on the first ring. At the end of August he came back to Cedar Rapids, for a family reunion. There were forty days until the fight.

Erik drove straight to Keoni's gym, and when he arrived all of his old friends were waiting to practice with him—DJ, Lonnie, Cliff, and Jared among them. The gym was clean. There was no cracked gilded mirror and there were no brass knuckles nailed to the wall, but this was as close as they would come to the nostalgic grime of Valhalla. They rolled for a full hour, Keoni leading practice, until the place was wet and limb slipped over limb with the same familiar intimacy. As the sun set, the light from the single window scaled the blue mats. Erik was face down on top of a face-up Cliff, white on black, their bodies at a forty-five degree angle from one another, like an open scissor set flat upon the mat. Erik wanted to sweep his right leg over Cliff's body and mount him, close the scissor, end up astride his friend.

This simple sweep, which the jargon-afflicted call "passing the guard," would have been among the first things Keoni taught Erik, and it was just as natural to Erik as walking. Even if a man is under you, as Cliff was under Erik, he is not securely held so long as his legs are free. To pass a man's guard is, in a single motion, to decommission a man's hips, trap his legs, make of him a helpless awkward merman in your grasp. It's the last motion in a tricky, trap-laden chain of dozens, and is invariably accompanied by the thought that here I am, I have arrived, that snap of satisfaction that comes with effort rewarded. Next to this, most everything short of a submission looks like a half-measure. And when it is successfully done there is the primal pleasure of finding yourself seated atop another, lesser man.

Erik lifted his knee and swept it successfully over Cliff's torso, whereupon his toes caught on a snag on the mat and his knee slipped ever so slightly inward, like a bike skidding on a bit of gravel before the wheels find traction. On top of Cliff Erik felt a champagnelike pop deep in the knee, and stopped the game to check on the joint while the others rolled around him, as if stepping out of scene for a moment. It wasn't painful, and he could ignore it as he ignored a dull pain in his stomach and a throbbing in a swollen elbow, and so he jumped back onto Cliff, submitted him ably, finished out the practice smiling.

The leg that called to him twenty minutes later, that demanded from him something he desperately did not want to give, was the same leg with which I had seen him, a month previous, fling his form into a pit of sand. It was the leg that he had swung in its swift arc so quickly that Francisco Rivera simply received the blow and dropped. The thick white band of fibrous tissue that connected the backside of his femur to the tibia that slammed into the face of Francisco Rivera did not, in Las Vegas, object to the way such force must have taxed its ability to keep the leg together, maintain the flowing grace of Erik's game. It waited until six weeks prior to the fight in Rio, during a simple sweep over an old friend, to call out, demand attention, assert itself as part of the cage that kept even Erik imprisoned. Twenty minutes after he mounted Cliff, the space around Erik's knee began to throb. By morning, his leg was hard and swollen, unwilling to bend.

Erik's father drove him to the hospital, where a nurse's tech listened and guided Erik toward a machine and disappeared for a while. Erik sat on the examination table, stiff leg straight, healthy leg swinging. He ran the flat of his palm over the knee, back and forth, and looked away. He was shivering. A doctor walked into the room where Erik and his father waited, folder in hand. She spent a very long time pulling out the X-rays, which wobbled in her hand. She pointed to a glowing mass, the thick swath of tissue half-torn at the top like pier-tied rope fraying from the pull of a ship.

Is there anyone less equipped to understand the will to escape embodiment, the deep longing for ecstatic release, than a doctor of medicine? Anyone more committed to the body as project, the cult of wellness, the pursuit of longevity at the expense of life? And it's this very myopia that keeps the doctor from understanding the very phenomena of which she speaks. To her the ligament is just a ligament, capable of no meaning beyond itself, emblematic of no cage worth escaping.

"You need four weeks of rehab," she said.

Erik's mouth contorted. He moaned and the moan turned slowly into a succession of sobs, first harsh and loud then soft, muffled by his father's shirt.

"It's not that big of a deal," said the doctor, confused, and indeed it was not, because the moment the ligament ripped Erik Koch was no longer the Rio-destined fighter for whom such an injury would mean the loss of a title shot, but another broken boy who made the mistake of going home.

Epilogue

DO YOU THINK ANY FIGHTER WILL BE surprised one day
to find his head grown soft, his strikes unblinkingly absorbed, his
legs dropping under him from the sinking force of a single kick?
Waking from a knockout he could not, having lost youth's alac-
rity, dodge, will he greet diminishment with denial? I am here to
tell you he will not. As was once thought that in the womb, the
fetus cycled through every stage of evolution before settling on its
modern form, men in the ring rehearse their inevitable atrophy
two dozen times before they retire. Think of it: what is aging but a
sealing in, a crude duct-taping of the box in which you are born;
and what is fighting but a mere acceleration of the battle we're all
doomed to lose? One day a pageant a dozen yards away proves
just so slightly out of range; the sound of your grandchild speaking across the room somehow fails to carry. The world must work
harder to find you. And as you lose the world, your own body
creakingly calls out louder and louder. Minor muscles, silent for

sixty years, grow suddenly conversational. Will any of this seem new to the man whose profession leaves him so bloody that he spends the third round blind in one eye, so weak on his feet that he must work to stand? Another man stamps on his toes, pulls at the backside of his elbow, knocks at his knees. Will sore joints thirty years hence be some kind of revelation? Age comes to the fighter not as a shock but as a memory.

The collapse of all I had worked for, and the interruption of my phenomenological study, brought with it a certain haunting clarity. In the mirror I saw brown irises shorn of their brightness, three tiny lines visible under the soft of each eye. I pressed my index fingers to the sides of my ski-jump nose and traced the deepening lines to the edges of my mouth. Soon my whole face would be cast in shadow.

There is an integrity in sticking by your fighter even when he proves himself injury-prone; even when he cannot take you to ecstasy because he brings with him an aura of worry; even when you can see, with a premonition clear enough to draw up a calendar of failures, how he will ultimately go down, grow soft, acquire children and a house and pay his taxes on time.

Erik did not have the courage to call me; it was my place to affirm that I remained loyal despite being failed. I thought to make up a list of men who had recovered from precisely his injury. I thought to sit down with him at his parents' kitchen table, his leg brace on, his crutches leaned against the wall, and watch with him video after video of his body in its glorious willowy symmetry. But I had nothing to say, except perhaps that I was thirty years old, and very afraid, and he couldn't help me anymore.

I pulled out one suitcase, and then two. I packed my notes, my books, then all my belongings. I got in the car without knowing where I was headed, but I drove south, in the direction of Corcovado. The cornfields faded into scrub and then into desert and the desert into lush wetland. I was in Texas, and tired of driving, when I stopped and found a place to stay.

For a long time I did nothing but read and reread my notebooks, my ninety pages of ecstatic observation. I thought about a gym Sean had once mentioned in the southeast part of the state, a strip-mall training ground started by a Miletich protégé, and wandered in one evening. When I opened the door a wave of wet heat washed over me, and I heard the shuffling sounds of men struggling on the ground, the occasional thump of a man hitting the mat, and I thought that perhaps I had come to the right place. But when I wiped the fog from my glasses and focused on the group of men tugging at one another's limbs at the far end of the single-room gym, I saw that all the men were Sean's age. On my way out the door I picked up a flyer for an event that evening—Legacy Fighting Championship 18—a few miles away.

I walked into the arena, slipped by some distracted ticket takers without paying, and set about finding the locker room. High above me, on the arena's uppermost floor, a group of men said something I could not hear to a guard and disappeared behind a door. I ascended to the top floor and feigned interest in some sound equipment adjacent to the room, thinking I might be taken for an engineer, turning this knob and that.

When an excitable fan tried to engage the guard in speculation about the night's fights, I appended myself to the back of someone's entourage and slipped finally into the locker room. Inside, pacing men shouted over one another, and in a corner, sitting on a cooler, a silent boy watched his father wrap his hands. He was just emerging from adolescence. His olive skin was as unlined as a child's, and his bright brown eyes, slightly too far apart, shined from either side of an unbroken nose. He was too young to be beautiful, but he would be beautiful soon.

I said I had come to watch him win.

His name was Charlie Ontiveros, he was twenty-one years old, and he was from Cleveland, Texas. He had never lost a fight.

Acknowledgments

For opening up their lives to a stranger, I am forever indebted
to three fearless and heroic men: Sean Huffman, Erik Koch,
and Keoni Koch. (Thanks also to Rocky for letting a girl
come over on Friday nights.)

For encouragement when it was needed, criticism when it was
merited, and kindness always, thank you to John D'Agata.

For her friendship, honesty, ear for Kit's diction, and refusal to
countenance a chowder, thank you to Kalpana Narayanan.
For their comments on drafts of this book, thank you to
Joe Wenderoth, Susan Lohafer, Elaine Stuart, Lina Maria
Ferreira Cabeza-Vanegas, Rachel Yoder, and Jen Percy.

In writing *Thrown* I drew inspiration from Jill Marsden's *After
Nietzsche: Notes Toward a Philosophy of Ecstasy*; I am grateful
for her insights.

For financial support, thank you to the Nonfiction Writing Program at the University of Iowa, in particular Robin Hemley.

Thank you to my courageous agent, Edward Orloff, who believed in the integrity of the manuscript from the beginning, and to Kristen Radtke and Sarah Gorham, two brilliant writers who turned that manuscript into a book.

Most of all I wish to thank my husband, William Wilkinson, whose support for this project began with a move to Iowa, continued through countless searching conversations, and never wavered in the face of Kit's fickle consciousness. May the worlds into which we are thrown always include one another.

Sarabande Books thanks you for the purchase of this book; we do hope you enjoy it! Founded in 1994 as an independent, nonprofit, literary press, Sarabande publishes poetry, short fiction, and literary nonfiction—genres increasingly neglected by commercial publishers. We are committed to producing beautiful, lasting editions that honor exceptional writing, and to keeping those books in print. If you're interested in further reading, take a moment to browse our website at sarabandebooks.org. There you'll find information about other titles; opportunities to contribute to the Sarabande mission; and an abundance of supporting materials including audio, video, a lively blog, and our Sarabande in Education program.